Montana,
Warts and All

Montana, Warts and All
ISBN-10: 0996745505
ISBN-13: 978-0-9967455-0-5

Copyright © 2015, Four Quarters LLC.
Story copyrights held by the individual authors herein and published with permission.

Book design by Craig Lancaster.

On the front cover: Wildlife biologist Randy Matchett works long nights preserving the endangered black-footed ferret in Montana's UL Bend National Wildlife Refuge. Photo by Thomas Lee.

On the back cover: Dusk envelopes mountains in the Lee Metcalf Wilderness Area. Photo by Thomas Lee.

Published in the United States by:
Montana Quarterly
P.O. Box 1900
Livingston, MT 59047
www.themontanaquarterly.com
admin@themontanaquarterly.com

CONTENTS

Truth Tellers

First Montanans

Pulling Together

Fiction

Contributors

Introduction

PHOTOGRAPHER THOMAS LEE HAS AN ELDERLY SAAB AND ONE OF ITS DOORS croaks like a sandhill crane, which makes me smile every time I open or close that door. It reminds me that sandhills have become common enough in Montana that most people recognize their call, whether the birds are lifting off or zooming in on some place of interest to them.

That's what we try to do at the *Montana Quarterly* as well: Rise above the fray to gain some perspective, then zero in for a good look around at a small town, a cool bar, an overlooked piece of history, or somebody who's trying to make the world a little better. Then we tell the story.

We've been at the job for ten years now and this book seemed like a good way to celebrate. We survived a recession, had to slap down some premature rumors of our demise, and came under new and independent ownership, which has helped us thrive. We've had a lot of fun at the magazine, made a lot of friends and stepped on a few toes. We didn't mean to, but that's part of the job and we're not going to back off. It's our editorial philosophy: Montana, warts and all.

While we're all proud and lucky to live in a place as big and open and welcoming as Montana, we try to keep our eyes clear. This isn't Shangri-La. Things aren't perfect and never will be. Warts are common. Some people are criminals, or greedy, or just bad neighbors. But I think they're overshadowed by the "and all," the people who get up every morning and do their job, who help, who wouldn't dream of leaving somebody stuck in a ditch, who share the *Quarterly*'s focus on finding ways to keep from screwing it up.

Those stories need telling. I'm glad we can make it possible. And I hope you enjoy reading this book as much as we did creating it.

Scott McMillion
Editor in Chief
Montana Quarterly

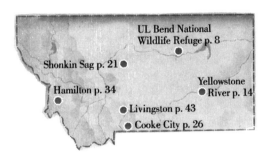

LIVING WILD

Montana is big and it's wild.
Nobody is here for the shopping.

Stuck in a Hole

By Scott McMillion

Winter 2013

CATCHING A BLACK-FOOTED FERRET ISN'T SO HARD. A long, narrow trap, made of steel mesh and wrapped in a blanket, will usually do the trick.

But you can't do that until you find the ferret. And that's the hard part. They dislike daylight and live mostly underground, coming out to see the world only during the blackness of night. You need a strong spotlight, a lot of coffee and plenty of patience to see a wild ferret. Cast your light everywhere, bathe the prairie with it, do it all night long, driving in circles, and maybe, just maybe, you'll get lucky. If you do, you'll spot the eyes first, licorice drops that flash green in the spotlight, that luminesce like pearls.

And when you do get lucky, your fatigue melts, your heart skips a beat. You scamper to the prairie dog burrow, the place where the ferret dens and hunts and sleeps. And there, three feet away, stands one of the rarest mammals in the world, bold and curious, staring back at you and wondering just how to make these large and pesky intruders go away.

Randy Matchett, a senior biologist for the U.S. Fish and Wildlife Service, knows this animal, both this species and this individual. He's caught it before and is reluctant to catch it again.

"That's a three-year-old wild-born female," he predicts. Then he waves his hand over her head, keeping her in the burrow until he can confirm his suspicions. He places a hard plastic ring over the mouth of the burrow and backs off a step until the ferret emerges again, a taut cord of muscle, about the same diameter from ears to hip, and the computer chip under her skin sets off a signal in the plastic ring. It's as he expected: this is ferret number 484.

He backs off, tells his crew to do the same, to retreat and watch. He hopes this one has kits somewhere.

"I'm looking forward to the time when I don't know everybody out here," Matchett says of the ferrets on the UL Bend National Wildlife Refuge in north-central Montana. But that day isn't likely to arrive any time soon. Despite two decades of labor and expense, black-footed ferrets still teeter on the verge of extinction.

It's 4 a.m. and he's in a 1,000-acre prairie dog town, just a quick shot north of the Missouri River, 50 miles from any pavement. Weather is coming to this wild place but it's not here yet and the stars astound in the clear sky. Matchett has been tending ferrets here since 1994, trying to foster a wild population, and he's frustrated. He's released 235 of them over the years and documented the birth of 291 more. At one point, in 1999, the population here rose to 90 animals, mostly wild born. But then it started dropping and by the end of his 2013 counting period, despite night after night of lighting up the prairie, he could confirm only three survivors.

"It's pretty bleak," he said, and he's not sure what happened to all of the UL Bend ferrets.

Black-footed ferrets live in a harsh world where half of newborns die in the first year and a four-year-old is an elderly individual. Rattlesnakes eat the little ones. Coyotes and great horned owls gobble any they can catch. It's all part of the complicated, intertwined relationships that swirl around a prairie dog colony, an ecosystem that some people compare to a coral reef because of the web of life it supports.

Despite that harshness, ferrets made homes in prairie dog towns for at least 100,000 years, evolution sharpening them into agile predators that can kill prairie dogs at will. But 97 percent of the prairie dog towns have been eradicated in the American West, done in by plows and poisons and bullets. And wild ferrets can't live without prairie dog towns.

While they will occasionally kill a cottontail or a mouse, ferrets are what biologists call an "extreme specialist." That means they depend on prairie dogs for food, and on their burrows for shelter from weather and places to hide from bigger predators.

"Their entire biology is built to survive in a tunnel system," Matchett says. "They're as agile upside down as they are right side up."

And then there is disease. Sylvatic plague, the same disease that wiped out so many Europeans in the Middle Ages, can kill a black-footed ferret three days after an infected flea sucks out a droplet of blood. It can empty thousands of acres of prairie dogs in a couple of weeks. A new vaccine renders ferrets immune to the disease, but it doesn't prevent starvation, which follows the plague when it decimates a prairie dog town. That's what happened to the prairie dogs and ferrets in the 40 Complex, a similar project a few miles north of the UL Bend, and in many other places around the West.

No prairie dogs, no ferrets.

MATCHETT AND OTHER SCIENTISTS AROUND THE WEST HAVE WORKED FOR years, trying to solve the plague problem, trying to think as big as a prairie. All the black-footed ferrets in North America descend from seven individuals captured near Meteetse, Wyoming, in the 1980s, the last members of the last wild population on earth. After some fits and starts, some bouts of disease, scientists figured out how to breed them in captivity. That part of the ferret restoration program works quite well.

Other aspects worked, too. Scientists developed an effective vaccine for plague, a disease that likely entered the country in rat-and-flea-infested ships from overseas, so all ferrets are vaccinated for both plague and canine distemper, a difficult process that is possible only because the ferret population is so small. Scientists also developed a vaccine for prairie dogs. It works in the laboratory but prairie dogs are too numerous to capture and inject individually, so a widespread oral vaccine is now undergoing testing, which means scattering peanut butter-flavored pellets over thousands of acres.

Biologists experimented with different ways of releasing ferrets into the wild, eventually learning that captive-born animals needed something like a boot camp if they were to survive. So they are "preconditioned," kept in a simulation of a wild prairie dog colony where they learn to hunt. The scientists tried using stuffed owls, a mechanical badger and live dogs to teach the ferrets to be wary of bigger predators, but that didn't work so well. Government shooters killed a lot of coyotes around prairie dog towns, but others replaced them soon enough. Crews strung electrified woven wire around prairie dog towns, to keep the coyotes out. It worked for a while, but the results were temporary.

And ferrets need a lot of room. A breeding age female needs about 100 acres of prairie dogs to make a living. And Matchett's charts show that, without at least 5,000 acres of prairie dogs, chances are slim for a sustainable population of ferrets. While Lewis and Clark and other pioneers reported prairie dog colonies that stretched for mile after mile, things have changed since then. Prairie dogs are constant gardeners, mowing around their burrows until the grass is as short as a putting green. Ranchers understandably see them as vermin, and many have done all they can, often with government help, to eradicate them.

Now, federal agencies are considering ways that would allow them to pay private landowners to foster prairie dogs, essentially renting that land from them. For some of those landowners, a program like that could produce revenue instead of the periodic expense of trying to control prairie dogs, according to Pete Gober, who runs the nationwide black-footed ferret program. A handful of such ranchers in several states could make a big difference, he says.

And some landowners take nontraditional views of prairie dogs, even welcoming them. Organizations such as The Nature Conservancy and the American Prairie Reserve, for instance, both own large properties near the UL Bend. Tribal lands also play a role, and the Fort Belknap Reservation recently accepted 30 new ferrets. There, people are hoping for a better result than they achieved in the 1990s, when 167 ferrets were released but none survived. This time, with help from the World Wildlife Fund, workers are dusting the prairie dog burrows with insecticide to kill fleas that carry plague, hoping to hold disease at bay.

Other landowners around the West are interested in hosting prairie dogs and ferrets, Matchett says, and plans are afoot to grant those people or organizations a "Safe Harbor Agreement," a set of assurances that, if, for instance, somebody runs over a ferret on private land, "the wrath of the Endangered Species Act won't fall on the landowners."

The Wildlife Service's 2013 recovery plan for ferrets says prairie dogs occupy about 3.7 million acres in the West today. If 15 percent of that land, about 500,000 acres, were managed to promote ferrets, the population could be recovered by 2040, the plan says. And other rare species that depend on prairie dog towns, such as mountain plovers and ferruginous hawks, would benefit, too. But that management won't be easy and it will be expensive.

Since plague is so widespread, ferret recovery means prairie dog burrows will need repeated dustings with insecticide. Ferrets will have to be captured and vaccinated. It will mean vaccinating thousands and thousands of acres of prairie dogs every year, assuming the new vaccine proves worthwhile in the field. It will mean constant monitoring of ferrets to see if all this work is working, if it's possible to push back on plague. Matchett sees some irony in all this: "We're using the highly endangered black-footed ferret as a medium to study bacteria."

The recovery plan estimates that costs—vaccinations, obtaining and protecting habitat, running the captive breeding facility, dusting for fleas, building partnerships—will total $150 million by 2040. That's an average of $3 million a year.

But as Matchett notes, the Wildlife Service has little choice but to do all it can to restore the species. He sees it as a moral imperative, plus restoration is the mandate of the Endangered Species Act and the black-footed ferret was one of the first species to be listed under that act.

"Those are my marching orders," he says. "To try to accomplish this."

Delisting the ferret will come only when 3,000 breeding adults live in nine states. At the end of October, after 30 years on the ESA list, there were perhaps 400 of them, mostly in other states with bigger prairie dog colonies, but places where plague is always a threat.

At the UL Bend, at the end of 2013, there were only three ferrets.

AFTER FERRET NUMBER 484 WAS IDENTIFIED, on that September night of astounding starlight, Matchett's crew spread out, blanketing the prairie with lights of its own. It was quiet, mostly, not much moving around except the pickups, a couple of coyotes, a badger and some deer. The burrowing owls had retired for the evening. Then the radio crackled. "I see a ferret. I think I see two of them," came a message from a pickup parked by research headquarters, the collection of camp trailers that locals derisively call the "ferret farm." Three vehicles converge, aiming spotlights, flashlights, headlamps. And there is number 484 again, trying to bring her kit to a prairie dog hole, where she likely has a fresh kill. Four bright eyes offer green luminescence as the mother drags the kit by the neck, pushes it from behind. Matchett watches for a moment, waiting, then hustles toward the animals; the kit is in a hole, the mother a few feet away. This is an opportunity. He stuffs the wire trap in the opening and wraps it in a blanket to block the light and make it seem like an extension of the burrow. Then, everybody backs off and 10 minutes later he has a ferret kit in the trap.

Then comes anesthesia, blood tests, the pulling of hair for DNA analysis, vaccinations for plague and distemper, the hypodermic injection of two microchips (sealing the tiny wound with superglue) and the application of some black hair dye on the neck and chest, so the animal can be identified later as one that needs no further capture. The kit is a little small for this time of year: 500 grams, about a pound.

Matchett returns the kit to the burrow where he captured it, pours a cup of coffee and grins. Then another kit pops up and he repeats the process. Two kits in one night. That's lucky, he says. Real lucky.

And a month later, they're gone. Both kits and the mother have disappeared.

"We pounded it for six nights" in October, he says, but found no sign of the family, though he spotted three other ferrets. Maybe the family moved. Maybe the luck turned in a coyote's favor. Nobody knows for sure.

Next year, more captive ferrets will be released at the UL Bend. Each will carry microchips under its skin, vaccines in its blood, more memory of man in its brain than of coyotes and owls and snakes.

"It's not very satisfying but that's the dance we have to dance," Matchett says. "But with this particular species and with this exotic disease (plague), I don't see that we have any options."

And without this dance, the ferret doesn't have any options at all. ◄

Bittersweet Ride

By Alan Kesselheim

Summer 2007

I N MY WILL IT STIPULATES THAT MY ASHES ARE TO BE SPREAD ON SOME appropriate piece of water. I leave the exact location to my survivors. Who knows what they'll want to take on, or which location will seem right. But when I conjure up a spot, it's the Yellowstone River that comes to mind.

I imagine my kids, a few relatives and friends, whoever shows up, camped on a gravel bar down around Forsyth, perhaps, or Rosebud, or upstream of Laurel. There is a fire going, stories are being told, the river ripples past, a train moans in the distance.

The Yellowstone is the river I know best, the river I've spent the most time on, where my kids became paddlers, where I go in my mind and in fact when I need the solace of current. Hearing the word, river, it's the Yellowstone that pops into focus.

As for my ashes, the Yellowstone seems suitable because it has had its share of fortunes: good and bad, glory and infamy, wild and tame. I could do worse than to mingle with that energy, to heed gravity as it does, to eddy out for a time and then move on again in the flood pulse. I could do a lot worse.

Last summer, for the second time in less than 20 years, I put a boat in the Yellowstone at the park boundary, just upstream from the Gardiner bridge, and aimed, non-stop, for the Missouri, 550 miles away. Like the first time, it was a family trip. The first time there were three of us, plus a bud. This time there were five.

When we floated the river in 1992, Eli wasn't yet a year old. Marypat and I were deep in an early phase of parental denial. Things weren't going to change just because we had a kid, by God, and we were going to prove it by going all the way down the Yellowstone. Eli was tethered to whichever one of us paddled bow. We were coping with teething, dirty diapers, and the demands of a nursing infant. At the start, we had no idea that our lives were about to get doubly complicated. Child number two, Sawyer, was busy doing cell division in Marypat's womb and had already been at it for more than a month.

This time Eli is 14, Sawyer is 13, and Ruby is just behind, at 11. We've succumbed to the reality of our changed life, but have somehow managed to embed adventure into the weave of family existence. The kids are more than game. In fact, the river reunion this time celebrates Sawyer's passage to adulthood. It's our way to mark his coming-of-age, on the same flow that he first experienced jostling around in amniotic fluids. Seems only appropriate to pay homage to his beginnings, to this great current, and to get a summer expedition in the bargain. Far better than mall-cruising, driver's licenses, or whatever else our culture offers up for a walkabout.

Where the Yellowstone crosses the arbitrary line at the boundary of Yellowstone Park it is as pure and untrammeled as any river in North America. It has already come roughly 100 miles, starting at 11,000 feet in the alpine tundra of the Washakie Wilderness in northern Wyoming. Trickling out of snowfields that linger all summer, the North and South Forks of the Yellowstone scribe dramatic, little-visited valleys around the flanks of Younts Peak, at the southern end of the Absaroka Range. The two streams coalesce to meander north through the remote, bear-filled meadows of the Thorofare and spill into the vast, thermally restless basin of Yellowstone Lake.

By the time the river pours out of that lake, it has real volume and power, enough to erode the Grand Canyon of the Yellowstone, plunging over Upper and Lower Falls, cascading through volcanic sediments where osprey and camera-wielding tourists perch. The water tumult continues, pounding down the Black Canyon, before emerging, silty green, battered, and roaring with throaty power, where we put in with a herd of inflatable boats towards the end of June.

There is no warm up at this launch. Gather yourself, cinch the life-vest, shove off and the dance is on. By the way, it's a slam dance, first with the wave trains and holes of the Gardiner Town Stretch, and then, a few hours downstream, partnered up with the boat-eating rapids of Yankee Jim Canyon.

Also right there at Gardiner, the pristine nature of the Yellowstone River abruptly ends. Within a mile of the park boundary, the river has been repeatedly polluted by untreated overflow sewage from Gardiner's antiquated treatment facility. Nothing intentional or malicious, always an accident, but nonetheless, the Yellowstone has been insulted by thousands of gallons of raw sewage on a handful of occasions.

For the rest of its course across Montana, the Yellowstone gets used and harnessed and confined and polluted. It may be revered, too. It may serve as the lifeblood of towns, industry, and agriculture. It may boast a rich historic and prehistoric significance. It may be valued and cherished for all of that. But none of it mitigates the fact of the onslaught.

We don't have time to think about sewage. Our send-off party, a parade of rafts and inflatables, bobs and slides through the rapids. Eli eats it in a side-curler, climbs back aboard his kayak and strokes towards another wave train. I see Sawyer disappear in a trough, then rise up again, a dot of red boat with a blue helmet, but I'm too busy controlling my own canoe to pay much attention.

It's a day to savor—for friends, for the warm sun, for the arrowhead Ruby finds at our lunch stop, and for the whitewater that never again will get this heady in the three weeks it takes us to get to the Missouri.

At the end of Yankee Jim we switch to expedition mode - traditional canoes and an inflatable kayak, five-gallon jugs of water, dry bags full of the food and gear that will sustain us across the state. Our friends wave and drive back to town. We drift down to a gravel-bar camp, fumble through that first set-up, remembering how things go. One door closes behind us, another opens. The echo of the day fades with the sun.

Frankly, I mean to dispatch with Paradise Valley as quickly as possible. It may be scenic as hell, bordered by the Absaroka and Gallatin ranges. It may have some charging sections of fun water. But around every bend there are driftboats. Highway 89 intrudes. Excessive homes perch on flood-vulnerable real estate, structural punctuations of pretension.

Most of all, Paradise Valley epitomizes the human urge to control nature rather than accept terms. In the last half of the 1990s, the Yellowstone served up back-to-back 100-year floods. Islands migrated, basements flooded, banks eroded in huge bites, bridges strained under the loads of logjams. At least one house had to be destroyed before it tipped into the brawny brown floodwaters. Awesome, terrifying, thrilling outbursts of raw power.

Landowners were understandably alarmed. Spurred by the very real threat, they went into action. The valley buzzed with heavy equipment. Residents riprapped the banks, fortified bends with boulders and barbs, walls and levees. The response was understandable, but the fact is that rivers flood. Periodically they flood with tremendous power. They change course, move the furniture around, writhe back and forth across the valley floor. It's what they do. We all know this and, to varying degrees, choose to ignore it. To expect immunity because you happen to own property in the floodplain is, well, presumptuous.

It's problematic, too, because reinforcing the banks of a river is a self-stoking activity. When an upstream neighbor puts in a section of riprap, the river speeds up and hits the next curve downstream with greater force and erosive power. Pretty soon that landowner is riprapping too. On it goes, until, eventually, the river becomes an armored corridor. Some argue that the upper Yellowstone has already become precisely that.

The valley remains beautiful, and I feel a bit elitist, but I yearn for the relative quiet downstream. We stroke from Yankee Jim to Livingston in a single long day, outrunning a black thunderhead in the afternoon, and camp on the outskirts of town.

From there the Yellowstone bends east. The days stay hot and sunny. Montana moves past in 25-mile chunks. Springdale, Big Timber, Greycliff, Reedpoint. We camp on sandbars and gravel islands. The kids develop a spirited and somewhat lethal game of baseball using driftwood for bats and river-smoothed rocks for balls. Bald eagles perch in snags, sandhill cranes call from fields, cormorants nest in cottonwood groves. Our sack of agates and petrified wood grows.

We raft the canoes together and drift for long stretches, reading out loud, retelling stories, making plans, letting the miles pass at the speed of gravity. Once in a while we hoist a sail and scoot along in front of a tailwind.

Despite the fact that the Yellowstone runs the gauntlet of I-90, railroad tracks, private property and towns, the river dimension exerts its hold. I notice cars going by at 70 miles an hour, I imagine those few passengers who look back, but they exist on another plane. Their concerns, their occupations, have nothing in common with mine. It's a testament to the seduction and embrace of this river that the round of existence we float past, close and observable as it is, familiar as it is, grows increasingly foreign. That it does is also a welcome benchmark, exactly where I want to be.

It's a tossup whether we swim or paddle more. The kids bob alongside like otters for miles. Camps are selected as much for the available rides in nearby wave trains as for suitable tent sites. Often as not, at the end of a rapid, we pull to shore, shuck our clothes, and run back up for a repeat ride, sans boats.

Traveling as we do, cooking on driftwood fires, letting the river rhythm assert itself, feels like a throwback to Huck Finn. As if we stole off in the dark, unloosed our homemade raft from the willows, and ghosted downstream past civilized territory, free and proud, even a little righteous.

And so, as the miles fall away in our wakes and the river embrace tightens, it becomes more and more difficult not to take it hard when civilization does intrude. On the outskirts of Billings we coast under Sacrifice Cliffs, where Indians threw themselves to their deaths in a vain attempt to appease the gods who had visited smallpox upon them. Just across the river the power plant squats, pumping up river water and belching steam. The interstate bridge arcs overhead, and right there we get ambushed by jet skiers.

Not many things provoke violent impulses in me, but jet skiers are one of them. They may be great fun for the rider ramming around in arcing loops and circles, but they ruin the day for everyone in a two-mile radius. One particularly obnoxious rider appears to think we enjoy his company. He circles us, a cigarette dangling from his mouth, follows us downstream, hounds us with his whining scream and foul fumes for half a mile. I distract myself fantasizing about bridge abutments and fireballs.

After the refineries and jet skiers, diversion dams are almost a benign intrusion. There are six major dams below Billings, starting with Huntley, which comes up about 10 miles past town. At each one, significant, stream-sized canals are diverted to supply irrigation across a vast swatch of eastern Montana. Some of the dams are identified by warning signs, some not. For the most part, paddlers are on their own to figure out where the dams are, whether they can be skirted, and how to portage around, if necessary. Running them is a dicey option, sometimes deadly.

The Yellowstone enjoys a reputation as the "longest, undammed major river in the Continental United States." Technically, that may be a valid claim. In reality, to call the river undammed is at best a narrow definition. Just ask the paddlefish or pallid sturgeon whose populations hang in the balance because they can no longer migrate upstream as they used to.

At Huntley we're able to sneak past the danger along a high-water channel full of snags. Right there the river starts to feel pretty rural. It winds through islands, past great blue herons and white pelicans. There are more bald eagles per mile than seem possible. The highway and railroad recede. The pace is bucolic.

For a time we encounter a diversion dam almost every day. At Waco we avoid it via another side channel. Below the confluence with the Bighorn we lift our canoes over the sidewalk-width barrier. At Meyers the water is high enough that we can run the dam far left. Coming into Forsyth we sneak along a narrow channel inside an island, and manage to fishtail over the far edge of the dam, literally bumping against shore as we go.

The only thing we have to stop for, every week or so, is drinking water. We fill the jugs at the campground in Columbus, at the Pompey's Pillar Visitor's Center, from someone's garden hose in Miles City. We'd just as soon stay on the water. Or in the water. The days continue hot. The kids accumulate a permanent veneer of river silt. We could have done this trip outfitted with nothing but a pair of shorts, a T-shirt, and flip-flops. Train engineers have come to expect us. We get regular toots and waves of recognition.

The first time down the Yellowstone I kept waiting for the river to lose its appeal, for it to get boring. It never happened. The land changes, opens, shades into the pastels of the badlands. The sky widens. Rattlesnakes swim the river. Cottonwood bottoms spread for miles. If anything, the valley becomes more evocative.

Our flotilla passes Froze-to-Death and Starved-to-Death creeks, Poverty Flats, Lost Boy Canyon, the Powder River, Valentine Flats. There are stories to imagine in those names. The towns are named after military men from the Indian Wars. I think almost daily of Clark and his return party, in 1806, pushing hard downriver in dugout cottonwood trees. Or of John Colter and Manuel Lisa. Of Chief Joseph. Of steamboats and wood hawks.

We stop for lunch at Buffalo Rapids. Not much in the way of whitewater, but the scene of at least one steamboat disaster. The rock ledges jut far into the river. The kids surf in the waves. The dome of sky arcs to the horizon. We are alone, in deep, loosed from the grasp of time.

One night, on an island downstream of Glendive, Marypat goes into pizzaria mode with some extra food supplies. The rest of us keep collecting driftwood and stoking the fire to make coals, and she keeps churning out Dutch oven pizzas until the sun goes down and we can't eat anymore. Somewhere in there, closing in on Sidney, Sawyer finds a mud wallow big enough to support full-body group baths that we emerge from like claymation figures.

After weeks on the water, boundaries begin to blur. Not just our awareness of time, but our sense of connection with the flow. The Yellowstone has become a companion, a force that carries us, speaks to us, that has, in some fashion, entered us. Our dreams are ambushed by its fluid cadence. Day on day the filaments of water communicate through the boat hulls, through the paddles, through our arms and knees and thoughts.

And here, near the end, the Yellowstone is telling us that it is exhausted. This message is direct, palpable and personal. With each stroke we feel it again. The mood infects us.

The river is warm and sluggish, thick with sediment and runoff, its flow unnaturally anemic. For more than 500 miles the Yellowstone endures our demands. It is siphoned off, barricaded, pulled into towns and fields and sugar beet plants, sullied by our wastes, loved and used to near-extinction. For the final week, our daily challenge has been to find camps out of earshot of irrigation pump motors.

It's as if we are in the company of an ailing friend. Finishing the journey becomes as much a matter of loyalty and obligation as the culmination of adventure.

We camp the final time within a few miles of the confluence with the Missouri, downstream of the old railroad bridge still outfitted with a drawbridge section to allow for the passage of steamboats. No one is hungry for dinner, so we make a pot of tea and call it good. The kids don't play their usual driftwood baseball games. We go to the tent early, thinking about being done.

At dawn I lie awake, looking at the mist over the turgid river. It's over, I think. A pheasant calls harshly from a nearby field. I strain for the whisper of current sliding past, for some echo of the rampant force surging out of Yellowstone Park, far upstream. The pheasant calls again, a metallic sound. Then an irrigation motor starts up across the channel, throbbing and insistent, nursing from the last, silent flow. ◪

The Shonkin Sag

By Ed Kemmick

Fall 2013

EXCEPT FOR A STINT IN THE SERVICE, Hank Armstrong has lived most of his 86 years in the house his grandparents built in 1910, seven miles east of Geraldine, Montana. He is the local historian, seemingly familiar with every square inch of land around his native hearth and the stories of everyone who has lived there over the decades.

The center of his world, the world he sees from the windows of his house, is Square Butte, a massive flat-top mesa that rises steeply out of the surrounding plain, with rampart-like tendrils of volcanic rock snaking down its flanks. Armstrong knows exactly how many times he's been to the top of Square Butte: 63.

"It's always been a part of my life," he says.

Dr. Gerald T. Davidson grew up in Harlem, Montana, in the shadow of the Bear Paw Mountains. Like Square Butte and a couple of other isolated mountain ranges in north-central Montana, the Bear Paws are made of igneous, or volcanic, rock. Early in life Davidson developed a fondness for what he calls "geological oddities."

"Geology is something you can't avoid if you grew up in Montana, which I did," he said.

After a 30-year career with Lockheed Martin in California, where he did mostly computational physics, Davidson retired to Red Lodge. In his retirement he has made an intensive study of one of the oddest geological oddities in Montana—the Shonkin Sag.

The Sag, as it is often called, is where the interests of Armstrong and Davidson intersect. The Sag itself marks the intersection of two of the most dramatic periods of Montana's geological history—an era of intense volcanic activity some 50 million years ago and the relatively recent era of the ice ages, which began about a million years ago and ended about 12,000 years ago.

The Shonkin Sag is a now-dry valley carved by river flow and glacial melt water during a succession of ice ages. It stretches for more than 60 miles from the town of Highwood, east of Great Falls, to the channel of the present Missouri River east of Geraldine. The valley is a mile or more wide and hundreds of feet deep, pockmarked by a chain of shallow, alkaline lakes.

Over hundreds of thousands of years, as the great glaciers of North America crept south and then retreated north before the cycle began again, these glaciers dammed precursors of the Missouri River and other streams, creating immense lakes. The freshwater seas would rise until they topped ridges or ice dams, spilling over and creating flow channels. The Shonkin Sag is one such channel. David Alt and Donald W. Hyndman, in their popular book *Roadside Geology of Montana*, called it "one of the two or three most spectacular glacial meltwater channels in the country."

The Sag happens to run through land rich in laccoliths, particularly striking remnants of volcanic activity. A laccolith is a layer of igneous material injected between layers of sedimentary rock. These are formed when magma pushes up from underground, lifting the strata above it. In some cases the overlying rock erodes away, exposing giant laccoliths such as Square Butte and the nearby Round Butte.

Other laccoliths were exposed by the cutting waters of the Shonkin Sag. The most stunning expanse of this formation is known as the Shonkin Sag laccolith, a few miles west of Square Butte. The dark, granite-like rock of all these laccoliths has been named shonkinite. The Shonkin Sag laccolith is a textbook example of igneous intrusion, where the shonkinite is interspersed with layers of pale Eagle sandstone, the same material as the Rimrocks that tower over Billings. That "magnificent exposure," to quote Alt and Hyndman again, "has made the Shonkin Sag laccolith the most thoroughly studied and best known igneous intrusion of its type in the country, perhaps in the world."

It was also the site of the Square Butte granite quarry, founded in 1914. Armstrong published a history of the quarry in 2000 and led a successful effort to have the site placed on the National Register of Historic Places.

It should not be surprising that so few people seem to know of the Shonkin Sag or of the old Square Butte quarry. Both are impressive, once you realize what you're looking at, but perhaps only someone with a keen interest in geology would be drawn immediately to either feature.

That is not the case with a portion of the Shonkin Sag known as the Dry Falls. For pure, breathtaking wonder, there is nothing quite like it in Montana.

The Dry Falls are about 10 miles northwest of Geraldine, surrounded by miles of gently rolling wheat fields and pastureland. You approach them on a narrow dirt road that can be impassable after a rain and park your vehicle in a wide spot in the road marked only by a nondescript sign advising you that this is private property, and to enter at your own risk. The Highwood Mountains—"shonkin" was supposedly the Blackfeet Indian name for the Highwoods—loom up to the south, and as you near the falls you walk through curious layered piles of rock covered in light-green lichen, looking for all the world like gigantic petrified cow pies.

After a walk of a quarter mile or so, you reach the rim of the Dry Falls, a horseshoe-shaped wall of shonkinite half a mile across, like the black walls of a great fortress. You look down 250 feet or more to Lost Lake, a long, fjord-like body of deep-green water. It is a dizzying, otherworldly spectacle. Verdant carpets of vegetation reach up the lower portions of the cliffs, creating the impression of a prehistoric rain forest or some South American Shangri-La.

Armstrong, standing on the rim of the Dry Falls last summer, spoke with wonder of the ice age marvel.

"It boggles your mind to think how much water came over this one spot," he said.

To imagine that volume of water, consider this: given the depth of Lost Lake, Davidson said, the falls probably dropped 300 to 350 feet when the Shonkin Sag was brimful and water poured over the top. At 300 feet deep and half a mile across, the Dry Falls would have been just about double the size of the largest cataract at today's Niagara Falls.

"It's one of the most spectacular geological sites in Montana and it really ought to be a state park," Davidson said.

The Lost Lake Valley also bisects another notable laccolith. The horizontal bands of intruded shonkinite on the north side of the lake are very similar to those at the Square Butte quarry.

Davidson and Armstrong have long been puzzled by the relative obscurity of the Shonkin Sag and its associated features. Early in the last century, as Alt and Hyndman indicated, the laccoliths in the area were extensively studied, particularly by geology students and professors from Harvard and Yale. But the Shonkin Sag itself seems to have been relatively neglected, the subject of more conjecture than research.

When Armstrong began studying the quarry near Square Butte, he said, "It was almost completely forgotten, even by people around here."

In a conversation once with Dick Berg, director of the Rock and Mineral Museum at Montana Tech in Butte, he learned that Berg had never heard of the quarry.

Davidson had similar experiences. When he worked for Lockheed in California, he used to attend the annual conferences of the American Geophysical Union. He made a point of trying to find geologists who knew something about the Shonkin Sag, but he never met anybody who had even heard of it.

"It's just so little known," he said. "I've tried to interest geologists in it, but they're just totally unaware. ... This is sort of off on the fringes, and nobody is doing anything that I have found."

With time on his hands in retirement, Davidson has tried to fill in the gaps of what is known about the Shonkin Sag. In popular accounts that mention the Sag, he said, there has been a tendency to simplify the geological history of the area. The descriptions generally speak of one or perhaps several catastrophic overflows of glacial Lake Great Falls, as the inland sea in this area was called, and they usually describe this as having happened at the end of the last ice age.

"I just wondered if the explanations of it held any water," Davidson said, and then he apologized for his small play on words.

His research, gathered through years of studying the landscape, reading published reports and creating detailed topographic maps of the area, has led him to believe that the Sag was the work of ages. He is convinced that different parts of the Sag were created during different periods of glaciation, and that the meltwater overflowed not just one lake several times, but several lakes on numerous occasions.

As ice age succeeded ice age, the ancient Missouri—which flowed north to Hudson Bay before the continental glaciers pushed its channel ever farther south—was dammed at different points, forming lakes of various sizes and shapes.

Davidson believes some parts of the Shonkin Sag could have been formed very early, many hundreds of thousands of years ago, while the relatively pristine channel seen near the town of Highwood was probably formed by the last overflow of the ice-dammed lake during the most recent ice age.

Topographical evidence seems to suggest that the channel that carved the Dry Falls and created Lost Lake was also formed in a later episode, maybe 80,000 to 200,000 years ago.

"Those are just guesses," he said. "I'm just placing them in the context of the ice ages."

For the modern visitor, it hardly matters how or exactly when the Shonkin Sag and its awe-inspiring Dry Falls were formed. And though Davidson likes to talk of creating a state park and protecting the landscape of the Sag, Armstrong points out that the whole area has so far been protected by its very obscurity. At the Dry Falls there are no signs, no litter, no evidence of people at all but for a few faint trails in the sandy soil.

In mid-June, Lucretia Humphrey of Great Falls and her sister Clarissa Metzlercross of Seattle were enjoying the near-solitude of the Dry Falls. Metzlercross had never visited the site before. Humphrey and her husband had seen it a year earlier for the first time, having gotten lost or turned back by muddy roads on two or three other attempts to visit the area.

"How can people not know about it?" Humphrey asked, gesturing to take in the whole vast scene. "There's so much in Montana. I mean, it's right under our nose." ◢

25

A Rare
and Ghastly Night

By Scott McMillion

Spring 2011

DEB FREELE WOKE WITH A FLITTER OF UNEASINESS. Something wasn't right.

Then, before she could even open her eyes, the bear chomped into her upper left arm. It didn't chew. It didn't shake its head. It didn't growl. It just kept pushing her into the ground, squeezing its jaws ever tighter, carving a furrow of flesh you could roll a golf ball through. She heard something crack. It was loud.

She thought it was a bone breaking. Later, she would learn the grizzly had snapped off a tooth.

"It was like a vise," she said of the grizzly's grip. "Getting tighter and tighter and tighter."

Freele screamed. She called out for help. "It's a bear," she yelled. "I'm being attacked by a bear."

But no help came, not for a long time. It was July 28, 2010, and she was alone in her one-man tent, her 13th night in the Soda Butte Campground a few miles from the northeast entrance to Yellowstone National Park. Her husband was in another tent about 40 feet away. But he'd been at the rum pretty hard that night and didn't hear a thing.

Yelling wasn't working, so Freele decided to play dead. The bear loosened its grip, only to snap down again on her lower arm, squeezing with its jaws and pushing, pushing down. She heard another snap. This time, it was a bone.

She wondered: "Does it think it has me by the neck? This thing thinks it's killing me."

Pinned on her side, she couldn't reach the bear pepper spray beside her in the tent. She couldn't strike out. She decided to go limp, thinking that, if the bear tried to roll her over, she'd have a chance to grab the pepper spray.

For maybe a minute, she suffered in near silence. She could see stars overhead and she could hear the bear's heavy breath, with blood or saliva gurgling in its throat.

Then she heard sounds from the next campsite. Voices in a tent. Feet scurrying to a vehicle. Doors slamming and an engine starting. Headlights flashed across her husband's silent tent.

And the bear went away.

"It dropped me and I didn't move an eyelash," Freele, 58, told me later from her home in London, Ontario. "I was afraid it would pounce on me."

The car from the neighboring campsite stopped and a window opened. "We're getting help," somebody said. The car contained a family with young children. Too terrified to leave the car, they drove around the campsite's upper loop, honking the horn and trying to rouse somebody. Most people ignored them, suspecting drunks or hooligans, likely.

And Freele lay there alone, in the dark, her tent demolished, her arm shredded like a chicken wing, knowing not where that bear had gone. She took the safety off her bear spray and sat partway up. It would be 20 minutes before the neighbors came back with help.

Freele didn't know it at the time, but she wasn't the bear's first victim. A few minutes earlier, at about 2 a.m. and a couple hundred yards upstream, the grizzly had attacked another tent. Though the tent contained two people and a dog, the bear moved it a few feet before biting through the fabric and sinking its teeth into the leg of Ronald Singer, a 21-year-old former high school wrestler who came up swinging while his girlfriend began to scream. The sharp blows and the racket helped the bear change its mind and it didn't stick around. Neither did Singer. His girlfriend's parents drove him to Cooke City, looking for medical help. Freele saw them drive by her camp, but they didn't stop, probably didn't even know the bear had struck again.

After these two attacks, the grizzly—a scrawny animal supporting three yearling cubs— kept moving downstream until she hit the camp of Kevin Kammer, of Grand Rapids, Michigan. All but three of the Soda Butte Campground's 27 sites contained campers that night, most of them in tents. Like Freele's site and Singer's, Kammer's site was a little isolated, with only one neighbor. And Kammer's site, number 26, was one of the most isolated. The closest camp stood 60 yards away, it was very dark and a nearby creek masked noises. Nobody saw or heard a thing.

And nobody found his body until a couple hours later, after campers had raised the alarm and a Park Count Sheriff's deputy, with a spotlight and a loudspeaker, began rousting campers, ordering them to leave. He found a ghastly scene. The bear had pulled Kammer from his tent by the head and shoulders and he bled to death within four feet of the tent, investigators determined. Then she pulled his body another 10 yards, and that's where the deputy found him, his torso partially consumed by mother and cubs.

By that time, game wardens, deputies, people from the Forest Service and the National Park Service, most of them armed, had sent the groggy campers on their way, most of them leaving their gear on the ground for the night. Dawn dragged its heels that morning.

"WHAT MADE HER CROSS THAT LINE THAT NIGHT WILL HAUNT ME forever," Kevin Frey told me. He is a bear management specialist in the Yellowstone area for the Montana Department of Fish, Wildlife and Parks. I've interviewed him many times in 20 years of reporting about Yellowstone and relied on him as a source for my book, *Mark of the Grizzly, True Stories of Recent Bear Attacks and the Hard Lessons Learned.* I've learned to count on him for honest, reliable information. Like me, he cares about grizzly bears and wild country. He finds no joy in it when he has to kill a bear.

And he works really hard. In normal years, he works with landowners to help bearproof their properties and, during hunting seasons, he crawls through dense brush, looking for a grizzly bear wounded by a surprised hunter. Last year, when a late spring meant poor crops of natural food and far-ranging bears, he worked well over two months without a day off, trying to solve problems.

He has investigated dozens of bear attacks over the years. He's trapped and handled scores of bears, tried to educate thousands of people about living safely in bear country. He said he's never seen an attack like this one. Analyze most grizzly attacks, and you'll find some sort of explanation: a surprise encounter: a hunter bounces one out of a daybed, a photographer pushes his luck, a hapless hiker winds up between the bear and its cubs, or between the bear and a carcass it is protecting, or somebody feeds the bear, teaching it to see humans as a source of food.

But none of that happened in this case. Frey's report, compiled in the weeks after the attack, pieced together what happened. But it couldn't tell us why.

"There is no clear explanation for the aggressive, predatory behavior," the report says.

It does rule out a number of factors. At 220 pounds, the bear was small, but not abnormally so. The cubs were undersized, too. But they were not starving. The mother carried an average load of parasites. She probably had lived near the campground for all of her life, at least 10 years. She knew where it was, had seen it and smelled it and mostly shunned it.

She was not rabid. She was not in the habit of eating garbage, or horse feed or bird seed or somebody's lunch. Relatively new technology means scientists can identify, through analysis of the isotopes in hair, the main ingredients of a bear's diet for the previous two years. She had lived almost exclusively on vegetation, unlike most of the Yellowstone area's meat-eating bears. Sometime in the previous couple of weeks, she'd been eating meat, though not much of it. She'd been a vegetarian, mostly.

None of the people attacked that night had any food or other attractants in their tents to tempt a bear's sensitive nose. Everybody in the campground had secured all their food and utensils in their vehicles or the bearproof boxes at each campsite.

The bear had never been trapped or tranquilized and she had no history of aggression toward people. The only known encounter had come a few days earlier when a woman, jogging on the highway near the park entrance, surprised the bear family along the road. The startled mother offered a bluff charge, then backed off when the jogger stopped running and started yelling at her, which is typical behavior. She was being protective, not predatory.

If anybody in the Cooke City area had problems with grizzlies grabbing garbage or other food that summer, they didn't report it.

Rumors circulated that a local photographer had been feeding the bears, which could have taught them to associate humans with food. Investigators chased leads but could find no evidence of such bear baiting. And the hair analysis ruled out any significant amount of human or livestock food.

While it took a while to sort out these details, the evidence that Frey and Warden Captain Sam Sheppard found on the ground made for a clear case, one as unusual as it was grim: this grizzly bear was treating people like food, like prey. And for that, she had to die. Anybody who pays any attention in grizzly country knows you should never, ever, give a bear a food reward. Don't do it on purpose. Don't let it happen accidentally. It just teaches them to look for more of the same. And this bear and her cubs had found a food reward in a person they killed.

By 6 p.m. on July 28, about 16 hours after Kammer's death, the bear had returned to his camp, where Frey had draped the rain fly from Kammer's tent over a culvert trap just six feet from where the father of four had died. She climbed in the steel tube, looking for more food, and the door slammed shut behind her. Within another 12 hours, Frey had captured all three cubs, too.

While Frey's team already knew this had been a predatory attack, an effort to make a meal of people, they waited for definitive proof that they had the right bear. The next day, some deft work by the crime lab in neighboring Wyoming made sure Frey and his crew had what they needed: DNA from hairs gathered at the attack matched DNA from the bear in the trap. Plus, the snapped tooth in Freele's tent matched a broken canine on the mother bear. Frey and Sheppard had the right bear.

Less than two hours later, a plunger dropped on a big hypodermic and the mother bear nodded into death. Her cubs will spend their life in zoos.

Frey and Sheppard said they have no regrets about the decision to put the mother bear down. Bears who learn to rely on things like garbage and pet food cause problems enough. A bear that has killed and eaten a person cannot be tolerated.

NEWS OF THE ATTACKS SPREAD QUICKLY AROUND THE WORLD. Media in Europe, China and Australia covered it. For some reason, lots of people felt more sympathy for the bear than for the man she killed. Some grew livid. Hundreds of emails poured into FWP offices, enough to clog servers. Some blamed Kammer for being there. Others put on a stupefying display of ignorance and fantasy.

"The bear had been to the area before the campers were there and when she noticed a strange presence she immediately went into survival mode, doing what was necessary to ensure the protection of her cubs," wrote one woman, who then offered to lock herself in a room with the bear to prove "it won't purposely kill me."

"What a bunch of morons!!!!" a man wrote. "The mother bear and cubs were simply looking for food in their natural habitat."

"I will always think of Montana as a backward, anti-animal state who will murder a mother bear, orphan her three cubs because stupid arrogant people have to holiday in the wilderness," wrote another woman.

"You will burn in hell for murdering God's beloved creations," wrote another man.

In the anonymity of the blogosphere, things got even worse. People even took shots at Kammer in the comments section of an online obituary.

Investigators saw it differently.

"That man deserves nothing but respect and sympathy," Sheppard said of Kammer.

I agree with him.

Kammer, 48, had taken a break from a career as a medical technologist to be a stay-at-home dad to his four kids, the youngest just nine and the oldest 19. Two of them attended a Christian school. His family chose not to comment for this story, but news accounts and comments from friends provide at least a partial picture: dedicated to his family, he was the kind of dad who showed up at school board meetings when a decision affected his kids. Affable and friendly, when coworkers had a bad day, they could count on him to elicit a laugh. He liked fishing and camping and kayaking, fixing up the house and relaxing in the hot tub.

His camp was clean. His food was properly stored. He wasn't in the wilderness, he was in a campground, a few feet from his car, a place with toilets and picnic tables and improved roads. Though surrounded by wild country, this place was built for people. He did nothing wrong. Yet doofuses on the Internet, cloaked in anonymity, felt free to criticize him.

Freele said she was in the ambulance on the way to a hospital in Cody, Wyoming, when she learned there had been more attacks, that a man had died. Until that point, she'd been feeling she was the unlucky one. She knew she was in bear country and had done everything right. She never cooked on the fire pit, not wanting to leave any food residue in there. She kept her campstove and food locked away. She poured her dishwater in the outhouse and even brushed her teeth there, to keep attractive odors out of her camp. She didn't use any lotions and she changed her clothes before going to bed. She kept her bear spray handy and if she found fresh bear sign on her daily fishing trips, she went somewhere else. She followed all the rules and somehow, the bear chose her tent that night. She has no doubt it was trying to make a meal of her.

Anonymous commenters on the Internet attacked her, too.

"That bothered me," she told me, but not as much as the knowledge that Kammer died nearby.

She wonders, now, if she couldn't have helped. She hopes he didn't suffer. She worries about his family. She wonders if she couldn't have tried harder to reach her bear pepper spray, if she couldn't have maybe chased the grizzly away, into the woods, away from people.

"Survivor's guilt, I guess," is the way she summed it up.

SOMEBODY GETS NAILED IN GRIZZLY COUNTRY EVERY YEAR. Almost always, they survive these attacks by animals that can take down a bull elk or an Angus steer, though the injuries can be gruesome. This, more than anything, refutes the myth that grizzlies are manhunters that lust for human flesh. If they wanted to kill us, they could do it in short order.

Attacks like the ones at the Soda Butte Campground remain incredibly rare. The last time anything similar happened in greater Yellowstone was in 1984, when Britta Fredenhagen, of Basel, Switzerland, died in the park's remote Pelican Valley. Like Kammer, she had kept a clean camp and obeyed the rules, but a bear dragged her from her tent and ate much of her body anyway.

"Bears very rarely exhibit that kind of behavior," Sheppard said. "But every one of them is capable of it."

And that's why the official response at Soda Butte was swift and immediate. Bear managers don't want to give bears a chance to repeat that kind of thing. Cynics respond that fear of lawsuits drives such decisions. I don't think it's that simple.

"There's a need to keep the community safe," Sheppard said. "We couldn't put a bear out there that we knew had cost somebody their life."

Not everybody buys that reasoning, as witnessed by the outpouring of invective over the death of the Soda Butte bear. Some people argue that killing an innocent man in a campground should not warrant a death sentence for a bear.

What these people fail to realize is that killing that bear might have saved other bears. Too often, hunters and hikers kill bears that seem threatening. In 2010, people killed at least 49 grizzlies in and near Yellowstone. That's nearly a record number (the record occurred in 2008) and at least

18 of those deaths remained "under investigation" by the end of the year. If the Soda Butte grizzly had been released, how many more bears would be killed by people convinced that every bear is that maneater?

Grizzly advocates—and I count myself among them—deserve to squirm over the events at Soda Butte Campground. Two people suffered serious injuries and a man died. None of them did anything wrong. These weren't garbage bears. It wasn't a surprise encounter. It was a deadly, predatory attack.

As we move on with the seemingly interminable disputes over Endangered Species Act protections for grizzlies, as we argue over which places and under which conditions the growing population of grizzlies should roam, as we contemplate mathematical models and political theories and a raft of other abstractions, let's keep this in mind: Kevin Kammer was a real person with a real family. He's gone now. And we don't know why.

That's not an abstraction.

It's as real as it gets. ◢

For Love of a Ditch

By Jeff Hull

Spring 2009

MICHAEL HOWELL'S VERSION OF THE STORY BEGAN ONE DAY IN 1991, when he was sitting in his Stevensville office at the *Bitterroot Star*, a newspaper he founded in 1985. Howell didn't know Robert and Randy Rose, but one day the brothers walked into his office and said something like, "You might want to come with us. It might be a news story."

And Howell asked something like, "What's the news?"

"We're going to go fishing."

"That doesn't sound like much news."

"We're going to climb a barbed-wire fence posted with 'No Trespassing' signs to do it."

"I didn't know much about the stream access law," Howell says now, standing in winter sunlight that pours through the big glass windows in the front of the Star's offices. "They showed me the law and I was impressed. I went along and took pictures."

The fence the Rose brothers climbed that day belonged to someone a lot of people know, or know of—popular rock 'n roll singer Huey Lewis. The water the brothers wanted to fish was called Mitchell Slough, a shallow, meandering waterway once so degraded by overgrazing and neglect that, 10 years earlier, most people considered it an irrigation canal, if they considered it at all. Back then, hardly anybody cared about fishing the Mitchell Slough on its 16-mile meander between Corvallis and Stevensville. But the Rose brothers wanted to make a little news.

The events that unfolded over the subsequent 17 years, leading to a decisive Supreme Court decision in November, 2008, have been reduced to shortcut storytelling in much of the local and national press—"wealthy, out-of-state" landowners (read: black hats) vs. good ol' Montana sportsmen (the white hats). But what's drowned out by the spatter of back-patting in the wake of the white-hat victory is that a lovely little stream, resurrected from dysfunction to become a vibrant fishery and potent contributor to the Bitterroot River ecosystem, is once again at risk.

H uEY LEWIS STARTS HIS SIDE OF THE STORY BY SAYING HE CAME TO Montana to fly fish as a young man struggling to make it in the music business. "I vowed if I ever made a dime I would buy a piece of ground in Montana and rehabilitate it for the wildlife," Lewis says. "I turned 30 years old with $300 to my name, and then I got a hit record, thank God."

After losing money to bad investments, Lewis made good on his word in 1987. He bought chunks of Bitterroot land from longtime ranchers Wayne Dayton and Steve Bingham. Lewis was told by the previous landowners that the slow, flat piece of water flowing through their properties was diverted water, and, therefore, an irrigation canal.

"The ditch was just that, a very muddy irrigation ditch," Lewis says. "It was super silty. You could barely walk through it. You'd sink up to your thighs in silt."

The mix of landowners along Mitchell Slough is unlike the demographics of most traditional Montana ranchlands. Some landowners ranch on the slough because their families always have. Some retired to the Bitterroot. Others arrived toting profoundly deep pockets. Most zealously guard the privacy the area affords.

A few of the wealthier landowners—notably Lewis, businessman Ken Siebel, financial services magnate Charles Schwab and Las Vegas casino developer Anthony Marnell—were keenly interested in restoring wildlife habitat on their properties (although Marnell's conservation ethic is obscured by the glass-floored wing of his home he built over a branch of Mitchell Slough, nobody's idea of environmental stewardship).

Lewis put a lot of thought into his place. He wanted the periphery of the property to operate as agricultural land, while still providing a haven for wildlife through the core of the ranch. Lewis turned his attention to transforming the slough into a viable fishery.

Lewis hired an excavator and filled in the edges of the slough's channel, making it narrower and faster. He built curves into the watercourse to create scouring current, and excavated deep holes for fish to hold in. He placed logs in the stream for cover. He laid gravel in the waterway, forming spaces for insect larvae and providing spawning beds for trout. It was not a sudden transformation; he did it piecemeal, touring with his band, The News, to finance the project.

"I did all that work on my own dime," Lewis says. "Siebel and Schwab are the rich, I'm the famous. Everything I've got is in my place. But it's so gratifying to do habitat reconstruction. It's as good as religion to me. I love the resource. I love to fish. I love looking at fish—and ducks and deer. It's so gratifying to watch the resource respond."

Trout had always drifted into Mitchell Slough with spring's high water, then slid back to the river as low flows left the ditch hot and full of silt and weeds. But as the rehab evolved, rainbows and browns and cutthroats dotted the gravel with spawning beds. Their offspring settled in the stream year-round and grew fat.

"Restoration is not a science, it's an art. You really don't know what's going to work," Lewis says. "That's what's so wonderful. Mother nature surprises the shit out of you all the time. And it's fantastic."

CHRIS CLANCY TELLS A STORY THAT ESSENTIALLY CORROBORATES LEWIS' account of the slough's pre-rehab fishery. Looking at fishing surveys done on the stream in early to mid-'80s, Clancy, a Montana Fish, Wildlife and Parks (FWP) biologist based in Hamilton since 1989, says, "there were pretty good numbers of fish in it, but a lot of them weren't trout.

"There were a lot of whitefish in the fall. A lot of suckers, northern pikeminnows—back then, we called them squawfish. You looked at it and thought, 'This data is from a low-gradient stream, a stream that gets warm. The work [Lewis, Siebel, et al.] have done, I suspect, has shifted the composition to more trout."

"I've talked to anglers and I've heard lots of things," Clancy says. "People have told me, 'We fished it and it was really good.' Others said it wasn't much of a fishery at all." The upshot, Clancy believes, is that before the restoration, "you weren't walking on the backs of trout in there."

But that's not the whole point, he says, because the less sexy side of the Mitchell Slough controversy was not about stream access. In 1975, Montana passed a law requiring anybody who alters a streambed or riparian area to apply for what's called a 310 permit from the local conservation district. In this way, the state is able to monitor and control how streams and rivers get manipulated. If Mitchell Slough is a perennial flowing "natural river or stream," it's subject to 310 permitting.

"From a 310 standpoint, the quality of the fishery means nothing," Clancy says. He issued his first 310 permit in 1980 and feels comfortable talking about what is or isn't a stream from a 310 perspective.

"If [Mitchell Slough] was not a stream," Clancy says, "then there are a lot of streams in this state—streams with fish in them—that we've done 310 permits for that are not streams."

Montana's Stream Access Law came a decade later, in 1985. That law states simply that anybody wishing to recreate on a stream in Montana may do so as long as they enter the stream through a public access and stay within the high water marks. If Mitchell Slough can be defined as a "natural water body," Montana's Stream Access Law applies to it.

And so the reams of data and torrents of newsprint generated about Mitchell Slough percolate down to one word: natural.

MICHAEL HOWELL COULDN'T BELIEVE MITCHELL SLOUGH WAS ANYTHING but natural. He'd watched the Rose brothers get cited for trespassing the day they scaled Huey Lewis' fence to go fishing, and covered their acquittal in a jury trial. The case turned on testimony by an FWP official who said Montana's stream access law covered the slough.

But seven years later, Howell found himself sucked back into the controversy. In 1999, knowing a Victor man had filed for a portage designation—a legal exemption on public streams describing how boaters and waders should bypass specific physical obstacles—for Mitchell Slough, and that the Bitterroot Conservation District had taken no action on the request, Howell asked to review the conservation district's full file on the slough. Right on top he saw a copy of a letter informing a landowner that the district had determined Mitchell Slough was not a natural stream and required no 310 permits.

"I thought, 'Why didn't I know this? When was the meeting and why didn't they tell the public about this?'" Howell says. "A decision was made with no public input and no official meeting. I said, 'You just can't do something of such great public significance without first having a public process.'"

Shortly thereafter, Howell huddled with other concerned citizens and formed the Bitterroot River Protection Association (BRPA).

"It wasn't like I decided to champion stream access law and decided to take this thing on. It started over the process, wanting it to be a public process with open records," Howell said. "Then it became an involvement to save the status of the river channel. That was our bottom line—the environmental protection for the watersheds of Montana. Then it became a fishing access issue on top of that."

The BRPA sued in District Court, arguing that the conservation district did not have legal authority to determine the status of Mitchell Slough. That case became Mitchell Slough's first appearance before the Montana Supreme Court—which ruled that the conservation district could indeed determine whether the slough was natural or not.

The conservation district took the task more seriously this time, holding public hearings, examining thousands of pages of documents, deliberating for months, then deciding again that Mitchell Slough was not a natural stream.

Next, the BRPA appealed that decision in District Court. Chris Clancy drove to Missoula to file papers necessary for the FWP to join the suit with the BRPA. But before he could submit the paperwork, he received a last-minute phone call from the department's legal staff—then-Governor Judy Martz's administration ordered FWP to stay out of it.

In July of 2005, District Court Judge Ted Mizner heard lawyers for the Mitchell Slough landowners argue that the slough's flows are controlled by a 60-foot wide headgate and delivered by a 600-yard trench, dug and maintained by four ditch companies. Mitchell Slough's bed, the landowners' attorneys said, is several feet higher than the Bitterroot River, and water doesn't flow uphill without human engineering. The slough was an example of the "genius of man," without which it would dribble to dry, abandoned as the Bitterroot River augered westward across its valley bottom.

The facts were clearly in our favor," says Ken Siebel.

Siebel's side of the story begins in 1979, when he bought over 1,000 acres along the Bitterroot River. "My parents both worked in factories," Siebel says. "My mom put 25 bucks a week away—she made 26 bucks when she started and 32 when she finished—so I could go to college. And when I had the good fortune to be able to acquire this property, I certainly should have the right to invite people onto it. I had 65 or 70 people who would come on and hunt and many, many more who would fish. It wasn't like I kept it for my own private domain."

Siebel hired a stream rehab consultant and dramatically narrowed the slough's banks, making it deeper, cooler and able to scour itself free of silt. At considerable expense, he brought in boulders, cobble, rootwads, and logs to create top-notch habitat, enticing migratory fish to settle in year-round.

"All of a sudden the spawning really picked up," Siebel says. "We got the depth of the water right and got the movement right, and we created a really nice nursery for the Bitterroot. People spent millions of dollars doing this, and a lot of time. Would we have done any of that if we thought there would ever be public access? The answer is a resounding no. Privacy is the most important thing to all of us."

Siebel and the other landowners along Mitchell Slough don't begrudge Montanans their right to access public waterways. They just very firmly believe Mitchell Slough is not a public waterway.

"When we bought this place," Siebel says, "this was clearly, clearly private property. Our land is on the Bitterroot River, and people float through, and that's great. People duck hunt on the river, and I help retrieve the ducks that come down on our land. That's fine. The river we understand is public. But we've been really good stewards of this other property. We, collectively, have been great stewards—not good stewards, great stewards—and all we've gotten for it is bad publicity."

Plus a few bad apples.

"People who have come up and down the Mitchell have been very confrontational with some of the landowners. Very confrontational," Siebel says.

Lewis concurs. He's heard of Internet chat rooms where people write about wanting to defecate on his property or stand in his front yard and flip him off.

"The people who come down to fish aren't really neighborly, friendly fishermen," Lewis says. "They're belligerent. I've had my life threatened down there. I care a lot about the resource but the privacy issue is much more important."

The irony, both Siebel and Lewis contend, is that had they never launched their stream rehab projects, the Mitchell Slough court case would never have happened. "No one would have ever wanted to fish it. They wouldn't have even thought about coming on, because there was nothing there and they couldn't walk in it because they would have been in mud up to their knees."

Siebel's story proved persuasive in Judge Mizner's District Court. In a 2006 decision, Mizner said Mitchell Slough's water was diverted, an exemption in the stream access law. Mizner also wrote of "clear and convincing evidence that if man had not manipulated the waters of the Bitterroot River with the Tucker Headgate and other diversions and also excavated the channel of the Mitchell Slough, the Mitchell would no longer flow and it would most likely be a series of ancient, paleo channels connected by man." By Mizner's reasoning, human activities had altered the slough too dramatically to call it "natural" now. He saw no reason 310 or stream access law should apply.

But Michael Howell had seen a certified copy of the original 1872 survey of the area by the General Land Office, precursor to today's U.S. Geological Survey. Completed prior to Montana's statehood, the survey is the original document to which all subsequent surveys must refer. Due to its primacy, it's held in a locked vault in Billings.

The map and accompanying notes—a record of what the surveyor saw as he walked the section lines—clearly indicate a natural stream where Mitchell Slough flows today. The surveyor called it the "Right Fork of the St. Mary's Fork of the Bitterroot River."

"We took the points where that river crosses the section lines and we compared them to modern USGS maps," Howell says. "Of the 23 points on the original map, 21 correspond to contemporary maps." Howell says this proves the Mitchell Slough is fundamentally the same waterway that flowed—naturally—through the valley in 1872.

If Mizner's decision had stood, Howell says, "it would have rendered 310 permitting and stream access law worthless, except for pristine wilderness rivers. It would have removed every stream from protection, because they've all been altered. It was kind of an all or nothing deal at that point. We either had stream access or we didn't. We either had laws to protect integrity of our riparian areas and fisheries values or we did not."

The BRPA appealed Mizner's decision, leading to the return of the Mitchell Slough fracas to Montana's Supreme Court. A new governor, Brian Schweitzer, unleashed FWP, which enthusiastically joined the BRPA.

Hearing the case in October, 2007, the Supreme Court accepted as fact the landowners' successful arguments from District Court. The justices also considered testimony from FWP hydrologists that Mitchell Slough is fed at its headgate by a flow of 15 cubic feet of water per second, but that its volume swells to 300 cubic feet per second by the time it rejoins the river 16 miles downstream. While some of that water might be irrigation return, clearly much of it, attorneys for the BRPA and FWP argued, is natural spring or ground water.

In late November, 2008, the Supreme Court issued a 54-page opinion, voting 7-0 to overturn Mizner. Mitchell Slough would be subject to both 310 and stream access law.

The justices essentially agreed with Howell. Speaking for the unanimous court, Justice Jim Rice wrote, "...[T]he District Court's dictionary-based definition, which essentially requires a pristine river unaffected by humans in order to be deemed "natural," results in an absurdity: for many Montana waters, the [Stream Access Law] would prohibit the very access it was enacted to provide."

FWP's CHRIS CLANCY THINKS THAT WAS THE RIGHT DECISION. "The thing that concerns me is the precedent that would have been set if it was decided the other way. It's not uncommon in our work for a question to come up, is this a stream or isn't it?" Clancy says. "This decision gave us better guidance on what a stream is and the guidance was consistent with what I always thought a stream was."

Clancy says the decision prevented the creation of an entirely new class of water—a sort of natural-but-altered subset—that could be privatized and removed from both recreational access and public permitting processes.

But lost in the celebration by anglers and activists is a more prosaic reality. Mitchell Slough is by all accounts a fragile resource, maintained in its revitalized state by the work and resources of private individuals. Anglers and hunters accessing the slough still have to wade within the normal high water marks, almost ensuring that, in the stream's most productive stretches, people will be mucking through trout spawning beds.

Early in his career, Clancy studied the effects of angler activity on cutthroat spawning in a private spring creek in the Livingston area. That study indicated that wading in small streams could be significantly detrimental to spawning success.

Clancy acknowledges what Lewis and Siebel claim—unlimited access on Mitchell Slough could damage the resource. "It'll come down to how many people are on [the slough] and how accessible the spawning areas are. If you do get crowding on it, it can only handle so many anglers from a standpoint of disturbance."

Still, Clancy said the department has no plans to limit angler numbers on the slough.

This disappoints the landowners. "The resource is the key and the resource gets killed in this particular case," Siebel says. "We helped create a wonderful habitat and that will be destroyed. FWP doesn't give a crap about that. If they cared about the resource they would have been working with us all these years."

Even more discouraging for the future of the fishery has been the landowners' reaction. Not all the Mitchell Slough landowners—not even most of them—are interested in stream rehabilitation. But most of them guard their privacy.

"We had a landowner meeting," Lewis said. "Most of the neighbors don't care really about the fish, but they don't want people in their front yard. And we don't want shotguns in our front yard.

"So the consensus was, quit feeding the fishery. We're going to shut off the headgates like we're supposed to and without maintenance and without cleaning, the slough will slowly go back to the mud ditch it was."

And then nobody will care about accessing it.

Michael Howell agrees it's possible the unlimited access he fought for may doom Mitchell Slough. He trusts the agencies—FWP, specifically—to react appropriately and in time to prevent that.

If they don't, and the slough's conservation values are sacrificed, Howell says, the fight was worth it. "What happens to Mitchell Slough—like with a lot of important issues—what happens right there in that spot over time may not matter."

And in this way, the story of Mitchell Slough comes full circle. ▉

The Death of Tim Cahill

By Tim Cahill

Spring 2015

J UST YESTERDAY, I was standing out in my backyard in Livingston, Montana, throwing a tennis ball on the roof of my house. My dog raced along the side of the house, listening to the thump and roll of the ball, then caught it on the fly as it dropped near the garbage cans. Dexter the Dog trotted back and dropped the ball at my feet. There was a brief contemplative moment. It was unclear who enjoyed roof ball more: me or the dog. It was a very simple pleasure to be sure. But if it is possible to be happy mindlessly throwing a ball, I had to imagine that, yes, I was happy.

Now, frankly, Dex and I have been doing this for years. I had never thought of our game as one small component of a life well lived. I suppose that is because I had never died before—and then been resuscitated—as I had been just a few weeks earlier. The experience might have made a philosopher of a finer man. Me? I just thought, "I never realized how much I like roof ball."

My death experience happened in the Grand Canyon, on the Colorado River, at Lava Falls, the nastiest rapid on the river. There were 16 people in my party and it was the 14th day of the trip. We'd navigated the other rough stretches with some ease. Crystal, Hermit and Granite rapids were all behind us. Lava Falls was the last big one, the most challenging.

Our party beached our five rafts and numerous kayaks just before the rapid, in the roar of surging water echoing off rock walls. We had to shout to be heard as we walked up the steep trail on the north side of the river to scout the rapid. And there we stood, all of us, staring down at an anthology of the dangers a river can muster. There was a pourover at the top and it dropped into a huge hole which had at its tail an enormous wave curling back upriver. This meant a raft or kayak or swimmer caught in the hole could end up endlessly circulating in a process some call being "Maytagged."

There were great curling waves to the right and the current, in places, jumped 10 feet in the air. Toward the bottom of the right side, the flow broke around a monolithic rock maybe 40 feet high. You didn't want to hit that rock. The river would crush you and hold you there. It's called being "postage stamped."

No, you'd want to avoid the top pourover by entering right, then you'd pull left because, near the bottom of the rapid, was another large hole, a last wily Maytag lying in wait. So it was abundantly clear that a river craft would have to pull very hard left to avoid the rock and then even harder left to skirt the hole near the bottom of Lava Falls.

We were done scouting but we all just stood there for another 20 minutes, staring and, in my case, feeling a little stunned. No one spoke much. I didn't know my team well, but I had noticed that while they sometimes cursed, they did so infrequently and appropriately. I liked that about them and, consequently, was making an effort to speak with a certain civility. So I looked down at the rapid that would kill me in about 15 minutes and whispered, "Gol dang!"

BACK IN OCTOBER OF LAST YEAR, I was invited on a private rafting trip though the Grand Canyon. I'd never been there but it was a place I had been endlessly told—you'll excuse me—of heart-stopping beauty. I did not know any of the other 15 river runners except for Harry Butler, the younger brother of a guy I hung out with in high school in Waukesha, Wisconsin. All the other participants were also from Wisconsin; they either lived there, or had some cheese-encrusted association with the state.

Harry was a cross-country skier and avid kayaker. We'd talked about that a bit when I had returned to Wisconsin. So, presumably, he figured that, even though I'd lived in Montana for 40 years, I might still understand Wisconsin folks (beer, cheese, Green Bay Packers). Moreover, he knew I'd spent almost 40 years traveling overseas, often in rough conditions, and consequently might even know what I was doing on a river trip. So when someone dropped out of this trip at the last minute, I was an obvious person to call: a guy who might be able to carve out the time and get his poop in a pile in 10 days.

Most of the party had kayaks, and I quickly realized that the five rafts were support for the kayaks. We—the rafters—would carry food and tents and sleeping bags. I was paired off with Bill Hobbins, who welcomed me with the information that, at 71, I was the oldest guy on the trip, an honor that had previously been his.

Bill did not inspire immediate confidence. "Ah, I don't know what I'm doing here," he said. Then he proceeded to load the raft, strapping down gear and rearranging things in such a way that we'd lose nothing if the raft flipped. Over the next few days, Bill proved to be a master. The raft packing was arduous and Bill wanted to do it himself. He was the captain of our raft and felt responsible for the gear. In the dry Arizona air, securing the gear with webbing straps and pulling them tight made his fingertips bleed. No matter. That's what Super Glue is for.

And then we were out on the river. The kayakers, to my untrained eye, seemed insanely talented. They spoke of rivers they'd run in the Midwest and the South and the West. Many had kayaked in Central and South America. They talked kayaking at a length that I found required several strong shots of Scotch for me to tolerate. After a few days, I asked the group whether they might be considered "elite." "Hardly," Harry said and there were some muffled chuckles at the idea. The talk turned to truly great kayakers they'd either known or seen. But they weren't fooling me: these guys were great in kayaks, but they weren't going to say it because cheeseheads don't brag on themselves.

My raft mate Bill Hobbins, for instance, who originally presented himself as a sort of doofus, was, in fact, both tough and omni-competent. It took days to drag all this out of him, but the guy was a kayaker, an open boat captain, a record breaking ice-boater, a guy who was offered a full ride to play hockey at the University of Wisconsin (he turned it down), a boxer and a judo instructor. And, though he was dyslexic, he held a master's degree in science and could read the river like a book, a skill he tried his best to help me learn.

It was a winter trip—from the end of November to mid-December— and the temperature at night sometimes dropped into the 20s. In the daytime, on the water, the temperatures might rise into the 50s or even hit the low 70s in the hour or so the sun peeked over the narrow rim of the canyon. Everyone wore dry suits, waterproof material secured by tight wrist and ankle bands and even tighter neck bands. I did not. I can't stand dry suits. The neck bands, called gaskets, choke me. I know they can be cut and adjusted, but they still choke me. I wore good waterproof gear over heavy fleece worn over expedition weight underwear. My dry suit languished in the bottom of my dry bag.

I guess I thought I was smart. The others were always pulling off the tops of their dry suits in the warmth of the sun or when they got overheated while paddling or rowing. I was perfectly comfortable, and in those times when I caught a chill, it was easy enough to row for an hour and work up a sweat.

But rowing was, in fact, more difficult than I'd imagined, even in the slower water. While I'm perfectly at ease rowing a fishing boat down the Yellowstone near Livingston, the Colorado was another matter altogether. The volume of water was astounding, as were the eddies. You could get trapped in an eddy and it might take 10 minutes of hard pulling to get back into the main current.

And that main current was something. Rivers are generally rated on an ascending scale of difficulty from 1 to 6, but the Colorado has its own system, and its rapids are rated 1 to 10. I could take rough water labeled 3 or 4 easily enough, but the 5s made me a little queasy and the one 6 I navigated was scary enough that I turned the rest of them over to Bill.

Then, on the 14th day, we found ourselves on a hillside, scouting Lava Falls, the rapid rated the highest on the river, a 9, and I just stood there, dumbfounded, looking down at all that hyperbolic water. "Holy cats," I muttered.

THE KAYAKS WENT THROUGH FIRST AND TOOK UP RESCUE POSITIONS NEAR the tail of the rapid. John McConville took the right entrance and pulled left neatly. Steve Smits followed. Justin Kleberg hit it perfectly and so did Dan LaHam. Four rafts through the rapids, all waiting for Bill and me.

I had stripped off my fleece, reasoning that if I had to swim, I didn't want a heavy jacket weighing me down. It may have been simultaneously the stupidest and smartest thing I did that day. Bill entered the rapid to the right and immediately pulled left. I was kneeling in the bow, holding the perimeter line. A wave curled up under the boat on the right and I "highsided" by leaning into it. Later, I saw a video of that run, shot from the bank by a group that followed us down the river. In the video some nasty bit of rogue hydraulics came up from the left and tipped the raft to the right. And all of a sudden I was in the water. At the top of Lava Falls. There was a lot more mean water below. This, I thought, does not bode well.

The video shows Bill being tossed sideways and struggling to regain the oars, which he did fairly quickly. But he couldn't see me and chose not to row and risk hitting me, probably in the head. An unconscious swimmer is unlikely to survive. Deciding not to row meant Bill hit the hole at the bottom of Lava Falls and was flung some distance to the right and out of the hole. A kayak picked him up in less than a minute. The raft made it through upright.

Meanwhile, I was somewhere in the rapid, under the water. I've studied the video frame by frame and have never seen even a hint of my blue rain gear. Anywhere. I know I must have been pretty deep despite my life jacket, because I recall looking up at a 10-foot-wide round hole. The surface seemed about 15 feet above and the center of the hole was so calm that I could see through it to the blue Arizona sky.

I swam toward the surface, glad that I wasn't weighted down with fleece. The rapid didn't much scare me. I swam varsity at the University of Wisconsin for four years. Even set a pool record at Notre Dame. (They tell me it lasted about a week.) In any case, I was a few feet from the surface when the hole started to fall apart in various shining ovals that dropped off on the downstream side while the rest of the surface looked like large shards of glass exploding in slow motion. It felt like swimming through a shining monochromatic kaleidoscope and I found myself thinking, "This is really kind of pretty."

And then the water dropped, as off a cliff, and I felt myself falling in air. That gave me a needed breath and I continued to fight my way through the shards of the kaleidoscope. I had no idea where I was in the rapid, but I wanted to thread the needle between the rock and the hole at the bottom. Perhaps I made it. In any case, I surfaced in the tail of the rapid where I managed to grab a rescue kayak. I don't know who was paddling, but I grabbed a back handle and kicked hard. The water was still rough and a dead weight on the back of a kayak will sink it.

The kayak pulled to an eddy where a raft was waiting. I grabbed the perimeter line, gasping for breath. When I looked downriver, another rescue raft, pushed by the eddy, was coming in fast. Too fast. These rafts are 18 feet long and weigh a couple thousand pounds. I didn't want to get crushed between them. So I ducked under and swam. But, moronically, I swam the wrong way.

Exhausted and disoriented, I swam against the strong current of the eddy. That meant I was all but trapped under the second boat. I recall taking a large involuntary breath of river water and thinking, "Well, that wasn't so bad."

The second involuntary breath was less pleasant. There may have been a third. All I know is that I came out from under the raft and Justin Kleberg and Rachel Butler yanked me into the bow where I lay gasping like a freshly landed tuna.

Justin rowed across the river to a large area called Tequila Beach, where groups that run Lava Falls typically stop to celebrate. I crawled off the raft and walked 15 or 20 steps over the sand. Roy Crimmins, a guy who'd paddled the whole river in an abbreviated canoe, handed me a beer. I sat down, passed out and died.

WHAT COMES NEXT I ONLY KNOW FROM WHAT I'VE BEEN TOLD. My boat mates said that I stopped breathing, turned blue, and then, they said, they lost my pulse altogether. The team sprang into action. They cut my life vest off with knives. Justin Kleberg, a wilderness EMT, started CPR. After 30 chest compressions, Steve Smits, a registered nurse, drew two rescue breaths and Kleberg started compressions again. Dan LaHam, at my arm, shook his head. Still no pulse.

Sometime during the sixth round of CPR, Bill Hobbins saw my eyelids flutter. "C'mon, C'mon, C'mon," he shouted. LaHam said he could feel a pulse. And then it was getting stronger.

And I woke to someone sitting on my stomach pushing my sternum three quarters of the way to my backbone. Was that the sound of my ribs cracking? What the hell?

Rachel Butler says, "You roared. It must have been some kind of rage to live. It was loud." I recall trying to wrestle Justin off of me and throwing a few ineffectual punches. "It took seven of us to hold you down," Bill Hobbins said.

And when I looked up at the people I'd just punched, I saw men and women wiping away tears. This seemed an overreaction. At the time, I thought I'd simply passed out for a bit. But up top, they'd seen a man die and then be brought back to life. The group that followed us was there as well. They'd run the rapid without incident. But this place had a special meaning for them: a friend of theirs had died kayaking Lava Falls and they were there to celebrate his life. Now, they'd seen another man go down. But suddenly that man was back, breathing and alive. Everyone was deeply moved. It didn't make any sense to me.

A National Park Service helicopter, contacted by satellite phone, was on the way. Since I didn't know my heart had stopped, it seemed like a waste of resources. The helicopter landed, a paramedic did a quick examination, turned to my team and said, "You guys saved a life today." I thought, "They did?"

I have to say that a helicopter ride over the Grand Canyon isn't much of a treat if you're lying on your back in a neck brace, staring at the ceiling. I was taken to the Heart and Vascular Center of Northern Arizona, in Flagstaff, where I was put into intensive care. I felt fine, except that Justin had done the CPR correctly and fractured a lot of ribs. I was coming to the realization that my heart had actually stopped for several minutes. I'd died. Tests, however, showed that I hadn't had a heart attack. Perhaps I'd simply drowned.

The care at the hospital was superb and I got to talk to a lot of doctors and nurses who simply wanted to hear my story. It seems that CPR isn't very effective in cases of cardiac arrest. There is something like a single digit percent of success. What the doctors said, what the nurses said, was that my recovery on Tequila Beach was "a miracle."

I began thinking of my boat mates as the "Colorado River Miracle Team." But miracle or not, I still didn't know what had happened. I have a theory though. The water was about 45 degrees. And I was swimming in it hard for 20 minutes, or so it seemed. In thin rain gear and without fleece. So there may have been a hypothermic reaction. I wasn't there for the exciting part (because I was unconscious), but I believe I may have gone into what is called the mammalian diving reflex, a condition in which the heart slows down in cold water. Blood, needed by internal organs, is shunted away from the hands and feet. Breathing slows and sometimes stops.

That all made sense, but then how I was able to get out of the water and walk?

I guess I'm just going to have to call it a miracle and live with that.

Still, I feel a little guilty about it all. I have little or no emotional investment in my death and resurrection. I wasn't there, after all. Intellectually, I wish I felt compelled to feed the homeless or cure cancer. To somehow devote my life to doing good works. But no, about the only thing I got out of the experience is a realization that I like to play roof ball with my dog.

What can I say? The river was deep, the guy in it was shallow. ◼

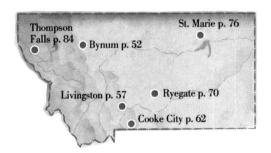

LIVING LOCAL

Small-town living.
It's all over the map.

No Child Not Dancing

By Alan Kesselheim

Summer 2014

FIRST THING IN THE MORNING. All 20 students at the Bynum school, just north of Choteau, gather in the old Methodist Church, now serving as the gymnasium, next to the two-story school building. Teacher Susan Luinstra cues up an ancient 78 vinyl LP on the equally ancient phonograph, and scratchy music from the 1930s fills the restless space—"Sally Goodin'," "Waltz With Me Darling," "You Are My Sunshine."

Shoes off, the kids pair up. Seventh-grade boys with third-grade girls, farm kids and kids from town. If there aren't enough boys to go around, girls join up. There is no awkward energy. They hold hands casually. Then they break into polka, the schottische, a waltz. The room warms up. The students, from first grade to eighth, glide and slide and hop and twirl around the small space. There is laughter. A sixth-grader asks Luinstra to dance and spins her in a giddy waltz.

Outside, the high plains swell toward the sunrise, the lonely cottonwood ribbon of Muddy Creek winds downhill, and the Rocky Mountain Front looms in the western sky like a tidal wave of rock about to crest. For the first hour of the school day, most every school day, music is the lesson plan, as it has been since the 1930s.

"You never know what kind of morning kids are having," Luinstra says. "But whatever you're dealing with, after you've danced for a while, it's all gone."

Next to the front door of the school building a black plaque reads, "In Memory of Mr. [Ira] Perkins— 1933–1986." In the corners of the plaque, the symbols of traditional school themes, Bynum-style—a trumpet, a book, a couple dancing, and a paddle. It is his legacy, and his inspiration, that has carried on for generations at this tiny, off-the-radar rural school. It offers a model that schools everywhere might take note of.

Perkins came to Bynum from west of Lewistown in the midst of the Great Depression. At that time, Bynum was a bustling town. The railroad ended there. There were three churches, grocery and hardware stores, hotels and homes. Settlers came and went. People used Bynum as a jumping off point and service center. Community dances were common and well attended.

Early in his time at the school, Perkins noticed a social phenomenon. When he went to the community hall dances, he watched as young people who knew how to dance engaged with older people, comfortable in the social atmosphere, having fun. He also saw the kids who didn't know how to dance. They were the ones out back smoking cigarettes, estranged from the community energy.

He thought about that for a time, then he took action. Perkins established a school mandate, much like the current spate of No Child Left Behind edicts. In Perkin's case, it was a single-school initiative, and, at first glance, it had nothing to do with the 3 Rs or keeping pace with global educational standards. Every student at the Bynum School would dance, Perkins vowed. Every student would also play an instrument and sing.

Turns out that Perkin's brainstorm had that magical quality of a simple idea with profound, long-lasting effects. And it stuck, in large measure, because of the ferocity of Perkins' commitment.

Perkins personally waxed the wood dance floor to a slippery, sometimes hazardous, shine. He rounded up instruments, solicited donations, convinced the school board, directed the band, entered students in local singing contests. Kids at bigger schools scoffed at the overalls of the Bynum country bumpkins, until they heard them perform. The fancy outfits sported by other schools paled in the face of Bynum's four-part harmony. Perkins, equal doses inspirational leader and dictator, demanded perfection and enforced discipline.

Luinstra first started teaching at Bynum in 1974, and overlapped with Perkins for five of her years there.

"Mr. Perkins came from a poor background," Luinstra says. "He was very sensitive about treating everyone equally."

"At the same time, he wasn't the easiest personality to get along with," she continues. "He could be pretty cantankerous, but we always managed."

"I didn't know how to dance when I came," she says. "Ira treated me just like one of the kids. 'You take Susan and teach her to dance,' he told one of the students. Talk about humbling!"

For more than 50 years, Perkins' musical tradition grew and flourished. The town of Bynum collapsed once the railroad pushed on. People moved houses away, businesses closed. Today there are a handful of residents, a post office, a bar, a dinosaur museum. The school remains the largest structure and most vibrant feature of the community.

"We had as few as four students in 2004," Luinstra says. "I was scared that year. In the '90s we had as many as 53. One year we had 12 girls and two boys."

"We are family here," Luinstra emphasizes. "When I go to other schools it makes me sad to see how uncomfortable some kids are in their own skins, and how awkward it is between sexes. If there were assessments for respect and cooperation and empathy, our kids would be off the charts.

"I still get people coming by who graduated 20 years ago and say that the most important things they learned were at Bynum School. Many of our students come from ranches miles away, or because their needs aren't met at the bigger schools, or because parents want them exposed to this musical tradition. Quite a few of those former students are still playing instruments, dancing, joining local bands."

Yazmin Bogden, a fourth grader from a farm near Choteau, is a case in point. She transferred to Bynum from a neighboring school district after having difficulty. She wears a purple coat and matching glasses, has an air of confidence and poise about her.

"My favorite dances are the 1-2 and then the waltz," she says.

"Music and dance are the best things we do," Luinstra adds. "I don't have the data, but I know it in my bones. The arts bring the whole child together. Dance and music exercise different parts of the brain, make connections work better. Students are comfortable with each other here as a direct result."

Luinstra and primary grades teacher Abby Armstrong combine to prepare Bynum students for high school and beyond. Their classrooms are a mix of old and new. The Palmer method alphabet is displayed on the wall, but there are also computer terminals and iPads. Old encyclopedia sets and wall maps combine with YouTube videos in lesson plans. Guitars, fiddles, brass instruments are always close to hand. Fiddles were donated by a music store in Great Falls. Trumpets were handed down from former students.

"We go hard until lunch," Luinstra says, "then we have a chat break. We talk about local news, or something I heard on NPR. If something's going well, we can let it go on. If things aren't going well, we can always push the desks back and do a little dancing or sing something to get back on track."

"It isn't that we don't have problems," Luinstra emphasizes. "We struggle with budgets, with personality conflicts, the same as any school. There are years when the music program fades, and others when it is really strong. Quite a few of our students come because they have social challenges or learning difficulties in different schools. Here they get individual attention, and they get the social acceptance that naturally comes when you interact the way we do. After you polka with someone in the morning, it's a lot harder to be mean to them on the playground."

Bailey Deshner, now in seventh grade, has attended Bynum School since second grade. She is an accomplished fiddle player, likes the schottische. Her family lives on the outskirts of Bynum.

"Her family enrolled her in Bynum specifically because of the music and other enrichment programs," Luinstra points out.

"Music is at the core of our school. We were so lucky to have had Ira Perkins," Luinstra continues. "But our main goal is to prepare our kids for their futures. To my knowledge, we've only had one student from Bynum drop out of high school."

ONE JANUARY DAY IN 2014, Rab Cummings, Adam Nordell and Johanna Davis come to Bynum to conduct a dance workshop. A busload of students from Choteau arrives after lunch.

"This Methodist Church was donated to the school," Cummings tells me. "It came with a stipulation that there would be no public dancing." Fortunately, school officials have negotiated an exemption from that edict.

At first the room is cold. The kids shuffle awkwardly, don't mingle much. Cummings introduces the music and dances. "These dances have been going on for hundreds of years," he tells the students. "They still exist for the same reasons they always did—to have fun, to learn and teach each other, to make friends."

Nordell (guitar, feet, vocals) and Davis (fiddle, feet, vocals), the duo who make up Sassafrass Stomp, dial up a tune, their instruments accompanied by the slap of shoe leather. Cummings starts to call an ancient dance full of swings and promenades and dosi-does. At first the kids are shy, embarrassed when they make mistakes. The students from Choteau take cues from the Bynum kids.

"We travel all around Montana putting on workshops," Cummings tells me, during a break. "Usually, when we show up at a school like this, it's like we've landed from Mars. In Bynum, it's just another day with some new dances thrown in."

Slowly the awkward energy melts. The room warms. Teachers join in. Personalities come out. For this afternoon, everything else in life recedes.

When it's over, the last couple sashays down the lines of dancers. A boy from Choteau does an exuberant belly slide finish on the slippery floor.

Cummings and the musicians pack up their gear. The Choteau kids climb back on the bus and head south. But the Bynum dancers won't leave. In fact, it is as if they have been waiting for this moment. They pull out the old trusty phonograph, the box of vinyl, start dropping the needle on records that have played in Bynum for more than two generations.

Whatever strained energy existed while the other school visited soon evaporates. Luinstra watches her students do the old polkas and waltzes.

"The first, most important thing is to love the music," she says. "We're winging it a lot of the time, figuring it out as we go. It's all so old and corny, but there is always this joy. And you realize none of the rest matters." ◀

Livingston, My Kind of Town

By Scott McMillion

Fall 2011

WHEN THE PREACHER TOLD MY MOTHER THAT DOCTRINE WOULDN'T allow my sister to join a dubious outfit like the Girl Scouts, the man learned something about my mother, who shut the door on that building and left it closed. And every time I walk past that church—it's a handsome structure with a new addition, so I guess they did fine without us—it reminds me why I so rarely tried to tell my mother what to do.

A busy supermarket stands just up the street, but there used to be a root beer stand there, which churns memories of my grandmother, generally a soft touch for a nickel to buy a frosty mug.

Around the corner is the tiny house Mom rented when she first moved us into town after her divorce, right across the street from the school where she taught first grade, the place where they told her that women teachers weren't worth as much money as men, a policy that turned her into a lifelong union member. Like I said, there wasn't much point in trying to tell her no.

On the other end of town, I often pass the house where I got my first real kiss. Though a passive player in that enterprise, and frankly a pretty surprised one, I cannot forget that moment. The taste of lips and the texture of tongue can sound pretty sour to the early adolescent mind, but Debby Sanders converted me.

When John Lennon died a few years later, I was sitting in a house on the corner of F and Geyser, watching TV with the sound off and the stereo turned up. It took a couple of minutes for the reality to soak through the fog.

These are the kind of ghosts I find on my daily walks around Livingston, Montana, my home town.

For a place with only about 7,000 people, Livingston is pretty well known. Celebrities hang around sometimes, and the scenery astounds. Three mountain ranges bulk up here, serving as a stop sign for the prairies that march all the way from Chicago. Millions of tourists pass through, usually on their way to Yellowstone Park, just up the road. They fill the bars and restaurants, at least in the summer, and they rarely cause much trouble. On the edge of town, the Yellowstone River shoulders by, mostly a delight and sometimes a menace but always a marvel, untamed in spite of us. We have an odd religious sect up the valley, but they learned to blend in, mostly, after doomsday passed without trumpets or bombs. We've got wildlife all over the place, from gophers to grizzly bears, though the latter shuns us, mostly. And we have our famous wind, the kind of gusts that roll semi trailers and motor homes, and once even a train, out by the truck stop.

Democrats and Republicans grab pretty even shares of the electorate, and we've learned to tolerate, even embrace, our kooks and eccentrics. Serious crime comes seldom enough that, when it does, it generally makes the front page of our afternoon paper. Still, two sheriff's deputies had to kill a man last winter. We live in the world.

A Google dump could tell you most of this. But it can't tell you who we are. That's what the ghosts are for, if you listen to them.

I've spent most of my life here, so I see these ghosts a lot. They don't pull at me, or make me particularly sad or happy. They just exist, like gravity, issuing reminders and providing weight. I'm pretty friendly with most of them.

It wasn't always like this. They used to scare the bejeebers out of me.

A generation ago, I returned to Livingston after a long stint of adventuring in foreign places, melting into the swarm of Asian cities, body surfing in New Zealand, learning that a dead chicken might not be worth much in a village market but can soar in value if you've run it over with a motorcycle.

I think the process of coming home started to percolate in Seoul, Korea, on a sunny afternoon when a little bird flitted over my head, and its shadow made me hit the deck. There had been riots, and I thought somebody was aiming a stone at me. Slogging through tear gas makes for a vivid memory, but what really struck me, after I regained my feet, was the rarity of birds in that city, that the flutter of wings could startle like that.

It took a while to come home for good, partly because when I got here, I found the ghosts, and they rattled me, made my feet itch for more travel. It seemed they were everywhere, peeking around corners, lifting a curtain to watch me pass, reminding me of their stories. Mrs. Working was a crabby woman, impossible to satisfy, while her neighbor, Mr. Hokanson, could always spare a minute for a kid. A giant boy named Phillip sat next to me in second grade and couldn't speak a word, but a shared crayon always made him smile. He liked the red ones. Leo Schaeffer had 11 kids of his own but loved an apple fight with the neighborhood hooligans. Willie Moffett, handsome and impish, joined the Marine Corps and I never saw him again. Perry Herbst disappeared, too. By the time Kenny Fleming died, he didn't add much weight at all to the first coffin I ever carried. I have no idea what happened to Debby Sanders, she of that first kiss.

In my vagabond years, I thought the best stories lay in unknown and exotic places, so that's where I sought them. Back home, the tables turned and the stories sought me, popping up everywhere, and I didn't know that familiarity could frighten so.

It took a while, but I learned to appreciate the stories, to realize they weren't assaulting me. Rather, they were part of me. Midge Taylor gave good advice to a lonesome young man at her cluttered table, and seeing her house on Ninth Street still provides a flicker of warmth. Mickey Livermore's giant fist taught me to watch my mouth. The bowling alley where I played pinball is now a mental health center.

Don't get me wrong. I'm fully capable of ignoring these ghosts, especially if I'm in a hurry or preoccupied. And I think most people have similar memories, but most people don't live in the town where they grew up, so their ghosts, like most things, suffer the erosion of time and distance.

My ghosts don't seem to fade, especially since, in recent years, I've been walking more, trying to wrestle back the middle-aged flab. And that means the ghosts get a better crack at me, a bigger share of my attention. They've taught me to see their stories as a sort of yardstick, a measurement of how things change.

On M Street, I remember how the kids ostracized Dolly McNeill, and I wonder if the modern ways of running schools could have nipped that in the bud. On Yellowstone Street, I recall the crush I had on Jill Glenn, the most beautiful girl I'd ever seen, and I wonder: If I had mustered the nerve to speak to her, would her memory remain so precious? Up by Winans School, I remember the satisfaction I felt when Benjie Schweniger knocked the snot out of the worst bully in junior high school. On Eighth Street, I remember the woman they called Dirty Mary, who raided garbage cans for food and suffered endless taunts. We didn't have a mental health center then, or a food bank either, though we probably needed both.

On some blocks, I can name somebody who lived in every house at some point in time. But on those same blocks, I often can't name anybody who lives there now. So I wonder: Do they know the stories of their homes? Would they care?

A great, scary, hairy man used to sit on his porch on the corner of Eighth and Clark streets, wearing a T-shirt and scowling at the summer hubbub. My friend Dave Eaton lives there now. He'd probably laugh at that story. But what about the house on F Street where a man impregnated his wife's 12-year-old daughter, with his wife's full cooperation? Somebody lives there now. The yard is neat, the dog barks in a friendly way, a tricycle is stowed on the porch and the walks are shoveled. I hope that reflects something good inside the house. So I'm not about to go knock on that door and spill those particular beans.

But the ghosts know. Like me, they've watched things change. They've watched our cruelties and our charity. They've watched us bicker over politics and they've watched us come together when the river floods or a house burns or cancer strikes. They've watched schools close down and new banks open up. They know that Livingston has more wealthy people now and fewer children, and I hope they see that there's something off kilter in that demographic.

This town has changed in so many ways. Most of the railroad jobs are gone and we have a dozen art galleries. The neighborhood grocery stores closed up ages ago, but we have better food now. A bin of avocados or a jar of kimchi no longer puzzles people and tuna doesn't have to come in a can. In many ways, I like my town better now. It's more open-minded and more generous, I think. We've certainly become more cosmopolitan, with creative people from all over the world coming through, some of them planting roots and living out stories that will be somebody else's ghosts someday.

But I'm glad my own ghosts are still here, the old ones telling their stories, reminding me of people now gone, people who died or chased a dream or maybe just found a job somewhere else.

They're okay, these ghosts. I'm used to them now. They can walk with me any time. ◢

Chilling in Cooke City

By Jeff Hull

Spring 2012

OOKE CITY, a one-horse, 140-horsepower town in the winter, is both one of the oldest settlements in Montana and one of the youngest. It has been continually occupied since 1870, but hardly anybody in town is second-generation. With few exceptions, most of the 100 or so people who live in Cooke City year-round arrived a decade or two ago, and, if history holds true, most of them will be gone a decade or two from now.

"You make a lot of friends here. But none of them are permanent," says Betty Sommers, 70 years old and Cooke City's longest continual resident.

Blame it on geography and geology. Cooke City is an isolated hamlet squeezed in a tight, high valley (over 7,000 feet) among towering peaks, surrounded by a sea of wilderness.

Those peaks, Baronette, Thunderer, Republic and Wolverine, rise to 10,000 feet, raking moisture from winter cold fronts. Living in Cooke City in winter is like living in a snow globe that somebody casually shakes almost every day.

Betty grew up on a homestead between Belfry and Bridger. She came to Cooke City to work in the summer of 1958, just before her senior year in high school.

"I made 50 cents an hour cleaning rooms," she remembers. "I went home with $250 that summer. More money than I'd ever seen in my life."

That summer she met Bill Sommers, a young outfitter whose family owned a motel in town, and after she graduated high school she married him and moved to the mountains for good, spending her first winter in Cooke City in 1959. For most of the early winters, Betty and Bill had a ball. "We played in the snow," she says. "After hunting season there was no way to make any money here. I like to snowmobile. I like ice fishing. When I was younger, I liked to ski and snowshoe and all the sports people do."

To Betty, the Cooke City area was a kind of wonderland. The danger of recreating in avalanche-prone mountains in the winter or fishing creeks frequented by grizzly bears in the summer never phased her. "You make sure you can take care of yourself and don't do anything stupid and you probably won't get in any trouble," Betty says. "I certainly never felt I was in any danger. You think about what you do. Knowing the country helps."

Betty raised her two children in Cooke City. Her daughter came home from the hospital by snowmobile. She can't imagine a better place to live, even though she remembers times when she'd have to shovel snow six times in one day, just to keep a passage open to her house. "You'd have had to live the life to know how much fun it was," Betty says. "Not many people would go back to their childhoods and do everything all over again just the way they did it the first time. I would do that in a heartbeat."

COOKE CITY BEGAN IN 1870 WHEN THREE PROSPECTORS— Adam "Horn" Miller, A. Bart Henderson and Ed Hibbard—struck gold. The three men staked claims and set up residences, despite knowing they were, technically, trespassing on what was then the Crow Indian Reservation.

Even by western mine camp standards, the outpost, first known as Shoo-fly, was remote in the 1870s—130 miles from the nearest settlement (Bozeman) and sealed off in winter by up to 30 feet of snow. Still, a collection of lives gathered here, chiseling the landscape in search of lead, copper, silver and gold. Eventually two smelters opened, and five sawmills, and the population swelled to nearly 1,000 summertime residents.

Miners eventually changed the town's name to Cooke City, flirtatiously naming it after a major player in the Northern Pacific railroad, hoping the railroad would lay a spur line to their claims. It would be hard to overstate the importance on a national scale of the man for whom the town was ultimately named. Jay Cooke, the son of a frontier lawyer from Sandusky, Ohio, rose to national prominence when he funded the Union's war effort in the Civil War, raising nearly $1 billion (in 1864 dollars) by pioneering the practice of selling bonds to the public.

Cooke then financed the building of the nation's transcontinental railroads. In the five years between 1868 and 1873, except for agriculture, railroads employed more Americans than any other business. Cooke's final turn on the national stage was less glorious. He triggered the Panic of 1873—which, until 1930, was known as the "Great Depression." When Cooke's ability to service his heavy investment in the Northern Pacific Railroad abruptly collapsed, banks fell like dominoes. The New York Stock Exchange closed for 10 days. In the next three years the unemployment rate would reach 14 percent. Cooke himself was forced into bankruptcy (though by the time he died, he had, through investment in silver mining, become a wealthy man again).

Prior to his bankruptcy, Cooke had been a vocal proponent of the foundation of Yellowstone National Park. Hoping to monopolize the tourist trade and other concessions—and receive private land titles within the proposed park—for his rail line, Cooke underwrote an East Coast lecture series by Nathaniel Langford. Langford was one of Yellowstone's explorers who became the park's first superintendent. Cooke also funded artist Thomas Moran's inclusion in the Hayden survey of 1871, making Yellowstone famous among people who had never seen its wonders. Moran's renowned painting of the Grand Canyon of the Yellowstone was unveiled in Washington at a Cooke-sponsored event in advance of a Congressional vote on legislation enabling the park's existence. "The press—the literati—the artists—all the rich people" came to view Moran's 7-by-12-foot canvas, according to the New York Tribune.

If Yellowstone owes its existence partly to Jay Cooke, today's Cooke City owes its continued existence to Yellowstone and the two national forests that surround it. Cooke City is a street of hotels, restaurants, and a couple of gas stations, backed by a few blocks of log structures and heavily insulated trailers. The mountains don't leave room for much else. It's a recreation town, dependent almost wholly on tourism, and in the winter, most of that tourism occurs on sleds. The winter soundtrack to Cooke City is similar to that of other mountain towns—chickadees chiming, boots squeaking on cold snow, the crackling of burning wood. But all of it is accompaniment to the angry-bee whine of snowmobiles.

I F YOU VISIT COOKE CITY IN THE WINTER, chances are somebody has just died, or somebody is about to die, or somebody's life is in danger and needs to be saved. Rescue is a fact of life here, in country that is both breathtakingly rugged and one of the nation's favorite playgrounds for high-risk adrenaline-addled activities like snowmobiling and back-country skiing. It's a rare winter that the Cooke City search and rescue team doesn't scramble out for compelling, spur-of-the-moment, life-and-death operations. That's life here in winter—long stretches of quiet time trudging through snow removal and visiting with neighbors over hot coffee, and then sudden, gut-wrenching need.

Jan Gaertner is part of the search and rescue team and the volunteer emergency medical service. Last winter she resuscitated a patient who had died in the ambulance, using defibrillator paddles.

"That's an incredible feeling," she says. "I was high on life for two weeks after that."

Jan, with her husband Leo, operates Buns N Beds, a restaurant and rental cabins. Rescuing people is a bit of an obligation when you live in a place like Cooke City, and Jan takes her role seriously.

"We're very proactive as far as training and knowledge, and our survival rate is pretty high because we have really good medics," says Jan, a ginger-haired woman, wearing rimless glasses over dusky blue eyes. She's animated by talking about rescue and the EMS.

"We do [avalanche] beacon training where someone will throw a beacon in a plastic bag, toss it out in the snow and say, 'OK guys, you've got 15 minutes to find it'," Jan says. She understands that adrenaline makes people do stupid things. But, like most people in Cooke City, Jan isn't judgmental about those who come here to have fun. "You can perish doing any sport," she says. "Even people who are doing things right can get in trouble."

Jan and Leo met in Chicago and worked in the hotel industry for years, landing in Billings. They used to drink coffee with a couple of guys who talked about snowmobiling in Cooke City. You have to go over the Beartooth Pass, the men told them.

"We came over the pass and we were in awe," Jan says.

The pass, the Beartooth Highway, is many people's introduction to Cooke City. A marvel of civil engineering and a monument of natural splendor, the highway delivers thousands of visitors to Cooke City—when it's open. When it's not, which is the majority of the year, there's only one road out of town, through Yellowstone on an ice-sheeted, bison-studded

56-mile drive to Gardiner. And then you're in Gardiner, still over 50 miles from Livingston and 80 miles from Bozeman, where most people go to "town" in winter.

Which is part of the reason Jan and Leo will leave Cooke City soon —that and winters and snow removal and Jan's progressively worsening arthritis. "I fell in love with the summers here," Jan says. "The seasons are totally different, two different worlds. Winter is very, very long."

B UNS N BEDS, it should be said, is one of several truly great places to eat in Cooke City, an oddity even for a tourist town of this size. Buns N Beds isn't fancy French dining, but everything you order is hearty and delicious. Bearclaw Bob's Café—where you would be a fool not to order the sour cream pecan cake—is another great place to eat, and while you're there you might stock up on snowmobile boots, goggles, engine oil and avalanche beacons.

The Bistro, just across the street and down a ways, actually is fancy French dining. Well, not fancy-schmancy, but French—it's one of the few places in Montana you can order escargot, which is, owner Richard Ducrot says, a surprisingly popular menu item.

Ducrot came to Cooke City from Cannes by way of the Caribbean island of Saint Maarten. Ducrot grew up in the restaurant business in France before opening a restaurant in Saint Maarten. He also grew up fishing. During off-season in the Caribbean—summer in Montana—Ducrot and his wife wandered into Cooke City, loved the place and arranged to move. In 1996 they bought some rental cabins for income, and in 1999 they sold the cabins to open The Bistro, an outpost of sophistication in the high mountains.

"It's a little like Saint Maarten's when we first got there," Ducrot says of Cooke City. "You didn't lock your doors. If someone came to see you and you weren't home, they'd come in and make themselves a drink and wait."

Adding to the international flavor, Ducrot hires young people from agencies that specialize in bringing workers from overseas to the Yellowstone area for seasonal jobs. On a cold night in January, he has a girl from Russia and another from Brazil helping serve a group of wildlife watchers. Every now and then, one falls in love—with the stunning mountain wilderness surrounding town, or with a member of the ruggedly single surfeit of men in Cooke City—and stays.

Soquel—pronounced So-Cal (ironically, she's from NoCal)—Snider didn't come from anywhere as exotic as France or Brazil, but she is in

Cooke City now, one year removed from California, acting as the town's schoolmarm. Though she'd visited with her husband Josh frequently in warmer seasons, Soquel has never lived through a Cooke City winter. So far, she's not intimidated.

The town's one room schoolhouse—formerly the Catholic church—occupies a log structure off the main street with a lovely view of Republic Peak. Inside, it belies preconceived notions of what a one-room schoolhouse might look like, with the same bins and art supplies and little kids' tables and chairs and big calendars and activity stations and dry erase boards and the teacher's computer and rows of books and a high-tech smartboard, and, of course, elegantly primitive children's art-work—colorful human figures with appropriately placed hearts and the words "I love God" or "I love Legos" or "I love riding my bike" splashed prominently across the page—as any elementary school in the country.

On a dazzlingly cold January morning when the temperature outside is 10 below zero, two young children—5-year-old Silas and his 7-year-old sister Stella—burst through the door, followed by a huge Saint Bernard. A few minutes later, once the dog has gone, 7-year-old Miles arrives, and the student body is assembled.

You could not imagine three more charming children, and their enthusiasm for the day's activities is palpable. Soon they're talking about the *Gingerbread Baby*. The older kids discuss what the problem in the story is and how the problem gets solved. Silas is responsible for describing the characters and the plot. It's like second grade anywhere in America. Except it's not. It's not, for instance, the intense teach-to-the-test pressure of California's education system, in which Soquel had taught for years and with which she had grown frustrated. And it's not a room full of kids who don't know what the natural world looks like.

Teaching three kids in a one-room schoolhouse is not without its challenges, either. "Teaching multiple grade levels is hard. What do I do with this kindergarten student while I'm working with the two second graders?" Soquel says. "I used to get a recess break, a lunch break. That's not happening here. I'm not used to being the janitor, emptying the garbage, vacuuming the floor, cleaning the toilets."

But Soquel is not complaining. She loves this gig. "So much of learning is not done in a classroom. When school started I took my kids for a hike every day, and I didn't have to fill out a dozen forms to do it. I'm taking them on a trip to the symphony in Billings, so I have a violin teacher coming up here four Fridays in a row for lessons. We have Family Art Fridays twice a month, where families with kids not yet of school age can come join us to make art projects. We still have standards. We still have textbooks, all that. I just have so much more freedom than I used to have."

All three of her students perform above grade level in standardized testing, which makes Soquel happy. Moving to Cooke City has made both Soquel and Josh happy. But she, too, will likely move on at some point. She and Josh have a 2 ½ year old son named Coltrane (yes, after the jazz great), and a unique problem.

"I can't see staying here Coltrane's whole life, because I'd be his only teacher," Soquel says. "Once he gets to about fifth grade, I want him to have other experiences."

EXPOSING HER KIDS TO OTHER EXPERIENCES WAS REALLY THE ONLY REASON Roberta "Birdie" Williams ever left Cooke City. Betty Sommers may be the longest continual resident of Cooke City, but Birdie Williams, 88, arrived in town first, in 1947, and she's still there—she just had to leave when the school closed in 1951, because she didn't believe in boarding out her children. "You don't let somebody else raise your second grade kids," Birdie says.

Birdie was born on a homestead in 1924 and did not live in a house with indoor plumbing until 1998. She started her married life living in a sheep wagon, and then had a little dugout house, built into the ground on the Crow Reservation near Lodge Grass. She and her husband Jack ranched and Jack worked for a while in the mines near Absarokee, but a cave-in crushed his spine. Afterwards, he could work for short stints, but then the pain would be too much. Birdie picked up the slack.

In the summer of 1947, Jack came to Cooke City with his father to build a house for a woman in town. He showed up back at the ranch on the flats in October and told Birdie they were moving to the mountains the next day. They did. Birdie remembers winters when only four people stayed in the silent town beneath those towering peaks, buried by snow.

"There were no tractors or anything to clear snow," Birdie says. "You had your webs [snowshoes], your skis and your snowmobile. We got mail once or twice a week."

In 1952, Birdie returned to the ranch at Lodge Grass so her daughters could go to school, but then she and Jack started drifting back to Cooke City, so that by 1978, they lived in town full time again. Before then, Jack had been laid up in bed for six months and Birdie decided to buy him a starter art kit. With no training, Jack began sketching and then painting. When the couple returned to Cooke City, Jack started selling his "primitive art," colorful, Edenic paintings depicting bygone eras. Tourists from all over the world bought his works, and CNN did a feature story on him. Today Jack's bigger paintings sell for $3,500 each.

Jack's health deteriorated until, in 1998, neighbors and friends rallied to build an addition to Birdie and Jack's original house—one with plumbing and a washer and dryer, a refrigerator so Jack wouldn't have to go to a care facility. He died the following year.

Birdie lives with grizzly bears on her porch ("you just holler at them, they go away"), epic snowdrifts (neighbors plow and shovel her out now), the coming of snowmobiles ("that changed everything"). Unlike the people who try Cooke City for a few years and leave, Birdie's made her life here.

"You go to [a bigger] town, your window is looking out at somebody else's window looking in at you. Here, you look out, you've got clear air. It's pretty. It's a good place to live. I've been here a long time. Where you gonna go?" ◪

Golden Valley Rider

By Alan Kesselheim

Spring 2011

A FEW MILES SOUTH OF RYEGATE, Robin Puckett pulls her small Mazda pickup abreast of a row of mailboxes. The sky is leaden gray, brooding with coming storm.

A woman is standing in the lee of another pickup, exhaust pluming into the cold morning air. She wears a winter coat, her head tucked away from the wind, waiting. Puckett idles forward. The woman walks to the open window, leans in to the warmth of the cab. Robin hands her the mail. They exchange good mornings, wonder about the storm—when and how bad—before she returns to her truck.

"People meet me at the boxes a lot," Puckett says. "It can be a four- or five-mile trip from the house for some. They'll give me money for postage. Sometimes they'll call ahead and have me bring them a priority mailer or some stamps."

"I suppose there is the human contact, too," she adds, watching the truck pull away down a long, empty dirt road.

Puckett has driven the Ryegate highway contract route for 28 years, since the early 1980s. Six days a week on the southern loop, three days a week up north towards the Big Snowy Mountains. If all goes well, she can do both routes in five hours. Today looks like five hours will be a hard target. This is Musselshell River country—Fish Creek, Rock Creek, Big Coulee Creek, Locomotive Butte, the bigger part of Golden

Valley County. It is a place where antelope and mule deer outnumber people and cattle by a long shot. Roads are more dirt than paved. Wind drifts snow in the hollows and rain turns hills into gumbo challenges; a place where, as Puckett says, "If you have to walk, it's miles and miles and miles to the nearest house."

Best to be self-sufficient. She carries candles, matches, water, energy food, sleeping bag, spare boots, a snow shovel. Before cell phones she had a ham radio in the vehicle, and her license plate remains her call sign—N7RLS. She wears her hair short, tightly curled, and has the practical air of someone used to figuring her way out of jams. "I can change out a flat in under 10 minutes," she claims. "I've learned a lot about fixing things on cars. I believe I'm on my sixth vehicle since I got the route. And this one, I hate to say, is a piece of crap."

Unless it's 20 below or colder, she drives with the passenger window wide open and the heat blasting on high. "I was blessed with long arms," she says, reaching across the truck cab and out the passenger side to feed mail into the next box. Although she has already "cased" the mail in order of delivery and laid it out in the metal tray she inherited from the last driver almost three decades earlier, she rechecks every bundle before it goes out the window.

"Don't like mistakes," she says.

What becomes clear, despite the miles between houses and the horizons of sagebrush and yucca and brown stubble that dominate the view, is that Puckett's route is an erratic, wandering thread stitching together an austere and far-flung community, and that she is continuing a history of human connections across land where loneliness is the norm.

She is the latest in a string of mail carriers going back over the past century. Betty Kunesh, now almost 90 years old, served as Robin's substitute driver for many years. Kunesh has spent her entire life in Golden Valley County, growing up in the upper Big Coulee and later moving closer to Ryegate. She remembers all the drivers back to the early 1900s, including her mother-in-law, who substituted for Elza "Dee" Iden, before the Depression. Iden's contract stipulated that he would have to travel three miles through pastureland along the route. He delivered the mail with a Whippet car and was famous for never wearing a hat, and for planting flowers by mailboxes.

"He wore a buffalo robe and nothing on his head," Kunesh remembers. "Back then, when the roads got really bad, they delivered the mail by horse and sled. They would stay over at someone's house in the Big

Coulee and take two days to do the route. We rode horses a lot back then."

Mailboxes are still miles apart. Often as not, the house attached to the box is out of sight down a two-track lane. Puckett's truck coming past is a faint heartbeat reaching out from town and the world beyond.

Herds of antelope look up from grazing, trot away through the sage. Rough-legged hawks rise off of fence posts. Narrow coulees scribe deeply into the bedrock valley bottom. Even on this cloud-bound day, the country is vast and exposed, shouldering away against the horizon. The weathered ruins of old homesteads settle into the landscape. She drives past the abandoned, one-room 79 School where she and her husband used to go to community dances. Rusted wagons and machinery punctuate empty fields. Buildings stand out, stark topographic features under scudding clouds.

It takes a certain personality to embrace this country, a person whose heart swells in the face of long distances, who is exhilarated rather than daunted in the middle of nowhere with a storm coming on. "I love the spring most," Puckett says. "It's so green everywhere. All the baby animals are out. The bluebirds and meadowlarks sing from the fence posts. Wildflowers color the fields. But there's beauty in the winter too." She points up to the distant rimrock that bowls the skyline above Big Coulee. "When the wind drives snow over the lip of rocks, it's like a waterfall coming off." It also means that there are likely to be drifts to deal with along the more remote and exposed roads.

Over the years Puckett has refined her backcountry driving technique. "I used to blast through snow drifts," she confesses. "Problem is, if you don't make it, you're high-centered in the middle and you have some serious digging on your hands. And sometimes the wind is drifting it back in as fast as you shovel it out. I've become a confirmed 'creeper' when it comes to snowdrifts. I'll just probe my way in, not too fast, so I can back out again and escape if I have to. Same goes for mud. Unless it's a pretty short stretch, I don't blast through anymore."

More important, she has figured out the alternate routes to avoid bad spots. She knows where to expect mud holes, where the snowdrifts pack in two feet deep, the hills where trucks slither sideways. She knows the secondary roads, the two-tracks through pasture that aren't on any maps, but that will get her around a flooded bridge along Fish Creek or avoid the bad hill with a 90-degree turn at the bottom.

Early in the route, past the Hutterite colony with its cute red box, Puckett delivers to a house that is regularly blocked by blowing snowdrifts.

"If it's bad, he opens up a gate to his pasture for me," she says. "He marks out a route through his fields so I can come up from behind and get to the box. Some years it's the only way to get to him for weeks."

The mailboxes along Puckett's route are as varied and idiosyncratic as the people. Many are mounted on platforms made out of old wagon wheels. A few sport the perforations of target practice. Some of the door hinges have rusted away, and Puckett has developed her two-hand techniques to get them closed. Another one, abandoned, with the door hanging, has succumbed to a second purpose in life as a bird's nest. She opens one with the flag up and letters waiting in a plastic bag.

"Not all of the boxes are waterproof," she explains, as she extricates the sheaf of letters and sets the bag back in.

At the top of a long hill that climbs out of Big Coulee, with a view back towards Locomotive Butte, Puckett pulls into a driveway and turns off the engine.

"I have some certified letters that need signatures," she explains. She reaches behind the seat and pulls out a handful of dog treats. "And I get to visit some of my favorite puppies."

Three dogs spill out of the doorway and come wagging up to her. She wades through them, dispensing treats, loving them up, trying to keep the mail clear of the melee. She could have had these folks come to the post office to sign their letters. Technically, she never has to leave her vehicle, but there is more than a business transaction going on here. There is warmth in the greetings, friendship and company in the middle of empty miles, that heartbeat of connection surging up strong.

By the time she backs out of the drive, it is snowing. At a "T" intersection on a high point, she extols the view, today shortened to a quarter mile.

"I've taken so many pictures from here," she says. "On a clear day you can see the Snowies to the north, the Crazies to the west, the Beartooths to the south."

Today she drives on. The wind is picking up snow; it writhes across the roads. A faint urgency takes hold. "Long as I can make out the fence line, I keep going," she says.

Repeatedly, when she stops, she has to turn off the ignition and restart the truck in order to get it into first gear. Puckett mutters at the vehicle. Then, on a steep, icy hill, the truck dies and won't start again. She cranks the engine, but it won't take hold.

"This happened once before," she says, pulling on the emergency

73

brake. "I need a pen." She rummages in the glove box until she finds an old ballpoint, gets out and walks around the vehicle. Halfway up a frozen hill, far from anything remotely like help, the sense of exposure is a cold embrace. From the passenger side she leans under the dash and rummages through the wires. "There it is," she says, and pushes at a connection with the end of the pen. Sure enough, when she tries again the truck fires up. She jams it into gear and grannies up the incline.

"I don't even remember how I figured that out," she shakes her head.

There are a great many regulations Puckett is supposed to abide by as a contract mail carrier. Out here, and especially on days like this, the force of those rules is as distant as the nearest mechanic. It is against the rules, for example, to leave anything other than mail in a box. That doesn't stop people from surprising Puckett with tins of Christmas cookies, or her from accepting the seasonal gesture. She is not obliged to leave the set roads of her route, but if she has to get around a flooded coulee, she'll find a way.

"Actually, I'm never supposed to 'dismount' from my vehicle," Puckett says. "I've had carriers I meet at conferences get all huffy when I tell them I get out to deliver mail. But hell, sometimes I've got a mud hole I'm not about to cross to get to a box 50 feet away. What am I supposed to do, turn around? How crazy is that? I'm going to get out, walk around, and deliver that mail. If that's a problem, I guess they'll have to fire me."

Late in the morning, snow falling thickly, Puckett "tiptoes" down a grade and back across the Musselshell into the old settlement of Barber. Like so much of this country, Barber is a shadow of what it was during the homestead era, when hundreds of people lived here, when churches, stores and schools flourished. Now it is a near ghost town, a few house lights still on along the highway.

Puckett regains pavement for a few miles, back to Ryegate, itself reduced to a couple of grain elevators, a café, county offices, a few shops and homes, and the post office. She heads in the back door of the small building and picks up the northern packet of mail, sets it in her tray. The building is quiet and empty. Colleen Smith, the postmaster who has split her career between the Shawmut and Ryegate offices, is away on her lunch hour. Puckett is running late. She has already called ahead to a few people she knows will be waiting for her at their boxes to tell them she's been delayed by the storm. Puckett's lunch hour will be spent in the cab of her truck, nibbling on snacks, heading north into the maw of white and wind under the pulsing light mounted on the truck cab.

Four miles north of Ryegate, a highway sign announces the end of pavement. Snow is spuming across the road like ocean foam. The fence posts are visible, but the snowplows haven't gotten out ahead of her. She points towards the Snowy Range, towards people waiting in the warmth of truck cabs for her. Her yellow light is visible for a hundred yards, a rhythmic beat against the gray swirl, then the storm swallows her. ◼

High Plains Adventurers

By Scott McMillion

Summer 2013

STAND BACK A MILE OR TWO AND ST. MARIE LOOKS NORMAL ENOUGH. Just another eastern Montana prairie town, up north of Glasgow, almost to Canada. Water towers. A few trees. Booming with quiet.

A sign greets visitors.

"Welcome to St. Marie," it says. "Home of the Adventurous."

It reads like a stab at irony until you pull in to town.

Up close, St. Marie looks like Chernobyl without the high rises; hundreds of empty homes that haven't seen a paintbrush or a new shingle in more than 40 years, tumbleweeds sprouting in the crumbling streets, trees clogging entrances to once-comfortable homes. The blight goes on for city block after city block. It looks like a ghost town with 1960s architecture. You could film a zombie movie there.

Adventurous indeed.

Somebody long ago busted the windows in the elementary school, where birds now nest in the light fixtures. A more reverent person sealed up the chapel. Likewise the bowling alley with its bar and restaurant, the hospital, the office buildings, the rows of barracks. Entire residential neighborhoods stand empty, the winding avenues and cul-de-sacs untracked. Under decades of neglect and tireless prairie wind, garage doors are the first to collapse. Windows and doors go next, letting the snow and wind inside. Roofs peel off, shingle by shingle.

Basement window wells overflow with snowmelt.

Deer take shelter in some houses. Feral cats slink about while curbside signs spell out that city buses once ran routes here. But there's nowhere for them to carry people now. About 500 people live in St. Marie today, many of them military retirees, but all the retail businesses fled long ago and there's not a gas station or a cafe in town. Not even a bar, usually the last thing to go in any Montana burg.

Even Pat Kelly, St. Marie's biggest booster for many years, agrees it "looks like a war zone" today.

It wasn't always this way.

The U.S. Air Force started building the Glasgow Air Force Base in the 1950s, supporting jet fighters and B52 bombers on Cold War patrol. At times it housed up to 10,000 people but in 1968, the Pentagon shifted gears, decommissioned the base, and flew the planes elsewhere, many to Vietnam. Still, construction didn't stop right away. Government contracts meant taxpayers kept paying people to build more houses and build them right: with strong bones, hardwood floors, full basements.

"The base was closing before it was actually finished," says DeAnn Ketchum, the no-nonsense director of the St. Marie Condominium Association, a group that residents call "The Condo." It's the one outfit in town with a track record of keeping things upright and functioning and the closest thing it has to a city government.

When you see a tidy, well-kept home in St. Marie, chances are it's part of The Condo, which also runs a "town hall" with an array of snapping flags, a meeting room, a post office and a business office with a wall clock that lists the time in Kabul, Afghanistan.

"We're a military community," says Ketchum, whose husband retired from a career in the U.S. Marine Corps. "Everybody here knows somebody in Kabul."

After the Air Force left, the town emptied and people tried a variety of schemes to capitalize on what looked like a fortune in government discards. (In 1962, the government valued its real estate there at $75 million, $580 million in today's dollars, and it wasn't done building yet.) There was a treatment center that brought in people with drug and alcohol problems, another one that taught living skills to the downtrodden, "hard luck people with lots of kids," as Valley County Sheriff Glen Meier describes them.

Those operations fizzled, as did plans for industrial projects. The county owned the town for a while and sold the hangars and the air strip—almost three miles long—to a subsidiary of Boeing, which still shows up now and then to test airplanes.

Other people and companies bought hundreds of houses, city blocks of them, and tried to get retirees, somebody, to move to one of the coldest, most isolated corners of the state, a place where six-foot snowdrifts linger into April. Many houses have been hauled away but roughly 1,000 still stand, only a small fraction of them occupied. Pat Kelly, an Air Force retiree, owned most of the town for a while and gave it its name, hoping to transform it into a Christian community. Then he sold it to a man who went bankrupt. Then he got it back, partly.

Over the years came a string of lawsuits, foreclosures, accusations, criminal charges, shuffled papers and shuffled blame, capped by the bankruptcy that tied things up for a decade while a judge parceled out the assets. Lots of people quit paying property taxes. Even for people willing to invest and sweat, a clear property title can be hard to find.

There is plenty of fault to pass around.

"There were all kinds of things that weren't done quite right," says Valley County Commissioner Dave Pippin. "He said, she said. Yadda yadda."

"It's a big-ass convoluted mess," is how Sheriff Meier sums it up.

He's worried the county will someday have to take back much of the town. If it does, county officials will have to figure out what to do with it: which houses to bulldoze, which it can try to sell, which ones it can rehabilitate, if it can find the money, if it can obtain clear titles.

"I see a great potential for it to harm this county," Meier says.

PLENTY OF PEOPLE HAVE OFFERED PLENTY OF PLANS FOR ST. MARIE. Now there's a new plan, one driven by the pile of money in oil and gas fields.

In recent months, 483 dwellings have gone up for tax assignment, a mechanism under which, if "Joe" doesn't pay his property taxes for a few years, "Jane" can pick up the tab and get Joe's property, eventually.

Over the winter, a company called DTM Enterprises paid $212,686 in overdue tax bills for those 483 houses, duplexes and fourplexes— about what you'd pay for one new home in Bozeman or Billings, if your tastes aren't too elaborate.

Merrill Frantz, one of the DTM partners, says he's looking to provide housing for workers in the Bakken oil fields, about three hours to the east, if the roads are good. He says he thinks his company can straighten out the title problems.

He says his group plans to rehabilitate the housing and put it on the market. The Bakken, he says, is "no longer a boom. It's an industry."

As of press time, tax deeds were being issued for about 120 of the houses, Valley County Treasurer Jennie Reinhardt said. That means DTM owns them, or soon will. County records show that DTM has transferred hundreds of other tax assignments to Missoula businessman Mike Mitchell, who shares DTM's goal of rehabilitating the housing, according to Frantz.

The only thing holding back energy development, Frantz says, is a lack of housing and St. Marie can offer "at least a partial solution."

But Kelly, who owns 370 of the dwellings now facing tax assignment, maintains that DTM consists of "Sovereign Citizens," a group with beliefs similar to those of the Freemen, the group of anti-government crusaders who holed up in central Montana in the 1990s. The FBI sent many of them to prison, but only after an 81-day siege.

Frantz says Kelly is wrong.

"I can't even begin to understand why he would say that," Frantz says. "We're trying to promote a positive image for St. Marie. I can guarantee you we're not one of them."

Around the country, people calling themselves Sovereign Citizens have landed in legal trouble, mostly for using what the FBI calls "bogus financial instruments." Some of them make their own license plates and refuse to use a driver's license. Some have been involved in violent crime, including murder, according to the FBI.

"The Sovereign Citizens are trying to take this over," Kelly insists.

"I don't know if I buy that," says Valley County Attorney Nick Murnion, who has close experience with anti-government groups.

When he was the Garfield County Attorney, the Freemen issued a wanted poster with his name on it and offered to hang him from a bridge. He stood up to men who threatened murder, tried to goad the FBI to move faster to arrest them, and earned a John F. Kennedy Profiles in Courage Award for his efforts.

He says the ideology of the new guys at St. Marie doesn't matter, as long as they obey the law.

"They've been following every step of the law," Murnion says.

Of his own politics, Frantz said he's a devout Christian who believes in the Constitution.

"We're going to try to promulgate the Christian religion," he says. "We're not going to shoot anybody."

Sheriff Meier says St. Marie has problems—he busted a meth house there about a year ago—but it is no hotbed of crime.

"I don't care who they are: Sovereign Citizens, black, Indian, atheist, Christians," Meier says of DTM. "They've not broken any laws we're aware of."

Still, eyebrows rose. Especially when the newcomers bought a newspaper advertisement last autumn, announcing plans to seize much of the town through eminent domain, a process that lets property be seized from unwilling sellers, usually for construction of a highway, a power line or some other public good.

Murnion and County Commissioner Pippin say that's just not going to happen, that the DTM partners don't understand the law in this case.

Still, St. Marie has been a constant drain on county finances for decades. Turning a few hundred houses over to new owners willing to pay overdue taxes might be an improvement, or at least keep the problems out of the county's lap.

"The tax deed process might be a blessing, in a way," Murnion says.

DESPITE ALL THE MESS OVER THE YEARS, St. Marie is far from dead. It's even grown over the past couple of years as the Bakken oil impacts ripple westward, providing jobs and money.

Sprinkled among the leaky roofs and sandblasted siding, the weedy and potholed streets, the basements without houses above them, the neighborhoods with no running water, you can find some gems; homes in good repair, places with proud owners, people who say they like it there just fine.

An influx of retired military people arrived in the 1990s and they fixed up houses and put down roots. Some of them served their country at St. Marie when it was an air force base.

Bob Anderson, now 78, was stationed there in the 1960s.

"This place was perfect," he said. Homes were solid, lawns were tended, friendships abounded. "By far, this was my best assignment. I always wanted to come back."

So he did so in 1991. He and his wife live today in a two-story duplex, an immaculate home filled with religious symbols. Some of their children also have moved to St. Marie and others are on the way.

"Where else can you buy a three-bedroom house for $20,000?" he says.

Living among all those empty shells doesn't bother him, though he'd like to see somebody fix them up before it's too late, before the prairie swallows them.

"I don't mind the ghost town," he says. "I've got my place here."

Clarence Guy, also stationed there in the 1960s, says St. Marie was the nicest base he ever saw, "and I saw a slew of them." He returned to stay in 1996.

"When we came here, it looked like a war zone," says Guy, but things have improved since then, at least in some neighborhoods, partly due to his efforts. An energetic man who enjoys model trains, he also works for The Condo fixing up some of its 251 housing units, as time and budgets permit.

Like other old timers in St. Marie, Guy and Anderson keep an eye on the DTM group, waiting to see what they'll do.

"We let them do their thing," Guy says. "Just don't mess with us."

"You'll find our mentality here is fairly jaded," says condo director Ketchum. People in St. Marie have heard a lot of big talk from would-be developers. She says she's watching DTM to see what their hands do, not what their lips say. So far, she hasn't seen much activity.

For a long time, St. Marie had drawn a trickle of people, many of them renters, who are "moving around to keep moving so they won't get caught for whatever," Ketchum says. But she sees that changing. Now, many of the newcomers seem solid, "people paying their bills and minding their Ps and Qs."

But others still struggle.

"THE MAJORITY OF PEOPLE HERE ARE PRETTY POOR," says Cindy Laffin, who came to St. Marie from Arkansas because she learned on the internet that Montana has good schools and St. Marie has really cheap houses. She, too, was shocked when she got there.

"I drove 1,806 miles for this?" she says of her initial response.

But she settled in.

Now her kids ride one of two buses that take St. Marie kids to school in Glasgow, 17 miles to the south. Her family lives in a house she picked up for $25,000. It came with a clean title and was fully furnished, right down to the dish soap and the toilet bowl cleanser.

"I thought it would be a good survival-type community," says Laffin, a self-described conspiracy theorist. "I walk a fine line between nut case and 'you really should listen to me.'"

She rattles off theories about FEMA camps and gas chambers and government plots.

"I really believe the world is going to hell in a handbasket," she says. "I want to build a self-sufficient community."

She's brought a half-dozen people to St. Marie from around the country. "I like to have like-minded people around me," she says.

She says she's not a Sovereign Citizen but shares that group's distrust of government.

She plants a big garden, puts up thousands of pounds of food and shares what she has because "in order to take care of yourself you've got to take care of everybody around you." She's got plans to raise goats and fish and put in a greenhouse. She doesn't have much money but says she doesn't need much.

"I don't have the expenses that lazy people have," she says.

She talks about her neighbors: who takes public assistance and who doesn't, the man who feeds the feral cats, the people who hauled in 14 horse-trailer loads of used clothing, to be ready for social collapse, and the "pink ladies," her term for the people who run The Condo and enforce its rules.

"People here really just want to be left alone," she says. "I think a lot of them are hiding from something."

She said she doesn't want to see a bunch of Sovereign Citizens move in.

"It just puts a target on your back for the government," she says.

Longtime residents like Guy say roughly 80 percent of the homes could be made habitable with a new roof, some siding and windows. But that won't be cheap. There are just so many of them. And who will live in them?

And the growth that has already occurred has posed problems.

Toni Alvarnez, who runs the Valley County Women's Resource Center in Glasgow, says she knows of seven families who've been abandoned in St. Marie, women and children left without money, food, transportation or friends because breadwinners "just don't come back from the oilfields."

Her office has opened a food bank and services 30 families a week, mostly from St. Marie. In the last fiscal year, her staff served 49 domestic violence or abandonment victims there. Alvarnez no longer lets her staff respond alone to calls in St. Marie.

"We go out in twos, now," she says. "You don't know if you're walking into crank or whatever."

Clearly, the community has problems. But it also has hope.

"I want to make this a beautiful place, and it's not, right now," says Pat Kelly.

DTM partner Frantz says he's confident the Bakken and other developments will provide the demand to fill the houses, giving oilfield and construction workers a reasonably close location for their families.

People like Ketchum remain skeptical, though non-judgmental, of groups like DTM. She understands the hurdles they need to clear and says The Condo will do what it must to protect its own property rights.

Murnion sees a possible bright side: at least some back taxes are being paid.

County Commissioner Pippin is just hoping the county doesn't have to take over.

"A lot of people are just hoping and praying it comes out well," he says.

Whatever happens, it could be adventurous. ◗

Born of Hard Work

By Jeff Hull

Spring 2010

Dick Vinson came to Thompson Falls from Polson in 1958 to fell trees on the steep slopes around town. He rented a piece of land on Blue Slide Road, and went rodeoing in the summer months. Pictures on the walls of Vinson's office—which sits snug on the banks of the Thompson Reservoir—show a strikingly handsome man, Clooney-esque in his secure smile. In the same pictures, Vinson's wife, Tricia, has the presence of a Nashville star.

Vinson's rodeoing ended the same year his marriage began. "I drove out of town from that last rodeo and I had won a round and that's how much money I had to my name," Vinson says. His speech is prone to long pauses, as if he's not interested in wasting words on things he's not sure he has to say. He has clear gray eyes behind wire-rimmed glasses and his hair has gone snowy white. "I think it was $286."

In 1964 Vinson bought 200 acres of the land he had rented, and by the early 70s he had acquired some machinery and gone into road-building. In 1974, Vinson contracted to haul timber pulp. Some of these ventures overlapped. He built a post plant and then a sawmill in Trout Creek and operated that for years before leasing it out and building a coal-fired power plant in Hardin in 2000.

Vinson is 73 and in the process of developing a sawmill and biomass power plant in Emmitt, Idaho, hoping to capitalize on the closure of several mills in that area. He also raises registered Angus cattle. In between all that, just for fun, Vinson and his wife hosted a PRCA rodeo on their property for 21 years. They brought in nationally known acts and champion riders—Shawn Davis, Larry Mahan—and staged a huge dance in their meadow. Thousands attended.

And that's kind of how things go in Thompson Falls: You work hard at one thing, then maybe you work a couple jobs at the same time, always looking for the next opportunity. You scratch and cobble and, in between, you try a few things you like to do, just for fun.

The people of Thompson Falls have never been afraid to take the initiative. The region's first settler of European descent, the Canadian explorer David Thompson, arrived in search of beaver pelts. He built a trading post he called Saleesh House somewhere near the eponymous natural falls in the Clark Fork River—there's debate about the precise location of the building—and spent the winter of 1809 here. His journals note a lack of game; he survived on dried meat obtained from native traders.

The town didn't get going until the arrival of the Northern Pacific railroad in 1883. According to one account, locals full of civic pride piled logs across the tracks to stop the train before it reached Belknap, a thriving station a few miles west. While engineers cleared the tracks, locals boarded the train and tried to persuade immigrants to jump off and settle right there in Thompson Falls.

Two years later the town site was platted and 20 saloons had opened to slake the thirst of miners headed for placer strikes in Idaho. Today Thompson Falls—and nobody local, by the way, calls it "T-Falls"; anybody using a nickname says just "Thompson"—is the seat of Sanders County. The mines played out, although some prospectors still wander the hills. The logging industry that employed so many shrank from three sawmills (including Vinson's at Trout Creek) to one. Thompson people learned to cobble together a living and persevere, just like Dick Vinson.

YOU'RE NEVER FAR FROM GEOGRAPHY IN THOMPSON FALLS. The mountains are not enormously high, but their slopes sheer steeply and they crowd in close, as if they're not going to let the town get away with anything. Upriver bare thrusts of pre-Cambrian rock, striations tilted skyward, line Highway 200. Perch on the canyon's edge below the long arc of the 60-foot high dam built by Pennsylvania Power and Light (PPL Montana) and you see the history of a river's power—the fractured, fragmented cliffs torn by high water pulses, some remnant plunge pools still 80 feet deep.

The dam is a hotbed of work activity, even on a freezing winter's morning when water pouring from gaps in the edifice's panels slips beneath a sheet of ice. PPL Montana is building a fish ladder to aid passage of bull trout and westslope cutthroats through the Clark Fork river system. The company is spending around $7 million and should have the ladder, which will consist of 48 pools in six switchbacks, finished by the time high water comes in the spring of 2010.

Thompson and Noxon reservoirs have been fertile fisheries for non-native species like bass and northern pike, although locals say the action has slowed considerably in recent years. The fish ladder isn't meant to address the declining bass and pike fishery, but rather to bolster populations of native species, says Jay Stuckey, who works for Montana's Department of Fish, Wildlife and Parks.

It's important for people to understand, Stuckey says, that not every fish is going to pass over the dam. The ladder's penultimate pool, Stuckey says, will be a holding tank from which FWP employees can sort out "desirable" fish to allow upstream. Pike and walleye will be washed back down.

Stuckey, a longtime fisherman, is another local resident adept at changing careers. He taught at Thompson Falls High School for many years—his wife, Eve, still does—but retired in 2000. He came to FWP in 2001, after working in watershed conservation. School, he says, had become too much paperwork.

LIKE MOST RURAL SCHOOL DISTRICTS, Thompson Falls' schools struggle with dwindling enrollment and funding. High school principal Don Jensen says that in the past seven years his enrollment dropped from 257 students to 197. Originally from Sidney, Jensen went to Montana State and wrestled on the varsity team back when there was one. He moved to Arizona to work as an administrator, then moved his family back to Montana in 1993, to Thompson.

Jensen—whose round, smooth face and head sit atop a muscular body that suggests a coiled quickness—could be 25 or 55. His teachers love him; they say he's quick to act on suggestions. Jensen faces a challenge not many other administrators deal with. There are now seven private group homes for troubled youth—spin-offs from the failed Spring Creek Academy—in the Thompson Falls area. Of the 197 students at Thompson Falls High, 42 are from group homes.

"In a small town in Montana, one new kid a year in the school is a big deal," Jensen says. "Most small town kids don't get exposed to a different worldview. They don't get to meet kids from outside and discuss how things are different in other places. Our kids get a lot more exposure to the world."

That's a double-edged sword. "There's a reason those [group home] kids are here," Jensen says. "They can bring the real world into your school, and that's not always a good thing."

But the group homes run highly controlled programs, and Jensen communicates regularly with their directors. Thompson Falls, Jensen says, is a very accepting community, and the group home kids do fine. The Thompson kids do fine, too. Jensen credits his teachers' "ability to relate to the kids."

"They're not authoritarians. They don't push buttons. They handle problems," he says of his staff.

Eve Stuckey, Jay's wife, is one of those problem-handlers. She doesn't stand in front of class and lecture. "I don't like hierarchy. I don't like podiums. I don't like anything that comes between me and [my students]," Eve says. "I'm not the be-all, know-all. I think they love the idea that 'Mrs. Stuckey doesn't know how to do that. I'll have to show her.' And they get real smug about it."

In her role as a multi-media teacher, Stuckey deals with the kinds of technology kids are often more adept at than adults. While university journalism programs around the country puzzle out how to teach college kids multimedia skills, Eve has just moved right ahead and done it at the high school level.

"I thought one better way of teaching would be to have the class do some video production and put a TV in the hall while the kids were eating lunch. I knew they'd be glued to it. They wouldn't care what was on," Eve says. She was teaching home economics then, so the productions were about how to shop, how to buy a car, how to gauge your sugar intake.

Eve understood the power of video as an instructional tool, and was an early fan of YouTube. "At one point I wanted to learn how to fly fish and Jay said, 'I'll teach you.' I said, 'You don't have to. By the time you get home tonight, I'll have watched all the best fly fishermen in the world teaching me how to cast,' " she says.

She started writing grants for video and computer processing equipment, building an impressive array of tech toys for her multi-media students. The students take the photo, video and audio production skills they develop on that equipment out into the world.

One of those students was Cody Best. After producing a video for a joint convention of the National Petroleum Management Association and the U.S. Air Force while still in high school, Best found himself struggling to pay for college. So he came home and started his own show.

Together with Justin Harris, Best writes, produces, stars in and edits "The Broken News," a wonderfully quirky community affairs program— Best's son Hayden, who is 5, has been submitted to the *Guinness Book of World Records* for certification as the world's youngest weatherman— broadcast by Montana PBS and available on YouTube.

"The Broken News" tries to handle contentious issues with true balance, Best says. "It's a small town. You don't want to step on anybody's toes, but it's tight quarters. On any controversial issue Justin takes one side, and I'll take the other, and we try to meet in the middle."

Best is 28, married with two kids. He's not looking to leave Thompson. "I love it here," he says. "It's beautiful. I love the people here. They're crazy and passionate and hard workers. We're willing to work hard for what we get."

HARD WORK AND THE ABILITY TO JUGGLE JOBS IS A GIVEN IN THOMPSON Falls. In addition to being a father and making videos, Best works at Little Bear, a slow-food restaurant (a sign on the door says "In a hurry? Please do not enter.") that serves the best soups, sandwiches and ice cream—made on the spot with an array of puzzlingly fresh fruits and vegetables—in northwest Montana.

"It's one thing for people to talk about your food being good," Best says of Little Bear's offerings, "but it's another when people alter their travel plans to make sure they stop in your shop," as visitors from Japan, Australia and all over the U.S. tell the Little Bear staff they do.

"They'll tell you the whole story about how their sister stopped here five years ago and still talks about how good the food is, and how, when they decided to go to Glacier, they arranged to take Highway 200 so they could come here," Best says.

Eve Stuckey works different jobs, too. Her fine art photography and pottery is for sale next to Little Bear at the Creativity Unlimited co-op, along with other local artists' work.

Annie Wooden worked around the country at big-city daily newspapers as an editor and a designer, but at the age of 29, she's back in Thompson, working as office manager at the *Sanders County Ledger*, the local weekly paper. Whereas when she worked at the *Dallas Morning*

News, Wooden's duties were well-defined, now she finds her tasks varied and unpredictable, and the hours long. Some of her work has little to do with journalism.

"I wanted to go out and experience the world, then come back and contribute to my community," Wooden says. "I want to see our community succeed, so I'm supporting it every way I can."

Wooden regularly attends community fundraisers and local sporting events. She also works at the golf course part-time.

"I could have stayed in Dallas and made a Dallas salary, but you make sacrifices if you want to live here," Wooden says. "It's not easy, but there are ways to do it."

Kris Anderson has narrowed her professional life to one pursuit for the past decade—Sherpa Cabins, prefabricated log cabins with beautifully finished interiors that she ships around the West—although her previous life was characterized by shifting occupations. Anderson was the first female electrical operator hired by Pacific Power and Gas in California, back in 1974. She sold sandwiches on the Alcan highway, and later opened a restaurant there. She worked as a bellhop in a glamorous New York City hotel. She worked as a poolside cocktail waitress in California.

She landed in Thompson Falls and opened a combination video store/tanning salon and rented VCRs when they first came out. When people first heard what she and co-founder Dennis Roberts were up to with Sherpa Cabins, they told Anderson she'd never sell one. In the 10 years since, she's built, sold and shipped 75 cabins (Roberts retired in 2003).

The collapse of the real estate market has slowed Anderson temporarily. She had to furlough her two employees, and at least a dozen local craftsmen and contractors who contribute to each Sherpa Cabin have felt ripple effects. Fortunately, Anderson shares a building with Sharon Pound that the two co-own. Pound owns a silk-screening business that's chugging right along, and the two have always pitched in to see each other through hard times.

Obviously Anderson isn't afraid of change. She anticipates business picking up again—she has two cabins on order for this summer—and once it's back to full production, Anderson might start examining other things that pique her curiosity.

"I want to learn how to weld. I want to be a personal trainer. I have all kinds of things I want to do," she says, which makes her a perfect resident for Thompson Falls.

BILL MEADOWS KNOWS ABOUT HARD WORK. He spent 42 years as a smokejumper and administrator, while also helping to run the family ranch. He built his entire house—a lovely two-story, 4,500-square-foot structure—himself. He framed it out and, when he needed help, he called family and neighbors to tilt the walls up and get them anchored. Then Meadows started on the interior walls. "I figured I painted three miles of sheetrock," Meadows says.

Meadows' grandfather on his mother's side homesteaded in 1884 the property adjacent to the one he lives on, in a drainage a few miles west of Thompson Falls. He bought the site of Meadows' house in 1902. The stories his parents—particularly his mother—told about making a home in this place inform Meadows' vision of it today. "The stories my mother told about growing up here and her father and how he worked...the biggest part was the interaction between the parents and the kids, and taking care of it all."

Meadows' grandmother milked cows and raised children and sold cabbages and other vegetables from her commercial garden. She proved up her own homestead and taught school. She served as the vice president of the Montana Farm Bureau. She lived through one of Thompson Falls' most memorable events—the 1910 fires.

"My grandmother was 5 years old, and her dad had gone into Thompson on the morning of August 21st to check on the fires," Meadows says. "The valley had been socked in with smoke for days. In the late afternoon the wind began to blow. My mother said it sounded like a freight train when the fire roared down. She said it was like standing in front of the blast of a cannon. It got dark at 5:30 in the afternoon.

"My grandfather hurried home on horseback, but met the fire at the top of the hill just between here and Thompson. My grandmother and the girl she hired to work the garden pumped water to put out fires on the roof of the house. They worked all day and saved the main house and barn. The next day, my grandfather walked back in here, thinking everything would be destroyed. He was thinking my grandmother was gone, and she was thinking he was gone. She saw him and fainted. He wept."

Meadows' wife, Helen, herself a descendant of homesteaders from the Wibaux area, understands the romance of loving a place created from blood, sweat and tears, too. She's co-written a book about the fires called *Flames and Courage* for young readers, and a historical book about the Montana Civilian Conservation Corps.

Now she's now working with the Sanders County Historical Society to produce an event in conjunction with the U.S. Forest Service to commemorate the 100th anniversary of the 1910 fires. Several places in Montana will hold ceremonies recognizing the anniversaries this summer, but Thompson Falls' will be the biggest.

The Meadowses have placed a conservation easement on their ranch, because they don't want to see the land watered by so much of their family's sweat split into somebody else's 20-acre dream of what Montana is like.

And when they leave this world of pine-robed mountains and lush narrow valleys, and their children face the challenge of keeping a ranch born of perpetual toil going, well...they'll just have to work it out. ◄

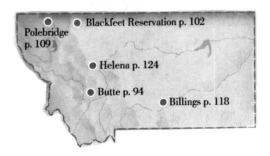

LIVING HISTORY

Because it still matters.

Butte's Bad Cops

By Ted Brewer

Winter 2013

O NE EVENING IN MAY 1980, Mickey Sullivan pulled a ski mask over his face, put on a pair of mirrored sunglasses, and walked into the Medicine Shoppe pharmacy on Harrison Avenue in Butte. Brandishing a .45, Sullivan forced the owner, his mother and two employees into a bathroom and propped a snow shovel against the door to lock them in. Customers watched as he filled a denim drawstring bag with prescription drugs and then pounded on the locked electronic cash register. That's likely what set off the alarm, connected to the police station. Had he been at work that day, he would have heard the alarm at the station because Mickey Sullivan was a shift commander in the Butte-Silver Bow Law Enforcement Agency, a lieutenant. But it was his day off.

According to the next day's *Montana Standard*, a man driving by in a pickup saw Sullivan fleeing the pharmacy on foot. The man drove after Sullivan. When police officer Larry Malyevac arrived at the pharmacy, he pursued the truck, thinking the man peeling away in it was the cause of the alarm.

Sullivan kept running. He passed the Met Tavern and several more bystanders before attempting to steal a car. Sullivan pointed the .45 at the driver, who ducked. Sullivan fired, shattering the driver side window but missing the driver. That's when Malyevac realized who was really the bad guy. Jumping out of his car, he ordered Sullivan to drop his weapon. Sullivan gave it up only when two more cars arrived carrying four more officers.

With their suspect belly down in handcuffs, the police pulled the mask from Sullivan's head.

"[The officers] were ... well ... flabbergasted," Sgt. Dan Hollis, who was filling in for Sullivan that day as shift commander, told *The Standard*. "It's really tough to have to arrest your own shift commander."

This was not the first time Sullivan had committed armed robbery, but it was the first time he'd been caught. It was also, as far as we know, the first of many robberies and burglaries where he acted alone. Partnering with fellow Butte police officers Clarence Delbert "Moon" LaBreche and John T. Sullivan (no relation to Mickey), and a civilian safecracker named Louis Jerome "Louie" Markovich, Mickey Sullivan had committed a slew of robberies and burglaries in Butte dating back to the mid-1960s.

But in 1980, after Sullivan had been arrested for armed robbery and aggravated assault, law enforcement had yet to discover the truth about him, his cohorts, and their responsibility for at least 15 years' worth of unsolved crimes. It would take eight more years, a seemingly unrelated robbery outside Fort Benton, and the work of a multi-agency, organized crime taskforce before federal law enforcement finally learned the truth and spelled it out in a court document chronicling the spree of crimes the crew committed, many of which were orchestrated from within the Butte Police Department. By then, Mickey Sullivan would be long dead.

NOT LONG AFTER HE JOINED THE POLICE FORCE IN 1964, Mickey Sullivan partnered up with Louie Markovich, a small-time thief learning to crack safes. They started with drugstores. With Sullivan on lookout, Markovich would break into the stores and collect the drugs. They eventually brought in Moon LaBreche, who had been in the department since 1951, and John T. Sullivan. Markovich would simply smash a window when one of the Sullivans or LaBreche was on duty and ready to respond to any alarm. Whichever of the three did respond would then bag the merchandise.

Later, the men moved beyond drugstores. In 1972, John T. disabled the alarm system at the police station and LaBreche kept lookout so Markovich and two other men could break into Christie's Warehouse and its loading docks. There, they hacked into a boxcar and made off with 254 cases of Pall Mall and Carlton cigarettes, worth an estimated $60,000.

With each successful hit, the crew's audacity grew. The Golden Rule department store was the unlucky three-time target of some of their most brazen heists. In each of them, Mickey was planner, LaBreche the lookout, and Markovich, aided by another man or two, the bandit. The first Golden Rule heist, in which Markovich peeled the safe, occurred in 1969 and netted them close to $20,000. That was before the store installed an alarm. The crew hit the store again in 1973. To get around the alarm, they grabbed the store manager at gunpoint.

That night, at his home behind the Golden Rule, manager Perry Kelly was asleep on a couch when he woke to a man kicking him in the arm. Wearing a ski mask and a snowmobile suit and holding a revolver, the man told Kelly that he and his wife and kids would not be hurt as long as Kelly cooperated. Another man, armed and dressed in the same wintry fashion, went into the bedroom and tied Kelly's wife's hands and taped her eyes and mouth shut. The children slept through it. One of the men was Markovich. LaBreche was somewhere outside keeping lookout.

The men walked Kelly to the Golden Rule and made him turn off the store alarm. Entering, they disarmed a security guard and took him and Kelly into the back office, where they forced Kelly to tie up the guard, open the safe and load three duffle bags with a total of $15,000. They then had Kelly carry the bags to a side door and left in a Ford Bronco that belonged to Kelly's wife.

Kelly would later tell *The Standard* that the men spoke with "heavy" Southern accents, and that he was certain they weren't faking it. "For big men these guys were extremely agile," he would also recall. "They moved very surely and quickly and when they walked they seemed to float across the floor."

The strong-arming continued. A few months later the police called Albertson's manager Gregory Salese down to the store because someone had broken a glass door and a big window after the store had closed. Shortly after he arrived, the police left to respond to a burglary call in another part of town. Since anyone could have walked in through the broken door, Salese decided to stick around until the baker arrived a few hours later.

"Glass was scattered all around near the door, and when I heard someone walking on it I thought it was the police coming back," Salese told *The Standard*. "The bandits came up behind me and ordered me not to turn around. They had a gun in my back." The bandits forced him to open the safe, which held only a few hundred dollars and a sheaf of traveler's checks. They emptied the safe and tied Salese up in the beer aisle before leaving in his Jeep Wagoneer. The bandits were Markovich and LaBreche. Mickey was driving around on lookout—in a squad car.

Mickey may have learned the next day in *The Standard* why there was so little cash in the safe: a Wells Fargo armored car had taken most of that day's receipts, as it did every day, before the store closed for the night. That might have given Sullivan the idea for what the crew did a few months later. This time, Mickey, John T., LaBreche, and Markovich all worked in concert. It would be their biggest, boldest heist yet.

One night in November, with John T. looking out, Mickey, LaBreche, and Markovich dropped in (as investigators speculated the next day in *The Standard*) through a skylight in the garage of the Metals Bank Building. They then broke into the bank's bookkeeping office by cutting through a plywood panel covering an unused drive-up teller's window. Once inside, they crouched behind a counter as two Wells Fargo drivers arrived with moneybags, deactivated the alarm, and opened the safe. Sullivan and LaBreche, both armed, stood up from behind the counter. They disarmed the drivers and led them to the back of the office and bound them with tape. Sullivan, LaBreche, and Markovich made off in a car they stole from the bank garage, with 18 sacks containing $140,000 in cash earmarked for several Butte businesses. They went directly to Mickey's house and split the money.

As the men polished their criminal skills, Mickey rose through the ranks in the police department. In 1974, after the four of them stole $50,000 worth of jewelry from Hanafin's, effectively putting the long-time jewelry store out of business, one of the two officers who led the investigation was Mickey Sullivan.

IT'S PERHAPS A TESTAMENT TO THE TIGHTKNIT NATURE OF BUTTE THAT MANY people contacted for this story declined to comment about the men known today as "the bad boys of Butte" (after a 2004 book of that title by Les Rickey, about Butte's panoply of infamous historical figures, including Sullivan and his cohorts). Those contacted spoke favorably of the men's family members and were afraid they might offend them by speaking ill of the men in question. Some even spoke favorably of the former cops.

"They were good guys," Rick Foote says. Foote knew LaBreche and the Sullivans growing up in Butte and also as a crime reporter and editor at *The Montana Standard.* He reported on several of the crew's crimes.

"To talk to these guys at the station, they were just regular-type cop guys.

"These guys were not wise guys. ... They wore uniforms and fought the city on union issues. They did the shit that union guys do to further their cause as police officers."

Bernie Hubley, a former FBI agent and a retired U.S. assistant attorney originally from Butte, bristles at the idea that the Sullivans and LaBreche were typical of what the Butte police force was like when the three wore badges. "Butte got a bad rap because of that," he says. "I think it does a terrible disservice to talk about these guys as the Butte Police Department. These guys were rogues."

They were also fathers and husbands. "Moon was a family man," Foote says. "He maintained a wife, two children, and a lawn."

In 1973, LaBreche retired from the police force and started selling cars. Mickey Sullivan retired in 1975 because he was suffering from back pain caused by several on-duty car accidents. He returned to the police force in 1979 (after the Butte Police Department and the Silver Bow Sheriff's Department had merged into Butte-Silver Bow Law Enforcement Agency).

Foote says that by the time Mickey Sullivan walked into the Medicine Shoppe in 1980, he was addicted to whatever he intended to steal and that his days as professional, methodical bandit were long over. Seven months after the robbery, before standing trial for it, Sullivan was found lying on a country road near Butte, the avid outdoorsman dead from an apparent self-inflicted, single shotgun wound to the chest. His shotgun was found leaning against a barbed wire fence about 10 feet from his body. The coroner ruled it an accident. Some in Butte continue to speculate otherwise.

John T. Sullivan retired in 1976 and died in the 1980s, but his criminal association with Mickey, LaBreche, and Markovich had apparently ended in 1975.

With LaBreche and both Sullivans out of the police force by 1976, Markovich and LaBreche no longer had police cover. They kept committing bold heists, and dabbled in other crime. But their control and calculation were already slipping. And they were getting nastier.

I N 1974, a sauna Markovich operated was peppered with bullets in a drive-by shooting, just missing some of Markovich's employees. After hearing a description of the car, Markovich suspected Dave Batterman, according to the court document that chronicles Markovich and

LaBreche's crimes and names Batterman as Markovich's accomplice in the Christie's Warehouse burglary and other crimes. Markovich confronted Batterman, who then threatened Markovich and his family and told him he better close his sauna. Markovich went to Mickey Sullivan, who told him to handle the situation himself. Markovich decided to kill Batterman—with LaBreche's help.

The duo hatched a plan. LaBreche lured Batterman to an abandoned mine yard, where Markovich was waiting. Markovich shot Batterman at least twice in the back. Batterman fled to a friend's nearby apartment and got a ride to the hospital. He survived, but refused to tell the police who shot him. The feud apparently ended there, as did Markovich and LaBreche's days as would-be killers. They went back to what they knew best. Working on confessions and witness accounts, federal prosecutors would later document their handiwork.

Working with new cohorts Daniel "Bones" Marquardt and Lefty Larson, LaBreche and Markovich burglarized two suppliers of vending machines. The two stole $65,000 from the local Buttrey's. With help from a local drug dealer named Thomas Hafer, they broke into a safe that legendary Butte madam Ruby Garrett kept under her living-room floor. They broke into the safe of a local gem shop and headstone provider. And they tried their hand at insurance fraud, providing some $50,000 worth of jewelry to a former Butte-Silver Bow auditor named Katie Murray. In on the scam, she insured the jewelry shortly before Markovich and LaBreche staged a burglary of her home.

They then branched outside of Butte.

"Criminals are greedy," former FBI agent Hubley says. "They keep it up, keep it up, keep it up, and they stub their toe, and law enforcement is there to see it."

In 1987, Markovich heard about a ranching family outside of Fort Benton that was growing marijuana to pay off a mountain of debt. He declared "open season" on the family.

Markovich, LaBreche, Bones Marquardt, and two other men went to the Kurth ranch first on October 16, 1987. Carrying some of LaBreche's weapons and possibly one of his old police shields, they arrived at the ranch posing as DEA agents. They roughed up some of the Kurths, tied them up, and stole a few plants. The next night they returned, minus LaBreche, to rob them of another 100 or more plants. Days later, one of the Butte robbers called the Kurths and told them that if the family didn't pony up $25,000, they would inform the police. The Kurths refused, and the Butte robbers made good on their threat. Acting on an anonymous tip, real DEA agents raided the ranch the next day.

Hubley, along with Assistant U.S. Attorney Jim Seykora as lead prosecutor, was a member of the Organized Crime Drug Enforcement Task Force of Montana, which started looking into the Kurth case.

"Information surfaced that there was a robbery and there were people with badges, and we got on it," Hubley says. The task force began what Hubley calls an "intense investigation," involving 10 different law enforcement agencies—city, county, and federal.

Seykora says that, during the year-and-a-half investigation, the task force collected a great deal of "fall-off, periphery type pieces of information" that involved other, non-drug-related crimes and took the task force in several directions. "We went where the tentacles took us," he says. One of the tentacles led to Butte, where Tom Hafer started talking after being indicted for selling cocaine.

He told law enforcement officials that Markovich had approached him about taking part in the Kurth robbery. He also told law enforcement that he had helped burn down the Cabin Bar in East Missoula at the behest of one of the bar owners, who wanted to collect the insurance money. Hafer named Markovich and LaBreche as his accomplices in the arson.

Investigators started poking into Markovich and LaBreche's past and began unearthing a boneyard of unsolved crimes.

"When you put together a good case and you have a good agent working on it, it puts pressure on people to cooperate and testify against other people," Seykora says. "And that's how the picture got painted." When the time came to interview Markovich and LaBreche, the task force investigators had a pretty vivid picture of their criminal histories.

"I just remember the way we were doing a lot of these interviews, late into the night and going into the morning as we were getting ready for trial, people would plead guilty and cooperate," Seykora says. "In a lot of the interviews, it took a lot of time and a lot of twists and turns. And you never ceased to be amazed, but then you never knew if you were getting a hundred percent either." LaBreche and Markovich would confess not just to the Kurth robbery and the Cabin Bar arson, but to a series of other crimes.

"It's fair to say," Hubley says, "that when people realize they're in a corner, based on the information that the investigator has that they're hard pressed to deny, they just give it up."

On August 10, 1989, the day before Markovich and LaBreche were sentenced in federal court, Seykora released a sentencing memorandum chronicling a series of crimes dating back to the mid-1960s, crimes also involving Mickey Sullivan, John T. Sullivan, and others. News of the memorandum filled the entire front page of the next day's *Standard* under the headline, "Cops' crime spree." The list of victims read like the Butte Yellow Pages.

Though the statute of limitations had expired on the old crimes he chronicled, Seykora thought it "only right and ethically fair," as he wrote in the memorandum, "that the citizens of Montana are informed of a long and wide ranging group of criminals before this court that have inundated, terrorized, mystified and existed in Southwest Montana, in particularly, Butte, Montana, for the past twenty plus years."

Even though Seykora recommended a lighter sentence as part of a plea agreement, U.S. District Judge Charles Lovell sentenced LaBreche to 39 years and Markovich to 40 for their roles in the Kurth robbery and in the Cabin Bar arson. Markovich would be released in 2000, LaBreche in 2002. LaBreche died six years later at the age of 72. No one contacted for this story knew Markovich's current whereabouts.

EVEN THOUGH HE'S RETIRED AND THE KURTH ROBBERY CASE HAS BEEN closed for decades, one particular footnote in the case still lingers in Jim Seykora's mind.

Before leaving Butte to help rob the Kurths, LaBreche programmed his VCR to tape a live heavyweight boxing match scheduled that evening between Mike Tyson and Tyrell Biggs. A few nights later, he played the tape for his wife, son, and some friends and duped them into believing it was a live broadcast. If ever LaBreche was a suspect in the robbery, his family and friends could thereby testify that he was home watching the fight on the night of the robbery. His son and two friends ended up doing exactly that.

"I said for many years that if I ever ceased to be amazed, I would quit," Seykora says. "I continued to be amazed the day I retired."

The Flood of 1964

By Butch Larcombe

Spring 2014

O N THE BLACKFEET INDIAN RESERVATION, creeks large and small drain the high country of Glacier National Park and the Rocky Mountain Front. They nurture crops and cattle and communities before blending into the Marias River, then the Missouri, then the Mississippi, sending Montana snowmelt to the Caribbean.

For many reservation residents, the creekside bottomland offers an oasis in the rolling prairie: shelter from the punishing wind, summer shade, wood for winter heat, water for humans and livestock. Brimming and turgid in the spring, the creeks drop quickly in the summer heat so dams were built long ago to capture water upstream, saving it for later use.

The system worked for decades. Then, in 1964, nature played a trump card. Spring was a cold one that year and followed a long winter. Mountain snowpack ran as high as 75 percent above average that May, one of the snowiest on record there, and temperatures in many places didn't crack 70 degrees until the Memorial Day weekend. Early in the month, a National Weather Service climatologist issued a statement: "We aren't in trouble unless we get a sudden warming and snowpack melts all at once. However, we don't look for that to happen—very rarely does snowmelt by itself cause flooding. But if we get rain on top of it ... then we're in trouble."

The trouble, first a trickle and quickly a torrent, came in the second week of June. At first, the rain was welcomed, after years of drought on the reservation, and brought visions of full reservoirs, bountiful hay crops and green painted across the rolling hills. "A million-dollar rain," some called it.

But optimism faded as the downpour clawed at the snow, rivers and streams rose, and the skies didn't lighten for days. "It came down as one pours from a cup, without stopping, all at once," a Blackfeet elder named Fish Wolf Robe told interviewer Helen West years later.

In roughly a 36-hour period, seven inches of rain fell at Babb, on the northern part of the reservation, while St. Mary saw 9 inches. Some reports said higher elevations received as much as 15 inches over several days. The rain hastened the melt and it all headed downhill.

HUNDREDS OF FAMILIES LIVED ALONG THE CREEKS ROARING FROM THE mountains. To the north of reservation headquarters at Browning runs Cut Bank Creek. Two Medicine Creek, with a dam up near the mountains, flows about a dozen miles south of town. Birch Creek marks the southern boundary of the reservation and in its upper reaches stood Swift Dam and an accompanying reservoir. Other creeks flowed between Two Medicine and Birch.

The first hint of tragedy came early on June 8 with a report of a man high in a tree surrounded by the surging waters of Two Medicine Creek. Rescuers were dispatched, along with school buses intended to evacuate people to Browning and Heart Butte, but deep water and washed-out bridges often stymied them. The telephone system on much of the reservation failed early in the flood so officials relied on two-way radios. Some folks on the reservation got news updates and emergency dispatches via KSEN, a Shelby-based radio station, while others on the sprawling reservation were left on their own, to do what they could.

RESERVATION ROAD SUPERINTENDENT ELMER MORIGEAU ENCOUNTERED a dramatic scene on the morning of June 8. Driving on a gravel road along Two Medicine Creek, he spotted a flatbed truck, loaded with people and making its way across the flooded bottomland, carving through water. Morigeau continued down the creek to gauge conditions and possibly warn others of the rising water. Retracing his route later, he saw the truck had stalled in a low spot, the water getting deeper and several people clinging to the vehicle. He radioed for help and asked for a boat.

Rescuers at one point knotted barbed wire to a tire and threw it into the raging current, trying to reach the stranded truck. They saved two people that way and a boat eventually rescued others. But nine members of a large extended family died in the vicious, frigid current. The youngest was two-month-old Terry Lee Guardipee; the oldest was 84-year-old Rose Grant.

One of the survivors told interviewers that she and other adults in the truck faced an unimaginable dilemma when the tire came close enough to grab. "The children were too little to send in alone [on the tire] and we couldn't go ourselves and leave them behind on the truck," said Fay Grant.

The horror of Grant and fellow survivor Lucille Guardipee, the mothers of some of the youngest victims, were later recounted by Nellie Buel in the pages of the Great Falls Tribune: "One by one, Lucille's children floated away," Buel wrote then. "The baby first, two months old, who had been clinging to Lucille's neck, and then the others. Then Fay's little five-year-old floated away."

An account by the Associated Press a few days after floodwaters began to subside told of a similar family tragedy on Birch Creek to the south. The just-the-facts story listed the names of those known to have died in the reservation flooding. It also listed the names of the missing and presumed dead including Dorothy Hall, 33; Thomas Hall III, 12; Marjorie Hall, 10; Kathy Hall, 6; Martin Hall, 4; Edward Hall, 2; and Judy Hall, 1. The Hall home, not far below Swift Dam, is believed to have been swept away by a wall of water. Linda Arnoux, 16, a guest in the home, also died. The only survivor among the immediate Hall family was the family patriarch, Tom Hall, Jr., who had gone that morning to Dupuyer for groceries. When he returned, he learned his family was dead, his home was gone.

NINETEEN PEOPLE DIED IN THE WATER ROARING DOWN BIRCH CREEK. Nine more died in Two Medicine Creek. All told, 30 deaths occurred in what became known as the Flood of '64, all on the Blackfeet Reservation. Of those deaths, 28 came in the wake of the failure of the Swift and Two Medicine dams on June 8.

Swift Dam was the first to be breached, likely during the late-morning hours. The dam on the Two Medicine didn't last much longer. Water cascading down from higher elevations put enormous pressure on the dams and later poured over the top, washing away rock and other fill before breaching the face of the structures.

The dam failure on Birch Creek became obvious within minutes. Abe

Rutherford, who lived with his family near the creek, shared the events of June 8 in a story published in Newsweek magazine a few weeks after the disaster. With water climbing fast near his home, Rutherford said he was preparing to move his family up a nearby hill when a boy on the hill screamed, "'The dam is busted.' We started to run. We got a little more than halfway up the hill when it came—a wall of water 40 feet high. It took out our house. We got away with nothing but what we were wearing."

Flying over the valley, shortly after the dam burst, pilot Jim Farrer of Shelby told of seeing buildings and livestock being swept downstream. "The most amazing sight was the crest taking away ranches and snapping telephone and power lines like matches. It was unbelievable." The pilot estimated the wall of water moved downstream at about 22 miles per hour.

One reservation resident, Woody Kipp, recalls listening to a remarkable account of the Birch Creek flooding on KSEN, which had hired the plane to survey the situation. The airborne broadcaster told of a herd of horses running down the creek bed, directly away from the fast-moving water, only to be overtaken and swallowed.

Many believe that the 19 victims along Birch Creek perished within minutes of the dam's collapse.

Patrick Wyse, the coroner in Pondera County, home to the dam and much of Birch Creek, said those who escaped reported a "tremendous noise" as the water roared eastward. "There was so very little warning that it was amazing how many people got out," he said a few days after the peak flooding. "The rubble is fantastic. The whole Birch Creek valley was swept clean of timber." The search for the bodies of the missing would cover an area 40 miles long and 5 to 15 miles wide.

The U.S. Geological Survey estimated the flow of water down Birch Creek after the dam break at 881,000 cubic feet per second, bigger than the average flow of the Mississippi River. But that measurement was made 17 miles below the dam and may have understated the peak volume.

WHILE THE GREATEST HUMAN TRAGEDY WAS UNDENIABLY ON BIRCH AND Two Medicine creeks, the tentacles of the Flood of '64 stretched well beyond the southern portion of the reservation. Woody Kipp, then 18 and headed to the Marine Corps, was living on the family ranch along Cut Bank Creek, northeast of Browning. There was no dam upstream, but the creek was a conduit for water gushing from Glacier.

"We had a big wall of water come down, probably from some of the big beaver dams up near Starr School," Kipp, now an English professor at Blackfeet Community College, recalled nearly 50 years after the flood. "They [the dams] held back the water for a while."

Kipp, along with his brother John and sister-in-law Mildred, filled sandbags for much of June 8. During a brief meal break, the creek rose to the doorstep of the family's home. The trio fled for higher ground, an escape aided by a four-wheel-drive truck, which, like a telephone, was a rarity in the rural reaches of the reservation in 1964. "Within a few minutes, the water was waist deep in the house," Kipp said. "We spent the entire night on about a half-acre of land that didn't get inundated," accompanied by chickens, pigs and other farm animals. "We had a whole menagerie out there with us."

A radio in the truck snagged the KSEN signal, sharing with the stranded family the news of the dam failures and the gloom of tragedy elsewhere on the reservation. The Kipps lost some livestock but the family home survived.

Similar run-for-your-life accounts unfolded in the days after the crisis. Numerous reservation families spent hours on hilltops and were later ferried to safety by helicopters from Malmstrom Air Force Base in Great Falls. Near Valier, a group of nearly 100 people found refuge from Birch Creek's rage in a rural schoolhouse. In Choteau, south of the reservation, the water overflowing from the Teton River corralled much of the community and forced 200 residents to evacuate. West of Augusta near where the Sun River leaves the mountains, water overtopped Gibson Dam. The concrete structure somehow held.

But below the dam, the Sun was forging a path of destruction as it made its way to the Missouri at Great Falls. West of Simms, the normally docile river carried dead livestock and debris and, according to one news account, a large barn that somehow remained whole. Forty miles east in Great Falls, the armada of junk included bathtubs.

West of the Continental Divide, the Flathead River and its tributaries rewrote hydrologic history, washing out bridges and miles of U.S. Highway 2 where it borders Glacier National Park, and dismembering large chunks of the Great Northern Railway line. An estimated 4,500 residents were driven from homes by the flooding in the Flathead Valley. Washed-out roads and bridges left Glacier isolated for days, and Highway 2 saw only limited travel for most of the summer.

The Flathead and Glacier flooding received lots of media attention. At the *Hungry Horse News* in Columbia Falls, editor-publisher Mel Ruder and the weekly's staff worked tirelessly during the flooding, producing three issues in four days. Each issue was loaded with photos taken from boats and airplanes and accounts of narrow escape. The reward: a Pulitzer Prize for local reporting—the first given to a Montana journalist or newspaper. KSEN, which broadcast what was likely lifesaving coverage around the clock for five days without any advertising, garnered a national broadcasting award.

All told, 15 Montana counties were affected by the flooding; eight of those were declared disaster areas by President Lyndon Johnson. Thirty were dead, 337 injured. On the Blackfeet reservation alone, 256 homes were destroyed. "It was the worst natural disaster ever to hit this state," Montana Governor Tim Babcock said at the time. Government estimates in 1964 put the tab at $62 million, $466 million in today's money.

WHILE THE DISASTER MADE THE FRONT PAGES OF THE *NEW YORK TIMES* and *Chicago Tribune* in days after the flooding and deaths, in the ensuing months the story was largely left to the *Glacier Reporter*, the weekly newspaper in Browning. The paper shared news of the search for bodies, typhoid inoculations, boil orders for drinking water, and the rush to rebuild lost homes before winter set in.

The newspaper also reflected grief and the post-flood rumor mill. Lucille Guardipee responded to gossip in a letter published in the Reporter on July 23. "I've been hearing rumors yet—people wondering why all my children drowned and I didn't. I wish some of those people had been in my place at that time—they'd know the reason," she wrote. "People are saying we were warned and why didn't we leave then. We were not warned. I sure wish people would quit talking because I feel bad enough and to hear these remarks and rumors makes me feel I am to blame for the death of my children. I tried my best to save them but God took them. No one will ever know how lonely I feel."

The Blackfeet Tribal Council declared June 8 a permanent day of mourning on the reservation. Ceremonies marking the flood and its human toll are held at the Museum of the Plains Indian each year. The tribal council also hired an archivist at the museum, Helen West, to interview reservation residents about the flood. Some of those interviews, published in 1970 in *Flood—The Story of the 1964 Disaster*, provide an intimate look at tragedy.

This year a handful of filmmakers and journalists hope to finish a film about the flood. The idea, says director Brooke Pepion Swaney, is to increase awareness of the flood and secure an accurate historical record

of the tragedy. Swaney, a Blackfeet tribal member who grew up largely on the Flathead Reservation, says, "Hearing about these stories has
been very difficult and emotional for me."

Out on Two Medicine and Birch creeks, there are no interpretive sites
or even highway signs recounting the deluge that some described as a
"500-year flood." Trees have grown back and the dams have been rebuilt.

For some, like Kipp, the memories of 1964 haven't been diminished
by the decades. "I would assume at some point, the rains will come
again," the college professor says wistfully. "We will see if the dams
can take it." ◪

Murder on the North Fork

By Myers Reece

Spring 2015

I N NORTHWEST MONTANA, an April midnight means darkness and mud in quiet woods. But in 1979, three Oklahoma fugitives shattered the calm with unspeakable bloodshed, and one man's midnight never turned to morning.

J.R. Fletcher, his wife Teresa Fletcher, and Ronald White, all in their 20s, had fled their home state and were aiming for the Canadian border. They drove fast and rested rarely, their heads pulsing with alcohol and a cacophony of drugs: heroin, cocaine, speed, marijuana, LSD. They stole cars and burglarized homes across the West. When they hit Montana, they were strung out and wild eyed. They had been awake for seven straight days.

In the earliest, darkest hours of April 7, they scrambled north on the rutted road that takes travelers along the North Fork Flathead River on the western border of Glacier National Park, past the tiny community of Polebridge and into Canada, weather permitting, though spring is rarely gentle in that country.

As the fugitives pushed onward, with no ID, in a stolen truck, they realized the border station might pose problems. So they hatched a plan to steal horses and ride through the backcountry.

When they spotted horses milling around in a corral, J.R. Fletcher steered their yellow Ford pickup, stolen in eastern Montana, into the driveway. But after a stint of outrunning the law, they discovered they couldn't outsmart the thaw. The pickup immediately mired in mud.

White trudged up the driveway to a trailer to ask for help. Roy Cooper, a 72-year-old rancher, answered the door. Then Cooper did what many Montanans would do: he helped. The generous act would be his last. By dawn, northwest Montana had lost a beloved native son.

CAROL HUGGINS, one of Cooper's two daughters and the only one still alive at 79, finds evidence of her father's kind heart even at his grisly murder scene. When investigators examined his body, his billfold contained three checks. Neighbors had given them to Cooper, a respected and knowledgeable horseman, to purchase three horses. The checks were signed but blank. They trusted him to find the best deal and fill in the amounts.

"He was an honest man," Huggins says. "He was a wonderful man."

A lot of people thought Cooper was wonderful. His funeral was among the largest ever held in Flathead County, with close to 400 people in the funeral home, and more huddled on the sidewalk outside. Farmers, loggers, hairdressers, bartenders, bankers, restaurant owners, out-of-state snowbirds, police, politicians, off-the-grid rednecks and off-the-rail hippies all mourned together.

"Everybody knew him and liked him," Huggins says. "I've always thought that it was lucky that Mom took care of the purse strings, because he would've given everything away. That's just how he was."

Cooper was born in Creston, near Kalispell, on Nov. 14, 1906. Growing up, he was as serious about work on the farm as he was about mischief off it, a big-hearted approach to life that never wavered through adulthood. In sixth grade, he and a few other boys were suspended for smoking cigarettes. He enjoyed the time off so much that, when the suspension ended, he stayed home. He never went to school again.

"He wasn't very educated but he was smarter than a lot of people with college educations, especially in math," Huggins says.

As a young man, Cooper met Adelaide Taylor, who had just earned a teaching degree from the college in Dillon, though the education gap wasn't wide enough to keep the lovebirds apart. They married on February 3, 1927, and had a daughter, Nora Grace.

Cooper worked a while as a logger, including a stint as the foreman of tree-clearing operations for the Hungry Horse Dam. When he heard that a coworker's wife had died and he was sending his kids to a children's home, Cooper volunteered to take in the youngest because the facility wouldn't accept infants. That baby was Carol Huggins.

"That tells you a lot about the kind of a man he was," Huggins says. "I was fortunate, very fortunate, to end up with him."

The Coopers farmed near Bigfork where Huggins and her father spent long days on horseback. Cooper earned extra money on the trading floor of a livestock yard, thanks to his quick-witted charm and his honesty. At the time, it was customary for a livestock buyer to name a cow after the seller's wife. Ranchers joked that damn near every cow in Montana was named Adelaide.

Cooper had a taste for beer and a wild side, too. He was a champion bullshitter with an extensive lineup of jokes, and he wasn't picky about conversation partners. Despite his active social life he remained a country boy, and sometimes it was clear that he understood mountains and horses better than bars and cars.

"One night he ran off the road," recalls granddaughter Linda Mc-Mannamy. "When he came home, he said, 'I'm trading that son of a bitch in. I don't have any use for a truck that can't find its way home.'"

The Coopers sold the farm in the 1960s and moved into a house in Kalispell, but Roy wasn't built for retirement or town life. So he rented a trailer near Polebridge, which proved to be the ideal base camp for a restless mountain man.

Cooper would spend days on end there, returning to his Kalispell home periodically to be with his wife and stock up on her premade meals. He volunteered to bale neighbors' hay, fix their machines, and tend their livestock, while working his own horses and cattle. He hunted and fished. He told jokes at the Polebridge saloon.

Cooper's nephew, Birch, stayed with him in the North Fork as a teenager, following his every move much like Jim, a grandson, had done as a boy. McMannamy called Jim her grandfather's "shadow," although all the grandchildren adored Cooper, and he loved all his little shadows.

"We were everything to him," McMannamy says. "He was there every holiday, at all of our plays. He was always there for us."

As with everywhere he went, Cooper befriended North Forkers of all stripes, even the mystifying hippie transplants. He liked to tease them about their long hair and beards, and he playfully threatened to introduce them to scissors and razors.

At the funeral, Huggins saw a group of men she didn't recognize. She pointed them out to a relative, who did a double take. It was the hippies. Their hair was short and their beards were gone.

GROGGY FROM THE LATE-NIGHT INTRUSION, Cooper ambled out to his tractor, fired it up and drove it down his driveway. He yanked the strangers' pickup out of the muck. The job was done.

The Fletchers and White have spun different stories about what happened next. The version that investigators and prosecutors pieced together, and to which the suspects admitted on the witness stand and pleaded guilty, begins with the night's first turn of violence, when White swung a rifle butt at Cooper as J.R. Fletcher pointed another rifle at him.

It's not clear whether the abrupt aggression was the start of a robbery or a response to Cooper noticing items in the pickup that had been stolen from neighbors' houses. What is clear is that Cooper's night was descending into terror.

For the next few hours, the fugitives held Cooper on his couch at gunpoint. They ate his food and drank his booze. At one point, they directed him outside to saddle three horses in the corral. They knocked out windows in neighboring houses, unoccupied so early in the season, and stole items for their pack trip: sleeping bags, canned food, kitchen utensils, guns, and lots of alcohol. Teresa and White took turns guarding Cooper at riflepoint.

Four months later, in Flathead County District Court, J.R. Fletcher testified that he entered the trailer to find a sleep-deprived Teresa nodding off and Cooper making a play for the rifle, though Cooper's family doubts this scenario. Fletcher grabbed a large knife from the kitchen and slashed at Cooper's throat. He couldn't remember in court how many times he stabbed him in the neck.

Prosecutors say Fletcher then ordered Teresa to stab Cooper so she would also be culpable for the murder. The attacks severed his spinal cord and nearly decapitated him.

Before departing, J.R. replaced Cooper's cowboy hat on his head and positioned his body upright on the couch, as if he were dozing. Then the trio hopped in their pickup and continued north before abruptly turning back south, their Wild West border crossing plans nixed by some combination of bad roads and impulsive violence and general madness. The horses neighed in the corral, still saddled, as daylight broke over the eastern mountains.

Neighbors found Cooper's body later that day. Detectives arrived soon after. Authorities put out a wire for murder suspects traveling with stolen goods.

The criminals darted over to Idaho, stopping to sell guns and camping gear at the Lumberjack Saloon in Lolo. They checked into a motel in Lowell, Idaho, a small river community 100 miles west of Lolo and nearly 300 miles southwest of Polebridge. It was still Saturday, not yet a day removed from the murder.

In Lowell, they met two men interested in purchasing guns. The prospective buyers wanted to test the weapons first, so White and Fletcher, leaving Teresa at the motel, traveled with the men to a spot in the woods.

Sheriff's deputies received reports of gunfire. When they neared the scene, a yellow pickup zoomed past them going the opposite direction. In the chase that followed, gunshots rained down on pursuing deputies, and the fugitives disappeared into the night.

At first light Sunday morning, deputies tracked down the pickup on a mountain road, and White and J.R. Fletcher finally gave themselves up as ammunition ran out. No deputies were injured but their cars were riddled with bullet holes. Newspapers reported at least 50 shots fired altogether. Teresa was rounded up later.

The story of the shootout and capture played out on front pages, though details of the murder wouldn't crystallize until courtroom hearings in August. The three suspects all initially pleaded not guilty to the same charges: burglary, aggravated kidnapping and deliberate homicide. But they changed their pleas as part of a pretrial agreement in exchange for reduced sentences.

The homicide charge was dropped for Ronald White, who pleaded guilty to aggravated kidnapping and received a 75-year sentence. Teresa Fletcher pleaded guilty to "mitigated" deliberate homicide because prosecutors concluded that she was a follower, not a leader, and was forced by her husband to wield the knife after the victim had already been repeatedly stabbed. She got 40 years.

J.R. Fletcher, identified as the ringleader and primary murderer, pleaded guilty to deliberate homicide and was sentenced to 100 years in Montana State Prison.

At their hearings, the Oklahomans showed no remorse, according to witness accounts and newspaper reports. Teresa smiled and laughed through her questioning. White shrugged off the judge's suggestion that he was treating the ordeal like a "picnic." J.R. flipped off cameras and swore at the crowd.

George Ostrom observed the courtroom drama as both a newsman and neighbor. Ostrom was covering the case for the *Kalispell News*, a newspaper he founded. He also owned a ranch in the North Fork, not too far from Cooper's trailer. He had teenagers who lived and worked there, and 35 years later he still shudders thinking how close the killers came to his property.

A hard-nosed Army veteran, Ostrom says Teresa "had the most foul mouth I've ever heard, and I've been around the world a time or two." But J.R. gave him chills.

"I kept staring him in the eye and I could see he was evil," Ostrom says. "You could see it. He was an evil man."

The word evil repeatedly comes up in conversations about Fletcher and in court documents. He did nothing to refute the label when he shouted at Cooper's family in the courtroom, threatening to kill them if he ever got out of prison. He was still yelling at anybody who would listen when he boarded a small plane to be transported to the state penitentiary in Deer Lodge.

The Kalispell *Daily Inter Lake* ran a front-page photo of Fletcher being escorted onto the plane by sheriff's deputies. He's standing with his chest puffed and face turned toward the camera. The caption proclaims that he remained "defiant to the last," shouting obscenities until the hatch closed and he could no longer be heard.

Sitting in a prison dormitory conference room in late January 2015, J.R. Fletcher is no longer shouting. He's been incarcerated in Deer Lodge since 1979. He looks nothing like the wiry young man with wavy dark hair in the *Inter Lake* photo. At 64, his face and body are swollen from age and poor health. He talks steadily, without emotion. It's the first time he's spoken with a reporter in 35 years.

Fletcher calmly suggests that he's not evil, nor is he even violent. In fact, he's now saying he never committed the murder.

Over the course of nearly two hours, Fletcher makes a case for innocence that is as full of complex specifics as it is blatantly full of holes, though not without a string of correlations and bizarre twists that often blur the line between fact and fabrication.

Fletcher presents a version of events far different than the one he admitted to in 1979. He offers a stack of documents, including two "affidavits," to support his story. The affidavits bear no official markings and are riddled with elementary-school grammatical errors. In November, 2014, he gave the same documents to the parole board, which denied him for a second time.

In his alternate depiction of April 7, 1979, Fletcher paints a picture of a peaceful evening, undone only by his wife's sudden violence. He says he had negotiated to buy Cooper's horses, not steal them, and was preparing the horses with White when they heard a gunshot. Teresa then emerged from the trailer, dragging a .30-06 at her side.

Fletcher says Teresa later admitted she "killed him just to see what it's like to kill somebody."

One of the purported affidavits is a confession signed by Teresa on June 10, 1982, in which she takes full responsibility for the murder and explains that she initially lied to receive a shorter sentence, for the good of her family. J.R. is portrayed as a martyr who fell on the sword to facilitate an early reunion between Teresa and her kids, one of whom was his. Though they had married four years before Cooper's murder, the Fletchers had spent barely two months together because J.R. was in prison for car theft and other crimes.

The other affidavit is signed by Ronald White and dated 1987. It gives a lengthy description of the night at Cooper's house. It also pins the blame solely on Teresa, stating that she shot Cooper. But Teresa's confession says that she stabbed him. It's as if the trio could never quite get on the same page, and even nuggets of truth are disguised by a shape-shifting carousel of distortions.

White had earlier presented Teresa's alleged confession as evidence in a request to change his plea. District Judge James M. Salansky said the documents lacked credibility. In his 1983 ruling, Salansky wrote that the three accomplices "repeatedly changed their accounts" and noted that White's lawyer said Teresa recanted her affidavit over the phone.

"[White] and his accomplices are playing games and making a mockery of the judicial system," the judge concluded.

Further convoluting matters, courtroom testimony raised the possibility of a rifle accidentally going off in Teresa's lap, though detectives never found a bullet hole on Cooper's body or in his trailer. On Cooper's death certificate, the coroner determined cause of death to be "stab wounds, head and neck area."

Fletcher now denies that he ever admitted to killing Cooper. He remains unfazed by facts. Instead, he claims he's a victim of a sprawling conspiracy that reaches untold corners of a government bent on destroying him.

"It didn't matter what the crime was. It was all about burying me."

But Ted Lympus, the county attorney who prosecuted the case, says it's not that complicated.

"He's the one who did it," says Lympus, now a district judge. "It was a cold-blooded event and he had a history. This is a classic case [in which] he definitely deserves permanent incarceration."

While most of the trio's wild inconsistencies stem from conscious manipulation, others are likely byproducts of their lengthy drug and alcohol binge. White and Teresa have both admitted to fuzzy memories, with periods of blackness, even if J.R. Fletcher has revised his autobiography today to exclude drug use.

Fletcher has made a lot of revisions to his story. There's not much else to do in prison, especially if you're staying out of trouble, which Fletcher has been doing for 10 years. As a reward for his decade without a write-up, he was transferred from the regular prison into a dormitory, where he sweeps and mops the hallway and lobby floors.

But sanitizing the past can't eliminate it. Fletcher tries hard these days to present himself as nonviolent. He concedes to a life of crime leading up to Cooper's murder, though he describes himself as a country bumpkin from Oklahoma who got caught up in car theft but never hurt anybody. While it's true that car theft was the primary reason he spent his 20s locked up, violence is the reason he spent the next 35 years in prison.

Count the parole board among the many who believe he's dangerous and untruthful. In a December 2014 disposition, the parole board dismissed Teresa's 1982 affidavit as further evidence that Fletcher refuses to accept responsibility for his actions. The board also cited the "evil nature of the horrific crime."

Teresa Fletcher and Ronald White have been paroled and released from prison. But at that last November parole hearing, Flathead County Attorney Ed Corrigan insisted that Fletcher should never again taste freedom.

"This man is a waste of space and organic molecules," Corrigan said, standing a few feet from Fletcher. "He committed a horrific crime. He is an evil man. There is no place in society for this individual."

RELATIVES BELIEVE COOPER HAD AT LEAST TWO MORE DECADES OF GOOD living. The family has a history of thriving into its 90s, and Cooper looked poised to carry on the tradition. He had lost only one tooth, despite a lifetime of chewing tobacco. His mind was sharp. He was still learning new jokes and breaking new horses.

"J.R. Fletcher took 20 years of fun times away from us," says Huggins, his daughter. "He stole that from us."

Cooper's legacy endures through a family tree that sprawls across western Montana. Nora Grace passed away last year, leaving behind five daughters and an army of grandchildren and great-grandchildren. Jim passed away two years ago.

Unlike her sister, Huggins hasn't added any branches to the family tree. She has never married and has no kids, maintaining fierce independence in a world that couldn't be trusted to protect a good man like Roy Cooper. As she nears 80, her appetite for college football and dark beer hasn't waned. She's sharp-tongued and tough and immensely likeable. She is her father's daughter.

But neither time nor toughness can fully erase grief, and her eyes moisten when she holds a photo of him, pointing it away from herself to show a visitor the can of chewing tobacco in his shirt pocket. Her finger covers his torso, as if wrapped around him. For a moment, it seems like she's holding more than a photo. ◣

The Wild Ride of 1894

By John Clayton

Fall 2008

THE OLD NORTHERN PACIFIC BOXCARS OVERFLOWED WITH UNWASHED, boisterous, and desperate men. Some miles behind them, a trainload of deputy federal marshals followed in hot pursuit, and nobody knew for sure when the looming confrontation would arrive. Yet in front of them, at the east end of the Muir Tunnel through Bozeman Pass, the rails were blocked by 30 cubic yards of rock, mud, and timber.

The men, about 300 of them, had stolen the train. There was no doubt about that. But they believed their cause was just, and the warm welcome they'd just received in Bozeman suggested that many Montanans agreed. But they hadn't counted on these so-called federal marshals, a group instantly deputized from what some people called "the scum of Butte" to do the dirty work of a large and greedy corporation. If that trainload of hired thugs caught these men before they'd cleared the slide, there was no telling what might happen.

Although this may sound like it's building up to the climax of a John Wayne movie, it is in fact a true story and a surprisingly overlooked piece of Montana history. The 300 men were part of a nationwide group called Coxey's Army, and they planned to take part in the first-ever popular march on Washington, D.C.

Problems had started with the Panic of 1893, so far the worst economic recession in the country's history. Across the nation banks failed, mines closed, railroads went bankrupt, and unemployment rates soared. Because Montana provided a huge portion of the country's gold, copper, silver, and lead, this state was hit especially hard. By January of 1894, 20,000 Montanans were out of work. At a time when the state's population was just 132,000, the ranks of the jobless may have included as many as one-quarter of all family breadwinners.

In Ohio, a man named Jacob Coxey decided to take matters into his own hands. Though wealthy himself, Coxey believed that men who wanted to work shouldn't be denied the opportunity, so he suggested the federal government initiate a huge road-building campaign. In addition to providing infrastructure, the program would put men to work and stimulate the economy.

To persuade Congress, Coxey urged 100,000 jobless men to present a "petition with boots on" in Washington on May 1, 1894. In late March, he started leading an Ohio contingent by foot.

In addition to being the first-ever proposed march on the capitol, Coxey's effort was one of the first big national stories to arise in a new era of journalism. Printing innovations and expanding literacy in the 1880s had led to new types of mass-appeal newspapers. The papers loved controversy, and for this story they practiced the "yellow journalism" techniques later perfected for the 1898 Spanish-American War.

Journalists painted Coxey's crusade in exaggerated images of warfare. The leader became known as "General Coxey" and his shambling men an "army." Sympathetic papers presented him as the hero of a "new French Revolution," while dissenters referred to his poverty-stricken followers as a "campaign of squalor."

Thanks to advances in communications—both in popular media and within labor unions—such accounts stirred emotions across the nation. "Coxeyites" sprang up in urban areas across the West, including San Francisco, Seattle, Portland, Tacoma, Spokane—and Butte. In April 1894, these men vowed to join Coxey in Washington. But given the vast distances, they knew they had to travel by rail.

In Butte, passions simmered through several public demonstrations in April. Butte merchants, supportive of the men yet tired of feeding them handouts, tried to persuade Northern Pacific to give them discounted passage to Washington. But railroads were among the hardest-hit companies of the recession, and the recently bankrupted Northern Pacific argued that its management no longer had authority to grant such a favor.

Finally on April 24, at 2 a.m., the Coxeyites commandeered an old engine and six coal cars. Playing the John Wayne role was William Hogan, a wiry, Shakespeare-quoting, 34-year-old teamster recently laid off from William A. Clark's Moulton mine. Hogan's men (including some knowledgeable railroad veterans) piled in and steamed up Homestake Pass. They nearly broke speed records on the 90-mile trek to Bozeman, covering the final third at almost 60 miles an hour.

In Bozeman the men were greeted warmly. Townspeople gave them two tons of provisions, and they were able to trade their drafty coal cars for standard boxcars. But there they also learned of the slide at the Muir Tunnel, caused by torrential rains. Northern Pacific personnel had started to clear the mess, but when they learned that the next train expected through the tunnel was a stolen renegade, they hid their equipment and pulled out.

The Coxeyites, however, were men who wanted to work. Arriving at the slide, they found the cached shovels and waded into thick, slimy clay up to their knees. When they had nearly cleared the track, the top slid in again and they had to start over. For almost six hours they toiled with shovels and dull axes, working in shifts because there wasn't enough equipment to go around.

They knew they had to hurry. In Butte, assistant U.S. Marshal M.J. Haley had struggled, in the labor-friendly city, to organize a posse to stop the Coxeyites. He eventually rounded up 80 men, only 15 of whom deserted before their train took off. By late afternoon the Coxeyites were still working in three feet of mud but knew they were running out of time. Their engineer backed up the train to get a full head of steam, blew the whistle, rang the bell, and blasted through the obstruction. Minutes later the Coxeyites arrived in Livingston, where locals donated another $75 worth of provisions.

Why were locals so eager to help? In part they wanted "Hogan's Army" to keep moving, so that any confrontation would happen in the next town down the line. But at the same time Coxey's populist cause had gained widespread support because of its ties to the Free Silver movement, which allied Montana's agricultural and mining interests against eastern banks and manufacturers. Indeed, once the train was stolen, Northern Pacific Division superintendent J.D. Finn had requested that Governor John Rickards call out the state militia, but Rickards refused.

If William Hogan is the populist hero in this legend, Finn is the corporate villain. In Butte he'd tried to stop the Coxeyites through numerous legal maneuverings, had routed trains away from the city so they couldn't be commandeered, and had pressured federal officials to assemble the ruffian mercenary "deputies." Now he decided to sabotage his own railroad tracks. Near Greycliff, he ordered a cliff dynamited, to spread more debris over the tracks. And for many miles to the east, he ordered that all trackside water tanks—used to replenish the steam engines—be emptied.

The Coxeyites easily removed the Greycliff slide, and then paused to restore the mess so as to slow their more-indolent pursuers, joking that they wanted to leave the track in the condition they'd found it. But the lack of water proved more crippling. Between Greycliff and Columbus the train had to slow to a crawl, with frequent stops so that men could hurry down to the Yellowstone River to refill the tanks with their single bucket. Finally, as they neared a bridge over the river, a light appeared on the tracks behind them.

It was 1 a.m., 23 hours after they'd left Butte. The Coxeyites now faced a showdown with the law.

Hogan stopped the train in the middle of the bridge. The deputies approached, now numbering about 60 under Haley's command. Hogan took his boldest move yet. He ordered several men to walk out into the headlight of the pursuing locomotive, armed only with flags of the United States and the Butte Miners Union. They dared the deputies to shoot.

Haley had to back down. How could his posse shoot at unarmed men assembled under the flag? (At the time the union was so powerful that its flag was nearly as symbolic as the stars and stripes.) The best he could do was to slowly follow his quarry and hope for another chance.

The Coxeyites creaked into Columbus, where friendly crowds greeted them. William Cunningham, a Hogan deputy and former union president noted for his oratory skills, led an impromptu rally. Soon the deputies approached, guns drawn, but the Coxeyites jeered and cursed them as their train pulled away just before a riot could explode.

At the next stop, in Billings, the fuse was shorter. Finn had wired Yellowstone County Sheriff James Ramsey with orders to arrest Hogan's force. But Ramsey, apparently following the mood of the townspeople, decided it was not his quarrel. He told his deputies they should plan to be "out on business" when the train came through. And so his undersheriff wired back to Finn, tongue perhaps slightly in cheek, "All of [our] able-bodied men are busy selling real estate. Stop Coxey's army at Livingston."

With little law enforcement present at the Billings depot, an "acting mayor" provided the Coxeyites with barrels of beef, bread and potatoes. A crowd of nearly 500 cheered, and as many as 100 volunteered to join the expedition. Then, amidst more speeches, Haley's pursuing deputies again approached, and this time their patience broke. They tried to fire on the engine, and in the general melee that followed, one of Haley's men fired into the crowd, fatally wounding a bystander.

The crowd turned on the deputies, disarming them and sending them scurrying for their lives back to their train. Some were beaten, and 10 were arrested. As the shooting victim neared death, Billings sought revenge—not on the self-described "honest workingmen on a peaceful mission to Washington"—but on the mob scraped together to pursue them in the name of the law.

Shaken, the Coxeyites continued eastward from Billings, still moving slowly with little available water. Hogan had led them through three unexpected escapes from the posse. He'd hoped that Northern Pacific, like Montana law enforcement, would choose not to interfere with his train. Now that such hopes were dashed, he may have understood that the next outcome would not be so favorable.

In the aftermath of the violence in Billings, Northern Pacific officials and Governor Rickards convinced U.S. President Grover Cleveland to send out the 22nd infantry, based at Fort Keogh near Miles City. Finn provided a Northern Pacific train to take the troops westward to intercept the Coxeyites near Forsyth. Hogan's men, who respected the Army much more than the posse, immediately surrendered.

The anticlimax continued in Washington, D.C. on May 1. Less than 500 men followed Coxey to his final demonstration. When they reached the Capitol, police arrested Coxey for violating the "Keep off the grass" signs. He served 30 days, long enough for his army to disintegrate and the newspapers to find a new sensation.

For his leadership in stealing the train, Hogan served six months in prison; several of his assistants got 30 to 60 days. (William Cunningham, who by then claimed not to be a Coxeyite at all, but an undercover journalist for an Anaconda newspaper, got off.) The rest of the men were released and—to keep them occupied and off the local welfare rolls—were actually given materials and provisions to head to Washington via rafts on the Missouri River. As they left Fort Benton at the height of spring runoff, their scows spun crazily, out of control. But the ragtag army made it all the way to St. Louis before having to face the fact that their cause was finished.

In the long run, however, Coxeyism proved not so much a failure as a crusade ahead of its time. In years since, we have come to adopt both Coxey's policies of federal work programs—a key response to the 1930s Great Depression—and his tactics of marching on Washington to protest injustice. Meanwhile, the Hogan episode demonstrated that, just seven years into statehood, Montana had fully entered the national stage. Its natives—specifically the hardworking firebrands of industrial Butte—had played the most militant and colorful role in what the day's journalists labeled the most important series of national events since the Civil War. ◂

Sometimes
a Great Document

By Alan Kesselheim

Winter 2012

A STATE'S CONSTITUTION IS ONE OF THOSE NECESSARY BUT CUMBERSOME documents that, more often than not, epitomize the timeless, staid, and perfunctory—in other words, Dead-Sea-Scroll boring. One of those parchments that every state might need, but that is destined to be filed away in dusty archives, vaguely extolled in speeches now and then, a lifeless and lawyerly drone of words someone had to string together back in the murky fog of history; and better them than us.

What you don't expect is a document with vision, with soaring language, and with living force projected through the decades to shape the course of lives. Nor would you expect a political process steeped in bipartisan fellowship, work sessions marked by respect and compromise, a unanimous conclusion, and a legacy that continues to inform the lives of its delegates forty years later.

You would not expect to uncover stirring drama, either; that the Constitution only barely squeaked through a narrow, fortuitous window of opportunity, and dodged a number of terminal pitfalls along the way. That it happened at all is a testament to the fortitude and timing and care of its delegates; and to luck. It was a far closer thing than we know.

Montana's original, 19th-century state constitution was more along the lines of what you would expect. It came into force in 1889, largely as a requirement of statehood. It wasn't the first attempt. In both 1866 and 1884 efforts were made to cobble together a document and pursue statehood. In '66, with the Civil War hanging over the continent like a dust storm, the hand-written document was lost on the way to a St. Louis printer. In 1884 constitutional momentum was blocked by federal legislative stalemate. Sound familiar?

By 1889 the planets aligned enough to allow passage of a constitution in conjunction with achieving statehood. The strife of war lay far enough behind the country to focus on expansion. The battle over slave and slave-free states had subsided and the frontier was closing fast. Women were still more than three decades from getting the vote. Resources, and especially mineral resources, were king.

Not surprisingly, the 1889 constitution reflected those times. It devoted an inordinate amount of attention to clearly establishing boundaries. It stressed the abolition of slavery. It gave tremendous advantages to the timber and mining industries, as well as bowing to the influence of agriculture. Public lands were seen as commodities to be harvested.

No doubt the constitutional delegates put earnest effort into the document, but it didn't soar. It wasn't dynamic. It lacked innovation or leadership. It was a legalistic document, a tool to gain statehood. As decades passed, it became less and less appropriate. By the mid-1900s Montana's constitution had become an anachronism.

Outdated though it was, the 1889 version had its share of defenders. The mining industry, for example, dominated by Anaconda Copper Company, along with the Montana Power Company, the state chambers of commerce, and the Farm Bureau all advocated for the business-friendly provisions and backroom political deal-making abetted by the original constitution. They liked the tenor and advantages of the previous century just fine.

In the 1960s it fell to the Montana League of Women Voters to agitate for change. Dorothy Eck, of Bozeman, was the president of the League. She spearheaded the effort and in 1969, after years of lobbying and public meetings, Referendum #67 passed the 42nd Legislature, requesting a Constitutional Convention. In 1971, much to the surprise of pundits, not to mention business interests who hadn't taken the campaign seriously, the referendum passed a popular vote.

Before the year was out, the Constitutional Convention was arranged and 100 delegates were elected. The very passage of the referendum, followed by the political vote to initiate a Constitutional Convention, was the first hurdle, and the first unlikely success.

Consider the tenor of the times. The Vietnam War was culminating in U.S. defeat. Counter-culture protests had reached a fever pitch. The sounds of Woodstock music reverberated on the airwaves. In 1970 students at Kent State University had been shot and killed protesting the war. Wallace Stegner would, in 1972, win the Pulitzer Prize for "Angle of Repose." The shenanigans of Watergate were hitting the news. Wilt Chamberlain was in his final basketball season. Nuclear tests were in full swing in the Nevada desert. The Dow Jones closed above 1,000 for the first time. The Clean Air Act was passed in 1970, followed by the Clean Water Act. *Ms. Magazine* began publication. Gold hit a record of $70/ounce. And Evel Knievel broke 93 bones in a jump over 35 cars.

That was the backdrop. America was a nation very much in flux. Environmental concerns were a gathering tide. The questioning of authority had reached a crescendo.

In the midst of all this, what stands out about the Constitutional Convention of 1972, in every phase, is the progressive, thorough, studious, and grassroots approach of its delegates. That tone was set well before the convention, during the political campaign, which was infused with the energy of a cadre of committed volunteers; people like Dale Harris, who, as an intern, held dozens of town meetings, spent months educating the public, and traveled around the state with his message. That groundwork and energy paid off with an overwhelming victory at the polls, and caught the opposition, including major corporations, napping.

The selection of delegates was calibrated to deny political office holders and other vested interests a controlling interest in the proceedings. Although delegates had party affiliations, they weren't entrenched politicians. Many candidates went out of their way to educate themselves on the constitutional process and the pros and cons of the old document. Paid researchers, including Dale Harris, compiled 2,300 pages of background information. Classes were offered through universities, including one that Dorothy Eck remembers taking from Professor Lawrence Pettit at MSU in Bozeman.

One hundred delegates were elected—58 Democrats, 36 Republicans and eight Independents. Among them were housewives, ranchers, a former Montana First Lady, businesspeople, educators, graduate students, a bee-keeper, a librarian and a retired FBI agent. Nineteen of the 100 were women. Leo Graybill Jr., an attorney from Great Falls, presided. In January of 1972 the Convention assembled and got to work, under Chairman Graybill's injunction to avoid partisanship.

Chuck Johnson was a 23-year-old Capitol Hill reporter for the Associated Press at the time. It was Johnson's first reporting job, and he had little appreciation for how momentous his journalistic debut was.

Looking back, forty years later, he remembers it fondly. "It was really a blast," Johnson says. "It was a mark of the times, and it opened the legislative door to a host of interesting people with good intentions."

"We were an exclusive club in Montana history," says Wade Dahood, now an Anaconda attorney. "And we presided over what was perhaps the most important political event of the last century."

Delegates certainly had their pet agendas—women's rights, the protection of the environment, more open government, Indian education, guarantees for business and agriculture—the sorts of issues that could have easily derailed the process. Several key decisions early on helped avoid those pitfalls.

Rather than depend on a process dominated by party caucuses and the bipartisan friction sure to follow, delegates chose to seat themselves alphabetically rather than by party affiliation. There was, as Ken Egan of Humanities Montana recently stated at the 40th anniversary of the Constitution, a resolve to "disagree agreeably."

At that same anniversary event, held in Helena, Montana's future governor Steve Bullock reflected on the awareness that the process was "greater than any individual, greater than any party affiliation . . . ," an atmosphere we could learn from today.

The various committees set up to handle major constitutional planks, from the Bill of Rights to the Executive, and from Revenue & Finance to the Environment and Natural Resources, were split up between the parties. If a committee had a Democratic chairperson, the vice-chair would come from the Republican ranks, for example. Small measures, but they led to a spirit of practicality and balance rather than one of divisive rancor.

The other sentiment that emerged as the convention proceeded was the need to avoid micromanaging the document. As the language of the preamble exemplifies, the constitution sets out clear, broad-stroke intentions, visionary ideals, and leaves the specifics to evolve over time in response to circumstances.

"We understood that there were inherent conflicts in the provisions we crafted, and we left the job of balancing those conflicts to the courts and the legislature," says Mae Nan Ellingson, who at 24 was the youngest delegate at the convention and is often credited, along with delegate Bob Campbell, with crafting the wording of the Preamble.

And so, as the weeks passed and language slowly clarified, phrases like "commitment to cultural integrity," the "restoration of full rights" to felony offenders after serving their time, the "inviolable dignity of the human being," the right of citizens to attend political meetings and the public announcement of votes at those meetings landed on the page.

Some of these were very pragmatic matters: the open meeting clause, which ended what had been a closed-door, secretive process of crony corporate politics, for example. Others were more visionary: the commitment to honoring the cultural heritage and right to education for Indian peoples, or the public ownership of Montana's rivers.

"The delegates had no way to anticipate many changes coming down the road," Supreme Court Justice Jim Nelson said recently. "Cell phones, the Internet, social media, none of that was on their radar. But because they wrote a visionary document, in plain and clear language, we can see their concerns and apply their sentiments to current situations.

"I frequently go back to the Constitution, and to the transcripts of the proceedings, to understand their intentions. It was not written like an insurance policy, thankfully. Because of that it is a living document that has lasted and will last through the ages, a compact with the people of Montana for just governance. And it is a great help in the balancing act required of the courts."

"We met for 56 days," remembers Dahood. It was a remarkably short and intense period. "Each committee prepared a pamphlet to summarize their section. Along the way, every single committee had vehement debates, real disagreements.

"What I'm most proud of is that, at the end, on March 24, 1972, we all walked up and signed the constitution. That unanimous signing gives me the greatest pride."

By that signing, and because of that process, the Montana Constitution survived another test, and skirted the minefield of political deadlock, partisan division, and outside meddling that could easily have defeated it.

But it was not a done deal. Far from it.

Betty Babcock, former Montana first lady, and one of six delegates elected from the field of 48 who ran in District 12, was a fierce defender of the Constitution, and is widely praised for her influence in bringing fellow Republicans along. "I'm a Republican," she said, recently, "but I wasn't very popular in Republican circles back then. I just felt very strongly that the people of Montana had a right to vote on this document that we worked so hard to create." The unanimity of the convention, combined with pressure from voices like Babcock's, had an impact on the legislature, which adopted the document despite severe misgivings by many members.

It still had to pass the test of a public vote, and by the spring of 1972, the entities with the most to lose had come to life. The Farm Bureau, the Chamber of Commerce, mining, timber and agricultural interests all lined up against it. They may have underestimated the process in its early stages, but by the time it was on the ballot, the opposition was awake and alarmed. They poured money and resources into a campaign against the new constitution.

Several side issues also appeared on the ballot, including abolishing the death penalty and legalized gambling. On June 6, when voters went to the polls, all the unanimity of the Constitutional Convention was a faint memory. The tenor was acrimonious, the airwaves buzzed with fear tactics, rumor and half-truth, and the vote was razor close. In Butte, while legalized gambling passed by a whopping 73% to 27%, the Constitution failed by a 53% to 46% margin. Statewide, however, the Constitution was adopted by a skinny majority of 2,500 votes.

Another mine avoided, but it still wasn't law. Immediately after the election the results were contested in court. Plaintiffs, the usual suspects, argued that the majority of Montanans hadn't voted on the constitution, only a majority of those who actually voted. Montana's Supreme Court reaffirmed the results of the election, but only in a narrow, 3-2 decision.

The plaintiffs pressed on, taking the case to the U.S. Supreme Court, where, finally, in the fall of 1973, the Montana Constitution was upheld. More than a year after the delegates of the Constitutional Convention put pen to parchment, the document became the official and supreme law of the state.

Nearly 40 years later, Montana's Constitution is still as visionary and inspired, pragmatic and careful, as it was in 1972. Indian education has benefited. Montana's environment has benefited. An open political process is now taken for granted. Outdoor enthusiasts enjoy the rivers and trails of the state as a right of citizenship. Individuals are awarded a high standard of dignity before the courts.

It is, indeed, a living document, one that is both extolled and challenged by turns.

"I find it interesting that most amendments brought up since 1972 have sought to weaken the document and take away rights of individuals," reflects Ellingson. "Initiative C18, in 1988, gave the legislature power to determine access to public assistance. CI 96, in 2004, denied the rights of the gay community. It's ironic. When the document is challenged, it always seems to limit rights."

Judge Nelson agrees. "Whenever I hear arguments like these, I'm always tempted to ask the plaintiffs, 'What individual right would you be willing to give up?' Whenever a right is taken away from a group, it is taken from all of us. People forget that."

Many of the delegates to the Constitutional Convention went on to make their mark in Montana history. Dorothy Eck became an influential legislator. "I was all set to study geology at the university," reports Eck, "but after the Convention I took up politics full time for the rest of my career."

Mae Nan Ellingson pursued a distinguished law career. Others became district judges, politicians, educators. To a person, they remember with pride the proceedings they took part in, and the legacy they left for the state of Montana.

"I feel even better about the Constitution now than I did in 1972," says Babcock. "It has stood the test of time. It distinguishes itself in comparison to constitutions of other states. I feel honored to have been part of that." ◤

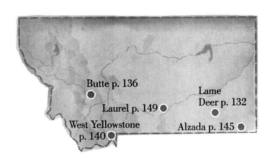

Butte p. 136

Lame
Deer p. 132

Laurel p. 149

West Yellowstone
p. 140

Alzada p. 145

EATING & DRINKING

Belly up. You've earned it.

The Toughest Bar in Montana?

By Scott McMillion

Winter 2005

L IKE A LOT OF SALOONS AROUND THE COUNTRY, the Jimtown Bar sells souvenir ball caps bearing the name of the bar. I've seen a lot of hats, but these are different. Embroidered on the back is a slogan: "Friday Night Special," it says. "Shot, Stabbed or Raped."

It's not really a joke. It's a sort of perverse pride.

I've heard for years that the Jimtown Bar is the toughest joint in Montana, the kind of place where the whupass can is always open.

Perched just outside the Northern Cheyenne Indian Reservation, which bans the sale or possession of alcohol, this rambling wooden structure overlooks an awful pretty stretch of Rosebud Creek. Everybody's welcome, but the bar specializes in scratching an itch for anyone willing to make the short drive or the long walk from Lame Deer, about four miles away.

For most of their long history, the Cheyenne were a warrior nation, a fact that Custer should have heeded. And the ravages of alcohol in Indian Country are well known, which is why the tribal elders have banned booze on the reservation. Violence erupts at Jimtown and everybody seems resigned to the inevitability.

So owner Mary Dillon does what she can to keep things under control.

"I've only had to shoot my gun a couple times," said Dillon, who has owned the place for 20 years. "And I've only been genuinely scared probably twice. But I buy pepper spray by the case."

She told me she's not afraid to use it, either, even if it means that "everybody's out of here, puking."

Vomit in the parking lot is better than a donnybrook inside.

Jimtown isn't really a town. It's just the bar, Dillon's trailer house out back and some outbuildings, where the yard is surrounded by 8-foot, chain-link fences and patrolled by seven Doberman pinschers and German shepherds.

"They respect my dogs," Dillon said of her customers. "If I raise my voice, those dogs are on somebody."

If she has to, she said, she'll handcuff a particularly truculent customer to a pole, where he or she awaits the police.

But those are extreme circumstances. Almost always, she or one of her bartenders can diffuse a situation before it gets out of hand.

"When the tone of somebody's voice rises, we get 'em out of here," she said. "It's my way or the highway, and they'd rather deal with me than the cops."

And then there are the everyday steps meant to fend off injury.

No drinks are served in bottles or glasses, because it's hard to do much damage with an aluminum can or a plastic shot glass.

All the barstools are massive logs, bolted to the floor and impossible to pick up and throw.

There's a pool table, but the cues and balls are available only upon request, and only after the bartender has given you the hairy eyeball, assessing your potential for destruction.

Brawls are equal opportunity events at Jimtown. The women fight, too.

"There's been enough hair pulled out in here to make a horseblanket," Dillon said.

That said, the place isn't as rough as it used to be.

"It's quieted down a lot since Mary took over," one lifelong rancher in the valley told me.

Still, gunshots sometimes ring out at night, usually just boozy exuberance, but that kind of thing always makes your ears perk up. Dead bodies have been found along the highway, boozed up pedestrians struck by cars.

And then there's the Time Tunnel.

Gary Spang, who calls himself the Mayor of Jimtown, showed it to me. It's about 300 yards north of the bar, and consists of a big culvert underlying Highway 39. A couple of mattresses lie moldering inside, along with lots of discarded clothing, empty liquor bottles and at least one used syringe. People sleep there when they're too drunk to get home. It's grim, but it sure beats becoming one of those crushed bodies on the highway.

"I lived here for a month one time," Spang said. "Sleeping with the rattlesnakes."

"And whatever," Dillon added, rolling her eyes.

"Sometimes we go cheek to cheek," he added, grinning.

IT'S NOT THE SAME PLACE IT USED TO BE," said Rosebud County Undersheriff Tom Skinner, who lives about five miles up the road. "And that's fine with me. You could get real tired of having to live there."

Skinner has been patrolling Jimtown for 33 years, and he said it's been at least five years since anybody was killed there. That case involved somebody speeding away from the bar with a sleeping drunk on the hood of his car. Even further back, in the 1970s, an off-duty bartender was beaten to death in the parking lot. And there was the time a white man got liquored up and stabbed a man in the parking lot because the man had taken his gun away from him.

"In the past, about anything was a possibility," Skinner said. "Anything that could happen would happen there."

So I asked him: "Is it still the toughest bar in Montana?"

"That was true in the 70s," he said. "Probably the 80s, too, and maybe into the 90s. Jimtown, right now, is the quietest it's ever been."

QUIET TIMES ARE JUST FINE WITH MAYOR SPANG, who has logged a lot of hours at Jimtown, both as customer and employee.

"I used to be an alderman," he quipped. "Now I'm mayor."

Half Cheyenne and half Crow, his duties include swamping the joint, fixing the plumbing, killing the rattlesnakes that slither onto the property ("I got 15 this year," he said. "Big ones.") and breaking up fights.

He's not a big man, and he'd rather laugh than scuffle, but he gets the job done.

"When it's between Cheyenne, he's Cheyenne," Dillon said of the mayor. "When it's between Crow, he's Crow."

"I watch things," he said. "I take care of people."

Spang impressed me: his matter-of-fact, warts-and-all telling of the

Jimtown story, his unusual pride in the house-sized heap of beer cans and liquor bottles in the back yard, a pile that started accumulating in the 1920s, back when Indians could only buy booze out the back door.

I admit I felt a little conflict about the bar, with the booze and poker machines, next to the reservation, with all the poverty and alcohol problems there. But the customers are free adults. They get to do what they want.

Plenty of Cheyenne avoid Jimtown like the plague.

"The people who don't drink, they say it's a hellhole," Spang said.

There are other types of people who probably ought to stay away, too. Smartasses, buttinskis and racists are all asking for trouble.

I was there on a Friday evening, when a woman came in and got justifiably loud with her husband for leaving her and a small child waiting outside in a car. He hung his head and followed her out, but he threw his eyes at me.

I turned mine away. He was angry and embarrassed and looking for trouble. I wasn't, but a smirk on my face might have fetched me some.

In the time I was there, most of the business came from people buying boxes of beer and bottles of booze, usually both. The drinkers at the long bar seemed like drinkers anywhere: talking, laughing, having a good time, minding their own business.

Still, there was that message on the hat.

By the time darkness fell on that Friday night, I decided I'd be better off down the road. The bartender had told me: "After 7 o'clock, anything goes."

I think almost anybody willing to watch his mouth could have a fine time at the Jimtown Bar and suffer nothing worse than a hangover. The chances of taking a beating are pretty slim and you might even make some friends.

I'd like to think the mayor would welcome me back.

"The Cheyenne never say goodbye," Spang told me. "Because you'll always be back. There's no such thing as goodbye."

But it might be a good idea to leave early. ◾

Another Round at Headframe Spirits

By Ted Brewer

Summer 2013

A CROWD HAS AMASSED IN THE TASTING ROOM OF HEADFRAME SPIRITS ON a Saturday evening, and fourth-generation Butte native Erin Garlinghouse sits at the end of the bar, sipping from a martini glass before heading off to her shift ushering at the Motherlode Theater.

"My father says he has a photo of me sitting at this very bar in Meaderville when I was a child," she says above the revelry at the bar. "The owners say they're going to hang it on the wall here whenever he gets around to finding it."

Before the Berkeley Pit swallowed it in the 1960s, Meaderville was a neighborhood on Butte's east side and the location of the Rocky Mountain Café, a nationally-lauded restaurant owned by a flashy Croat named Teddy Traparish. Bedecked with columns, cornices and other architectural flourishes, the restaurant's bar serviced drinkers for nearly half a century. When the pit came creeping and the restaurant prepared for demolition, Traparish donated the bar to the World Museum of Mining, which 50-odd years later loaned the bar to Headframe Spirits.

Reflected in the bar's mirror is Headframe's still. It stands on the floor of what originally had been Montana's first Buick dealership and what later became a Cadillac showroom, a floor Teddy Traparish trod annually for decades, kicking the tires of the next new Cadillac he was about to buy.

Headframe's co-owner John McKee relishes telling the story of Traparish's annual visit to the building that would decades later house his bar. "There is a cycle of history in Butte," John says. "We've had people walk in here ... who mucked that bar as children or had their first drink at it."

Headframe Spirits produces eminently drinkable gin, vodka, whiskey, rye, and cream liqueur—each of which is named after one of the city's old mines or a headframe (the tower above a mine shaft, often bearing the same name as the mine) and labeled with historic photographs of its people, miners especially. And its tasting room does a brisk business selling carefully crafted cocktails mixed with its products. But what Headframe may sell more of than anything else is Butte, America, cyclic history and all.

DURING PROHIBITION, there were so many people producing illegal liquor in Butte that the city engineer warned the mayor that the city's sewer could break down from all of the rye, wheat, grapes, plums and other types of discarded mash clogging the pipes.

"I can guarantee you that in all of the production we've put out thus far, which is a lot, there was more spilled in this town before we ever became a legal distillery," John says.

Before he and his wife and co-owner Courtney opened Butte's first legal distillery, John worked for a different kind of distillation business— one that made biodiesel from vast quantities of discarded grease, fats and oils. The business was sold in 2010, leaving him unemployed. One night in bed while discussing his prospects, Courtney floated the idea of starting a distillery of spirits. John thought about it for a moment, then got out of bed and started writing the business plan.

But the bankers the McKees approached didn't quite share in their enthusiasm, perhaps because it was 2010 (a time when banks weren't exactly tossing out loans) or because the micro-distilling industry was so new that there wasn't much data with which to evaluate the business plan. All of them wished the McKees best of luck at another bank.

"It eventually took everything we had to close on the building and then hope that someone would want to finance us," Courtney says. The McKees, who are both in their late 30s and have two children, went eight months living on ramen and on Courtney's not-so-regular income as an IT consultant.

"[Practically] all we had was the building and a hell of a business plan," she says.

A friend finally pointed out that the couple was selling their idea all wrong, that what they needed to do was approach an agricultural bank, not a traditional one, with a plan for "value-added agricultural manufacturing." It worked, and in February 2012, Headframe Spirits opened its doors under the Montana law that allows breweries and distilleries to sell a limited amount of product directly from a tasting room (two drinks and two bottles per person, per day in the case of distilleries). The business took off. In four months the McKees paid off their operating loan. In a year they had 19 people on the payroll.

Before opening, John realized that in order for the business to be viable in the long run he would need to figure out a more efficient way to make liquor than by using a conventional pot still, which entails boiling, draining, cleaning, refilling and reheating, then repeating the process over and over again. So he convened four or five engineering buddies from his former job and, over the course of a weekend and a few cases of beer, they designed a continuous-flow still that would fit under the ceiling of the old Cadillac showroom. It was basically a small-scale version of the still at any mass distillery. Unlike a traditional pot still, the continuous-flow still runs almost on its own, enabling Headframe to make about 800 gallons of 100-proof liquor in a week, enough that the business spends only 10 days a month producing all it needs for bottling and barreling.

Having won several national awards for its product and gained the recognition of other distillers, Headframe is also now manufacturing copies of its still for other micro-distilleries.

THE SHORT AMOUNT OF TIME IT TAKES HEADFRAME TO PRODUCE ITS MONTHLY quota frees John and Courtney to concentrate on the aspect of the business they seem to enjoy the most: marketing the company's brand—that is, telling the story of Butte.

"When we decided we were going to make hooch and started off with the plan, we very quickly came to understand that what we were doing here was opening a marketing company that happens to make hooch," John says.

Co-branding their product with Butte no doubt left the McKees open to accusations of appropriating the city's history. It didn't help that neither John nor Courtney was, technically speaking, a native. John moved to Butte at age six when his father got a job teaching at Montana Tech. Courtney moved from Connecticut in 2001, seven weeks after meeting John at a wedding in Missoula.

Butte-Silver Bow Community Development Director and Headframe regular Karen Byrnes says the McKees weren't the first to walk into her office with ideas of starting an Uptown business that capitalized on Butte's history. But the McKees were different.

"You can tell when people have their act together," Byrne says. "These guys were just so motivated and driven they were never going to give up."

After the business opened and word spread that John and Courtney weren't out to swindle anyone, former Butte miners started showing up at the tasting room with their old helmets, lanterns and picks, asking if they could give these objects to Headframe. The tools are now on display in the tasting room, along with an antique pot still that a man donated, a still John thinks was forged in the tin shop of one of Butte's mines. And 10 or so people have offered to share hooch recipes passed down in their family history. John plans on making samples from these recipes for an event he and Courtney want to hold next year, to which they'll invite these same people to tell the stories associated with the recipes.

John says that people brought all of these valuables on their own, without being asked. "That to us is very special, because it means we're doing something right with how we're telling the story of Butte, with how we're keeping its history alive," John says.

HEADFRAME'S BARTENDER, mixologist and otherwise all-rounder Matt Sargent waves goodbye to Erin Garlinghouse as she heads off to the Motherlode, then goes back to muddling, shaking, pouring and keeping patrons lubricated. When he returned to Butte a year ago after losing his job in San Francisco, he planned to stay for a few weeks, send out some resumés, and hopefully land a job somewhere else. Sargent is from Butte, and staying didn't interest him until he started having cocktails at Headframe and seeing what John and Courtney were up to. They offered him a job, and he stayed.

"I absolutely do feel differently about Butte since working here," he says. "I feel like I've reconnected with the town."

Sargent slides a cocktail to Mike Nance, who is well underway celebrating his birthday with some friends. Director of the local children's theater and a Colorado native, Nance says he enjoys going back to Denver, ordering a cocktail mixed with one of Headframe's products, and telling people that he lives in a city that makes the best liquor there is.

"Because of places like this I get to be a snob and say I'm from Butte, and those two never go together," he says. ◀

High Tide
at the Happy Hour

By Megan Regnerus

Fall 2006

BE CAREFUL IF YOU EVER VISIT THE HAPPY HOUR BAR & RESTAURANT, 15 miles northwest of West Yellowstone on the shore of Hebgen Lake. Things tend to happen there.

Step inside and you'll see 20 years worth of ball caps tacked to the ceiling and a few liberated bras dangling from the rafters; drag your eyes down the walls and you'll see Polaroids everywhere—one wall covered with the bare breasts of headless patrons, another covered with distinctly male behinds. Behind the window in the men's bathroom is a nude female mannequin whose adornments change with the seasons, though last time I peeked she still sported a St. Paddy's Day necklace and a detailed sign requesting help. A deer mount on the wall occasionally has a microphone rigged near its mouth, a sign that folks have gotten a little silly with the Karaoke machine again. There's a three-man water balloon launcher that might earn you a free drink if you nail someone and Rin Klungervik or Tahni Longworth —sisters who help run the bar with their folks, Bud and Karen Klungervik—think it's funny enough. Although ever since some locals accidentally nailed a cop car and ran for the closets, they try not to encourage mischief that might get anyone arrested.

The first time I visited the Happy Hour was with a group of runaway moms on a Nordic ski weekend in West Yellowstone. It was dark, the snow swirled and landed in dusty piles, and inside the bar was warm and packed with an eclectic mix of snowmobilers, old timers and locals ranging from 21 to 70 years old.

I ordered a drink from Rin, a tall, permed, blonde woman wearing shorts and a baggy sweatshirt, then turned around to find one of my friends already dancing cheek to cheek near the jukebox with an old man wearing lots of jewelry. I introduced myself to some snowmobilers, filled them in on how the skiing had been. One of them narrowed his eyes at me. "I'll bet you drive a Subaru," he said.

A park ranger told him to be nice and over the next drink I managed to get the ranger to tell me exactly how far over the speed limit I could drive in the park before he'd pull me over. At one point a guy came over to the bar and informed Rin he was going to get a game of Twister going. "Nope," she said, staring him dead on. "Nobody plays Twister 'til I say so."

Rin and Tahni are tall and take after their father, Bud, more than their tiny mother, Karen. The one time I asked them if they ever had any trouble with drunk patrons giving them guff, they seemed confused.

Anyway, the guy skulked away and before long, one of the sisters had the tables pushed aside and a whole-bar game of musical chairs started. Not playing didn't seem to be an option. I watched as if on some surreal movie set as my friends and everyone else were gradually weeded out of the game, singing and dancing all the while. I eventually found myself the sole competitor against a woman who looked like my grandmother. Country music played in slow motion, all eyes on us as people cheered on the older woman. When the music stopped she cocked her hip to one side and then unloaded it, sending me flying across the room before smugly plopping in the last remaining chair and raising a victory fist.

"That was Carleen," Rin told me this past summer when I revisited the Happy Hour. "She's a regular. That's funny—we were just remembering that game this past week."

Beyond these anecdotes, good luck getting any incriminating stories out of the Klungervik family. "We don't pour and tell," said Rin. Despite the fact that Rin is only 38 years old, she's helped her parents run the bar since the day they bought it 20 years ago. In a sense, she and her siblings have grown up at the Happy Hour.

"Iris [the former owner] would let us sneak in here and play asteroids," said Rin, referring to the days when her family lived in Utah and came up to vacation on Hebgen Lake every summer. "Then if things got too busy she'd kick us out."

"She'd feed us Shirley Temples and we'd play pool," said Tahni.

"The Happy Hour was originally an old summer home," explained Karen. "When the earthquake hit [in 1959] it ended up in the lake, but then got pulled back out. Iris McNabb bought it in 1972 and started running the Happy Hour Bar during the summers."

McNabb was a little red-haired spitfire who let the girls help out around the place as they got older, then one year Rin and Tahni sadly recalled that something wasn't right with her, and they ended up running the bar by themselves for a whole week. The next summer the doors to the bar were locked when they arrived. "Iris came to the door and said, 'I've been diagnosed with Alzheimer's and I want you folks to take the bar,'" said Karen.

Tahni and Rin remember fondly the early days of running the bar, back when boats would pull up at the deckside dock and one of them would hop in and go water ski during their shift. The Happy Hour Web site states, "The Happy Hour Bar & Restaurant is the only bar accessible by boat, car, or snowmobile."

"Back then if we had a hundred dollars in the till we were doing well," said Tahni.

"As we got busier and busier sometimes we'd still sneak off and go water skiing. But we can't do that anymore," said Rin. "I remember sometimes even mom would be in the kitchen, and you'd bring in an order and she'd be gone."

"People ask us why we don't advertise. We don't need to; we're busy enough," said Rin, pausing to explain that they run a full-menu kitchen where everything is homemade and even steaks are hand cut. "It's a small little joint and we like it that way."

But plenty of people have heard of their small little joint, including Charles Kuralt, Henry Winkler and Heather Locklear.

"Most of the time we don't know 'em and we don't care," said Bud of their more famous patrons.

"What he means is we treat them just like anyone else," said Karen.

Like the time a Hollywood-type walked in the door on a busy night when Rin was behind the bar. "I was balls to the wall in here and this star—I won't say who he is—tried to get in front of everyone and order from me. I told him he needed to wait his turn and I'd get to him when I could," remembered Rin. "So he says, 'Don't you know who I am?' and

I said, 'Do you know who I am? I'm your (expletive) bartender, which makes me the most important person you know right now. I'll get to you when I can.'"

Still, the family means for everyone to have a good time—even when they present a demanding customer with a Burger King crown. "If I have a high-maintenance customer sometimes it even helps me to lighten up when I put a crown on their head," said Rin. "We say, 'You think you get it your way here? You're at the Happy Hour, princess, not Burger King.' I've turned some of the grumpiest SOBs around."

And they've seen some pretty conservative folks cut loose. Hence, the body parts adorning the walls with captions like, "Thank-you Doctor Morgan, $4,500 later."

"I think the fun thing about the boob wall is that we have people in here from all over the world—some of them with high-powered jobs— and they can come here and do something they'd never do in real life," explained Tahni.

"I love when I see people come in and have a good time," said Karen, who at 63 years old has such a maternal sweetness to her that she could just as easily be talking about hosting a church potluck.

Which perhaps isn't too far off the mark. The family hosts several "theme parties" a year, including Christmas in August, where they hold a big fundraising dinner with donated turkeys and trimmings, and have created an account to help needy families in their community. To hear all that Karen, Bud, Tahni and Rin do and to see them rushing around on a normal night at the Happy Hour is enough to make a person tired.

"We are tired," admits Karen.

Tahni and Rin each put in 60 hour weeks without blinking during high tourist season. "As anyone in this town knows, we have two seasons to make money; that's six weeks, twice a year," said Tahni.

"It's been a hard year for everybody here in West because we're all busy and there's not enough help," said Karen.

The Klungerviks may be tired, but not too tired to rally when a couple of Happy Hour "virgins" walked in the door, just as I was leaving. It was two fly-fishermen who admitted they'd been coming to West Yellowstone for 15 years, but had never been to the Happy Hour. Tahni heckled them a bit, then coaxed them into checking out the view of the night sky from the deck.

"Can you see Venus over there?" she hollered out to them. "Get over to the edge where it's darker and you can really see it."

She looked back at her dad Bud, who was ready at the helm of the bar, hand on a big air horn.

"Okay, Dad," she said, and he gave them a blast.

Both guys jumped and came back inside laughing.

Tahni handed them each a sticker that is only given to customers who earn it. It says: "I've been Honked at the Happy Hour Bar." ▉

The Stoneville Saloon

By Ed Kemmick

Fall 2009

GROWING UP IN SOUTHERN CALIFORNIA, Diane Turko's only ambition was to be a beach bum.

Some years later—her age is none of your business—she's the sole proprietor of the Stoneville Saloon in Alzada, Montana, about as far from an ocean as you can get in this hemisphere. It's true what it says on the promotional gear sold in the saloon: "Conveniently located in the middle of nowhere."

Or, as Diane puts it, "This is not a destination. This is a stop on the way to wherever."

Lucky for her, one of those wherevers is Sturgis, S.D., 70 miles east of Alzada. In the first full week of August, during the annual Sturgis Rally, there are so many motorcyclists on the road, either heading for Sturgis or taking day trips outside of Sturgis, that Diane sells enough food and drink to carry her through the rest of the year.

Last year she sold 297 cases of beer and 83 twelve-packs of pop during the rally. It's also the only time of year she hires help. The rest of the time, seven days a week from roughly 11 a.m. to 11 p.m., Diane's behind the bar.

"Every day," she says, half proudly, half wearily. "If I'm not here, the place is not open."

Diane was on her way to Sturgis herself back in 1990, riding motorcycles with her boyfriend, Rob Peterson, and another couple from

California. The wide-open spaces and endless sky were something new to them. As Diane tells it, "one of the idiots" suggested it might be fun to live in Montana.

They looked around for a business to buy and settled on the Alzada Bar and Café in the far southeastern corner of the state on Highway 212, three miles north of Wyoming and 20 miles west of South Dakota. Diane was doubtful, but she figured she'd give it at least a year.

As it turned out, the other couple left after a year and a half, and she and Rob hung around. Nobody ever mistook them for locals. Rob, who died in 2001, wore a beard that hung below his belt buckle and favored sleeveless T-shirts, the better to show off his tattoo-covered arms. Diane has her own tattoos, including a feathered necklace design encircling her neck and a three-headed dragon that climbs up her left leg and thigh. Her bleached-blond hair nearly reaches the slinky black dress she often wears on the job.

When they bought the Alzada Bar, Rob said years ago, it was "one of those one-light, local, don't-come-in-here places." Rob and Diane went to work to change that image, putting in a wooden floor, raising the ceiling and creating an Old West look out front, complete with a barn-wood façade, a porch and hitching rails.

Inside, Diane covered the ceiling and walls with antiques. She didn't have to go far to find them. The bar came with 21 acres that were strewn with 30-some dead cars and the sort of debris that seems to grow as thick as weeds on some patches of rural landscape. Diane salvaged the best of it and hung it up inside the bar—license plates, skulls, horseshoes, cigar boxes, tractor seats, bullet-riddled cans, buckets, pickaxes, a battered 12-string guitar, saddle tack, a rusted tricycle and a mailbox.

"The ranchers all thought I was nuts," she says. "They said, 'What are you hanging all this junk up for?' I said, 'This stuff is cool.' I didn't grow up around here."

One major renovation was prompted by events beyond the control of the bar owners. On the Fourth of July, 1997, a man drove his pickup into the saloon at an estimated speed of 60 or 70 miles an hour. The impact shattered an ornate old tobacco cabinet, busted up the Brunswick back bar built in 1865, smashed a mirror and broke every liquor bottle behind the bar.

"He was trying to commit suicide," Diane says. "He was a local crazy. He didn't want to die unnoticed. He could have driven into a bentonite pit, but nobody would have found him for a month."

The driver lived through it, though, and none of the six or seven people

146

in the bar had more than minor injuries. As part of repairing the damage, Rob and Diane moved the back bar, which used to run down the middle of the building, up against the west wall of the saloon. The move opened the place up considerably. A friend who did woodworking repaired the damage to the bar and painstakingly rebuilt the tobacco cabinet.

The other big change was to the name.

"Rob read every book he could find about this area and he found out this town used to be called Stoneville. That's where the name came from." Diane laughs and adds, "It has nothing to do with smoking pot."

Fittingly, Stoneville was named for Lou Stone, a saloonkeeper in the earliest days of the tiny town that sits on the banks of the Little Missouri River. The town came into being when the government was building Fort Keogh near Miles City in 1877-78 and wanted to establish a telegraph connection with Fort Meade, under construction in South Dakota. Stoneville sprung up at the point where the telegraph line crossed the river. Later, after it was determined that another town in Montana had a similar name, Stoneville became Alzada, named for Alzada "Zadie" Sheldon, the wife of a pioneer rancher.

There's a photo of Zeke and Zadie Sheldon, taken in 1888, on the wall of the Stoneville Saloon, given to Diane by a great-granddaughter of the pioneer couple. Under the photo the great-granddaughter wrote: "Zeke was really a lazy bum. Zadie was just this side of a saint and earned a reputation for setting broken bones and tending shotgun wounds."

Rob moved back to California in 1999 to work as an electrician. He died two years later, electrocuted in an on-the-job accident. So Diane has been working the Stoneville by herself for almost nine years now. Sometimes she can't believe it herself.

"If you would have told me when I was 16 that I would be living in the middle of nowhere . . ." Her voice trails off and then she adds, "I would have said you're insane. My goal in life was to be a beach bum."

Her doubts are strongest in the winter, when the temperatures drop and the winds seem to howl nonstop.

"Every winter I say, 'It is insane that anyone lives here. What in the hell am I doing here?'"

Since Rob died, Diane has scaled back a few of her activities. She used to give tattoos up on a stage in the back of the bar. Patrons, most of them local ranch kids who'd had a few drinks, would sit in an old barber chair while Diane decorated their flesh with ink.

Working by herself, she said, "something had to go. I couldn't do it all. And when you're doing tattoos, you have to give your full attention."

One sideline she still indulges in is selling prints of her paintings and drawings, examples of which decorate the walls. There is a dragon, resembling the one on her leg, a few cowboys and cowgirls, an old pickup truck in front of a barn, a crusty old-timer drinking out of a fruit jar and a startlingly realistic pair of wolves.

"Anything you can do here extra to make money is a plus," she says. "And you need something to do when it's slow, so you don't lose your mind."

She also sells used clothes—most of them her own cast-offs. She does her own alterations on a sewing machine that occupies the spot on the stage where the barber chair used to sit. There are a few used cassette tapes for sale, and (in June, at least) there was a box containing two hats for sale at $2 each. One was a Miller Lite hat; the other, a dusty camo job that bore this inscription: "Joe Curry Jr. 2nd Annual Memorial Fishing Tournament."

And of course there's the victuals. Since the Stoneville Saloon opened, its motto has been, "Cheap drinks, lousy food."

"They're both a lie," says Shane Mulkey, who's come down from his place on a local ranch on this hot late-June day to put away a few Budweisers. "The drinks ain't cheap and the food is good."

There's a lot of regular fare—burgers, chicken-fried steak sandwiches, BLTs, mozzarella sticks and corn dogs—and a few unusual offerings like taquitos, Rocky Mountain oysters and crab cakes. The best-seller has always been the chili, based on a recipe developed by Rob and sustained by Diane.

"People rave about it. Personally, I don't care for it, but people rave about it," she says.

Nearly all of her business comes off the road. Whether it's truckers, tourists or bikers, she hopes enough people will notice the odd-looking saloon in the middle of nowhere and give it a try. So many people stop just to relieve themselves that she posted signs in the restrooms, asking folks to buy a can of pop at least, or just make a small donation.

Mulkey says not too many other locals frequent the Stoneville, but he likes it for the chance to meet strangers.

"It sure makes for good conversation on an afternoon to meet people from here, there and everywhere. Everybody has a story."

Diane is probably going to be there to listen to those stories for a long time yet, despite her misgivings.

"This place is too cool," she says. "If I was to leave here, I would lose my identity, or this bar would lose its identity." ◄

Enough Spice to Go Around

By Scott McMillion

Fall 2014

AFTER 23 YEARS OF WAITING TABLES IN HER FAMILY'S RESTAURANT, Mabel Torres has seen it all.

But my friend Bob stopped her in her tracks. He'd just ordered a second plate of *ropa vieja*, a succulent blend of braised beef, vegetables and spices that serves as comfort food all over Latin America. It's rich and filling and delicious. And it's not a Lay's potato chip. It comes with beans and rice and tortillas and most people can barely eat just one. But Bob wanted two.

And that's what made Mabel pause. Had anybody ever eaten two of them before? She took the question seriously. She thought for several seconds.

"No," she said. Then she went to fetch Bob's second load.

Mabel (pronounced Ma Bell) is the public face of Café Mabel's, a funky-looking joint on the industrial east end of Laurel, which is a fragrant neighborhood. Coal and oil trains bake in the sunshine there, and moving them around creates a lot of diesel smoke, which almost overwhelms the creosote oozing from all those railroad ties. And there's usually a hint of refinery wafting in from the big smokestacks down by the river.

But Mabel's is a rose among these thorns. In the potholed parking lot,

you'll get a whiff of what you came for: garlic and beef, pork and potatoes, chicken and chilis. It's a heady blend for a hungry traveler.

But first you have to find the place. Drive to the middle of Laurel,
cross beneath the railroad tracks to the north side of town and turn east on
Main Street, past the bars and junk shops and storefront churches. When
you see an old motel the color of Pepto Bismol, you're getting warm.
Watch for a nondescript gray storefront on the north side of the street,
sandwiched between a brace of convenience stores. That's Mabel's. Find
a place to park (mind the potholes) and haul your appetite indoors, where
you might catch a faint whiff of bleach, depending on how recently Mabel
cleared and swabbed your table. She keeps the place very clean.

Overhead, a pressed-tin ceiling resembles an avocado skin. The walls
are mango. The carpet is a little frizzy and the table-tops are Formica. A
velvet Aztec adorns one wall and giant picture windows offer a commanding view of those trains parked across the street. In the corner there's a
gumball machine, another that sells temporary tattoos and ornamental
stickers, spelling out that this is a family joint. There isn't a speck of dust
anywhere. Not much noise, either. Everybody's too busy eating.

And then comes Mabel and she is impeccable. She doesn't walk so
much as she glides, servicing a dozen or more tables and running the
cash register, too, making it all look easy. Smiling beneath horned rim
glasses and a perfect crown of steel gray hair, she brings chips with salsa
of her own making, the kind with a little effervescence in it. She brings
menus, tells you beer is available in the convenience store next door and
goes about the business of easing hunger, one table at a time, as she's
done for all these years. The Mexican food she brings is the real stuff,
not some Tex-Mex hybrid, which isn't bad but it isn't what Mabel's is
about. She's a trained chef. So is her husband, Joel. They serve the kind
of food Mexicans serve their holiday guests, or order in fine restaurants.
Fresh ingredients, plenty of lime and cilantro, and not too much heat,
unless you want it that way.

A sign outside describes it as both *nuevo Latino* and traditional
Mexican.

"You can go somewhere in Mexico and find the same dish," Joel explains. "We try to cover all five regions of the country."

You can get a burrito or a couple tacos if you want. But that's not why
you're here, not when you can get a plate, or two, of that *ropa vieja*. In
English, that means old clothes, but it's really a pot roast, in a sauce Joel
and Mabel created. Like everything on the menu, except the tortillas

and chips, it's made by hand, in-house and from scratch.

Pot roast isn't your style? Try the *pollo al cilantro*. Or the steaks rubbed with Mexican spices. The house chili loaded with beef and beans. Or the pork chops sautéed with garlic and black pepper and green chiles. Or the *gordo* salad, which means fatboy, because it's topped with a grilled ribeye. Or you can get it topped with shrimp, instead. Both, if you're feeling especially *gordo*.

The menu has something for everybody, except vegetarians, though the crew will work with you on that.

And then there's "For the Adventurous." That's a menu item. Honest. You never know exactly what you'll get. Just select a type of meat and announce your tolerance level for peppers: poblanos for the dyspeptic, habaneros if you've got a leather gullet, somewhere in between for most people.

"Your choice of meat, your choice of heat," the menu says.

"People who are adventurous pretty much let me do what I want," Joel says. "In 20 years, nobody's been disappointed."

So I figured why not? I ordered chicken, shrimp and chipotles. It arrived mounded with Mexican *queso fresco*, papayas and peppers. A spare plate held the rice and beans.

Portions are big at Mabel's, the service is prompt and the prices are reasonable. Lunches run about $10, dinners about $20, mostly.

Both Joel and Mabel were born in Mexico, but Joel quickly points out that he's all American now. (There's a map of Mexico on the wall, but there's an American flag next to it.) He first came to Montana to study at Montana State University Billings, where he later taught culinary arts, and brought Mabel up from Arizona for a visit in 1980.

"I loved it," she said. It reminded her of her childhood home in the Sierra Madre foothills of western Mexico. In 1989, the Torreses returned and set up their own business. The mountains drew them, Joel said, but he didn't want to get locked in to a seasonal resort economy. So he settled in Laurel, a blue-collar town where he could distinguish himself and his menu from the chain restaurants and Tex-Mex places that dominate shopping strips in bigger cities.

He and Mabel started out selling takeout food and making deliveries but his business quickly outstripped his workspace so he moved to the current location, once a bakery and before that a grocery store, paying off the mortgage in three years. His kids worked there until their educations priced them out of that kind of work. "I couldn't afford them any more," Joel says with a proud smile, but a 13-year-old grandson now helps the kitchen crew, most of whom have been with the Torreses for years.

"I pay my help well and they work hard when I need it," Joel says. "So far, it works."

The crowd is mostly local, mostly blue-collar, but you could see almost anybody there: Billings bankers on a lunch break, workers from the refineries or the nearby farms, a young couple celebrating their first anniversary, travelers detouring off Interstate 90. But they all have one thing in common: If they leave hungry, it's their own fault.

Which is something my friend Bob didn't do. On a second trip, he ordered the *ropa vieja* again.

"*Dos, por favor.*"

Mabel just rolled her eyes. This time, she'd seen it before. ◪

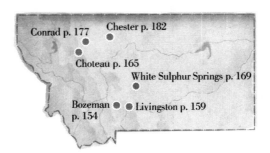

TRUTH TELLERS

*Stories shape us all. But who
shapes the stories? Who tells them?*

Being Floyd DeWitt

By Alan Kesselheim

Spring 2015

FLOYD DEWITT IS NOT A MAN OR ARTIST YOU COME TO KNOW, as much as a man and artist you experience. Like weather.

As with a storm, DeWitt is unpredictable, powerful, fitful, intimidating, challenging and very real. Also, like a storm, and despite the apparent chaos of forces, he adheres to certain patterns and rhythms, themes that keep surfacing out of the mix, clear and fundamental. And it is that mixture of chaos and pattern that emerges, powerful as a microburst, in his art.

DeWitt doesn't stick to the topic in conversation. He refuses a linear discussion, but instead veers off into stories and memories, reveals the epiphanies that stand clear in his life. He quotes Aristotle, Frost, Hesse, Twain, leaps decades, confounds chronology, employs metaphor.

"If I could tell you what it is I do," he blurts out, "I wouldn't have to do it!

"How a kid from Roosevelt County, Montana, came to be the artist I am?" he shrugs, smiles.

"I have a kind of passion," he goes on. "That makes me difficult for some reason. I've always been different, kind of an oddball, and there is a price to pay for that. It took me many years to understand. I remember even when I was a kid in Wolf Point, I was asked to leave the Cub Scout pack because I wasn't going to fit in. The den leader talked to my mother and told her it wasn't a good idea.

"Same thing happened in the Army," he says. "I was the one nobody urged to re-enlist."

Now entering his 80s, DeWitt is perhaps the oldest working sculptor in Montana. His house, outside of Bozeman, is full of his work. Horses everywhere. Headless horses and horse heads, riders on horseback, a stunning rendition of the Four Horsemen of the Apocalypse, a piece DeWitt calls *Weightlessness*. His studio is crammed with sketches, busts, nudes, a figure of a symphony conductor, his father's old barber chair, a full-sized ewe called *Mother of the Ram*, a bust of his daughter he has been working on for 30 years.

"Maybe I don't want to finish her, because then I'd have to let her go," he says.

"My parents were hard-working people," DeWitt says. "My mother was a nurse. My father was a full-time barber. I went to school. I smoked cigarettes and got into mischief. I found magazines lying around and started copying the pictures. I liked the Indians around home, mostly because they liked horses. It was all really about learning to be a man. By the way, I finally gave up on that," he says with a laugh. "I got handy at drawing, started doing some landscapes, little studies, playing around with ideas. Like I said, I was an oddball."

He leaps again. "You have to open the envelope of who you are." DeWitt rounds his aged hand around his coffee cup. "Find out who you are, find your way to God, whatever you decide that is."

After growing up in Wolf Point, DeWitt enlisted in the army, traveled to Europe. "There was no compatibility between me and the military," he says. "But I was in Europe and that opened my eyes. Europe is full of epiphany. The air is thick with it. You put your hand on an ancient stone bridge and think about all the other hands that have rested there. That's something."

DeWitt remembers visiting St. Peter's Cathedral one time on leave. "I was walking around and not thinking much of the art. I was a young fool looking for Charlie Russell or Frederic Remington in the face of all that great stuff. There was a door marked 'Do Not Enter.' Of course that was just an invitation and I walked right in. It was an alcove full of hedges, patterned in a maze. There were monks strolling around in robes, meditating. I sat on a bench. Gregorian chants were playing. No one bothered me. I'd never heard anything like it, never been anywhere like that. It was a revelation. Talk about magic!"

One of the themes that surfaces again and again out of the confusion of DeWitt's life is the edict to study nature, not copy nature. "Study nature," he emphasizes, "don't copy it. Do you see what I mean?" he leans in, intensity emanating like heat.

Somewhere in that distinction is the leap of abstraction, the quality that separates DeWitt's work from the cliché of wildlife sculpture outside of bank buildings. That unnameable element that marries the true experience of observation, the synthesis of emotion and humanity and contemplation, and then expresses something fresh and authentic in a piece of art.

"We lack humility," he says, reflecting on current trends in art. "There is none of that in most gallery art. There is no humility in university art schools. So much art, now, is crass commercialism. And the rich people buying art have no appreciation or understanding of it."

On the center of DeWitt's dining room table sits a sculpture of a baseball pitcher, caught in the crescendo of a windup, a figure about to explode, tension like the sizzling air before a lightning bolt.

"I was sitting in a bar in Livingston," DeWitt remembers. "Just me and the bartender. There was a baseball game on, but on the other channel the news was showing troops marching into Iraq. We started arguing about which channel to watch. Finally we struck a compromise—three minutes of baseball to one minute of news.

"This piece came out of that moment. I've never pitched a baseball in my life. But that's me. I became that pitcher. That's the terror and tension of humanity. That's the appalling realization that watching baseball was more interesting than men going to war."

DeWitt starts to sketch the lines of the pitcher with his hands in the air, following the flow of the piece, connecting elements, noting how the light falls here and there, leading the eye, how it all adds up to unity.

"It's not a conscious process," he says, looking at the figure. "You begin with humility. You go out and observe, come back with material. And then there's the magic of that synthesis coming out.

"I can't stop. It's in me. It has to come out.

"Read Frost's poem, that's my life in a nutshell," DeWitt says.

In the poem "The Road Not Taken," Frost wrote,

"Two roads diverged in a wood, and I—
I took the one less traveled by,
And that has made all the difference."

For DeWitt, that road started with time back home in Wolf Point, working as a cop, breaking horses, drawing landscapes, seeking.

"After the army, and ever since, it's been a swamp of confusion and enlightenment all jumbled up," DeWitt says.

"I look at it as a series of rebirths. I was reborn when I came back from Europe. Then I went to the Minneapolis School of Art, and was reborn. From there I got a scholarship to the Royal Academy of Fine Art in Holland, an offshoot of the Beaux Arts Academy tradition in France. Reborn again."

DeWitt spent six years studying at the academy, and several subsequent decades working in Holland as an artist. His art is showcased in European museums and private collections, owned by members of the Danish royal family, and has been installed as public monuments. When DeWitt first arrived in Europe, one of the first instructions he received was the life-changing edict to study nature, not copy it.

For DeWitt, the challenge, the magic, is to truly inhabit a subject, to get at its essence. His *Mother of the Ram* was provoked by a visit to a ranch in Paradise Valley. "This ewe, a really defenseless creature, was standing there, so defiant, so protective, so unequivocal. She was nature standing up for itself.

"We all have access to the same visual experience," DeWitt emphasizes. "An artist like Van Gogh had the ability to express that experience like a poet does. Frost said that he wrote poetry that was hard to get rid of. I guess that's what I try to do."

DeWitt tends to sleep until midday. He has a cup or two of strong coffee, something to eat, and gets to work some time in the afternoon. Then he works late into the night, often after midnight.

"I am a great consumer of time," he admits. Much of that time is spent mulling, looking, getting at feelings, moving around through the clutter of pieces in the studio, losing himself.

"People think I'm difficult," he says. "They say I'm complicated and hard to understand. Really, all of my work is just a big thank you. My pieces are eulogies, statements of gratitude to nature. That's all.

"A lot of it is subliminal," DeWitt says. "Changing perspective, working with the masses, balance, seeing where the light falls."

As he talks he points to the details of pieces, how a shoulder leads to the torso, how lines and shapes reinforce each other, how a complex mass of running horses all rests on four points, everything building toward unity.

He notices a sculpture of a yoga instructor he is working on. "It feels like her," he says. "I call that the music of a piece.

"I did a bust of Gustav Mahler once," he said. "I didn't know anything about him. I started listening to The Titan to get a sense of him. Mahler didn't particularly like that piece. To tell the truth, I didn't much like it either. But I listened to it, nonstop, for 14 hours a day. Again and again. I got so I could smell Mahler's armpits.

"You don't really know when you're done. You just decide you've finally done all you can. At the same time, you can ruin a piece in 15 minutes if you go too far. It's a helluva tough thing."

Late afternoon, the light gray, DeWitt stands in front of the nearly life-sized symphony conductor, a work in progress that began with a study of Bozeman conductor Matthew Savery. "This isn't Matthew anymore," he says. "You can make it Matthew if you want, but it's not." He looks up and down the figure, the upward surge from the tiptoe stance to the bent wrists, full of the tension of the symphonic moment about to burst forth. You can almost hear the rising music, like a wave about to crash.

"You see?" he says.

Tracing Parks Reece

By Myers Reece

Spring 2010

FOR MY FATHER, artist Parks Reece, the transition into finger painting was inevitable. He loves to use his hands, particularly when eating at nice restaurants. It is a curious phenomenon, sadly overlooked by "Planet Earth" producers, to observe a wild Appalachian hillbilly in feeding. I knew it was only a matter of time before he poked those greasy fingers in paint. That time has come.

But the origins of my dad's finger painting extend beyond basic prehensile urges. Finger painting is in his blood and in his training. As a boy, he trained under Ruth Faison Shaw, who appears in art history books as the "First Lady of Finger Painting." Shaw is credited with introducing finger painting as a fine art medium—and a psychiatric therapy method—to the United States.

Through her therapy work, Shaw met Gwyn Finley Reece, my grandmother, and in turn opened the world of art up to a boy. That boy grew up to be my father.

There are so many moments that influence an artist's evolution, so many points in his timeline that help give us context. With artists, we seek context. With Parks Reece, it's hard to find. By nature, his art seems to exist in a world that is out of context. Fish smoking cigarettes. Ranchers shaking hands with wolves. Flying buffalo.

Occasionally a painting can be traced to a specific instant or period.

Jurassic Pork, in which a massive pig hovers over fleeing humans, was born out of a suggestion from my fifth-grade classmate. Generally, however, the inspiration is far more nebulous. But if identifying the inspirations that shape his evolution is difficult, identifying the moments that mark it is a bit easier.

In my lifetime, I can pinpoint several such moments: the opening of his own gallery, the start of his Web site, his transition into lithography, his book's publication and, now, finger painting. His art has come full circle; he has summoned his roots.

"Finger painting helped make me who I am," he told me recently. "It kind of gave me my view on life."

Before you can understand Parks Reece the artist, you must try to understand Parks Reece the man. I have spent my life observing this phenomenon, taking mental notes like a diligent behavioral anthropologist. He too fancies himself as somewhat of an anthropologist, as he often compares the miracle of my birth to the arrival of a pet monkey into the house.

His art, like the man, defies classification, but many critics give it a whirl anyway. The Los Angeles Times said he is an "alchemical artist" with "an untamed imagination." The Chicago Tribune called him a "natural surrealist." He has also been described as "Van Gogh meets The Far Side."

But his favorite has always been from a friend, writer Tim Cahill, who described his art as "an altogether peculiar perception of our natural world." My dad considers "peculiar" a distinguished compliment.

Critics glom on to both the artist and the mystique that is Parks Reece—raised in the mountains of North Carolina, a world adventurer, an anti-establishment folk hero living in a Montana log cabin, and a lovable hillbilly who cares deeply about good art but couldn't care less about the stuffy "art world." My dad may appear to run in circles at times, but art circles aren't typically among them.

The only way, of course, to truly understand Parks Reece is to spend time with him. It doesn't have to be anything special, but it always includes random encounters with art. For instance, let us describe what might happen on a typical stroll down the street with him.

He is walking and something shiny catches his attention. He crosses the street to observe the shiny object, but is distracted by another shiny object. A car. This shiny thing carries people in it, so he stops for a chat. They talk, in the middle of the street, until people in another shiny car grow impatient.

My father then approaches the other people to tell about the original shiny object he spotted. He explains that he doesn't yet know what it is because he got distracted and, anyway, how are you? Their impatience dissipates and they too grow eager to chat, in the street.

They talk about art, though they don't realize it. They just think they're talking about shiny things. My dad, meanwhile, has already identified 17 more shiny objects in their car and wants to talk about them. Later he tells me about a new painting idea he thought of, just strolling down the street. He is shiny and happy.

If you stop to tie your shoes, by the time you stand up, my dad has found art. He finds art everywhere: tree stumps, garbage, constellations, dead animals, pranks gone wrong and the world's shortcomings. Everywhere. When I was a kid, he particularly liked finding art on the way to school when I was already late. Pulled over on the side of the road, he would dangle out the driver's seat window to snap photos of the sunrise.

"Do you see how much it's changed in just a few minutes?" he would ask.

"Yes," I replied. "Do you see what time it is?"

He didn't. He was already out of the car and on the hood, seeking that ever-elusive "better angle." But when Parks Reece is your father and chauffeur, you don't need a note if you're tardy. It's already understood.

More than ever, much of his life now revolves around his house, where his studio is located. It is a beautiful log cabin outside of Livingston surrounded by mountains and, more recently, big rocks. These massive boulders, unearthed from his property two miles down the gravel road, are arranged in various ways in both the front and back yards. He has placed them amid his many planted trees, which include cherry, pear, apple and conifer.

One stone arrangement is in the shape of a giant serpent, slithering down the hill. Each stone in the serpent's body weighs about a ton. Also, there are surprisingly comfortable stone seats, a fire pit and a performance stage, with underground wiring.

He loves creating new worlds. He built this rock world, with the help of backhoes and months of manual labor, as a tribute to his father, who passed away in April. He calls it "The Flintstones' Living Room."

And if it feels like you're being watched, you are. Lodged in the stones' cracks are eyeballs, purchased from a taxidermist. They're artificial eyes, but they're always introduced to strangers as the real thing.

"That one's from a marlin," he told my girlfriend upon her first visit. "It's keeping an eye on you."

When I stopped by for Christmas, I noticed with some astonishment a new addition to the landscaping. In the ditch below the house was a 1993 Toyota Camry.

"I left it in neutral a few days ago and it rolled down the driveway into the ditch," he explained. I was left to assume he would retrieve it when he got around to it.

In one section of the house is yet another tribute, to his mother: a wall covered with her photographs and paintings. She died from diabetes-related complications in 1973. In the years before her death, she had submitted herself to hospitals for a variety of treatments. At one of these hospitals, she met Ruth Faison Shaw, who was exploring the possibilities of healing through finger painting.

Shaw taught finger painting in Rome in the 1920s and then incorporated it into psychiatric therapy in the U.S. The free-flowing expressionism of finger painting, where the artist actually feels the paint, comforted and inspired shell-shocked veterans, the mentally ill and the blind, among others. And moreover, with its non-toxic formula, kids loved it. My dad was one of them.

"Finger painting," Shaw said, "gives color to thought for which children often know no words."

Gwyn Finley Reece, the grandmother I never met, was already a talented artist when she met Shaw. Her diabetes was particularly debilitating, attacking her body and mind. But in finger painting, she found solace. I have a piece of hers hanging on my wall and, surrounded by my father's paintings, it is the most discussed artwork in my house. It's gorgeous, and people notice.

When my dad was 6 years old, he spent a summer finger painting with his mother and Shaw, who had become close friends. He sold his art at shows, sometimes raking in $200 as a first-grader. An artist was born.

He carried Shaw's teachings with him through grade school and on to art school at East Carolina University and the San Francisco Art Institute, through his Pan-American art studies in Costa Rica and on his many world travels.

Even today, in all of my father's art, Shaw's free-flowing finger painting fundamentals are evident. While the individual figures of his acrylic paintings are detailed and often realistic, the backgrounds are colorful worlds unburdened by premeditated shapes and lines. He applies the background's paint without prejudice—he lets the art become itself. Characters, shapes and new worlds then emerge.

This is how he views life: freedom of expression, art in the most un-expected places and funny shapes.

In 2008, he was asked to teach a finger painting class at Livingston's Center for Art and Culture. Having not finger painted for over 40 years, he naturally agreed. He began practicing and rediscovered the sensation that first prompted him into art as a boy.

When finger painting, he recalls Shaw's lessons: "You never sit down, you stand poised and you're balanced. Then you kind of dance. You move fluidly. To loosen up the paint, you add water and play. You have fun."

"That's part of the therapy," he says.

And since you don't use brushes, precise details aren't—and shouldn't be—expected: "You abandon the idea that you're going to make it photo real." He uses his palm, his forearm, his fingers, his fin-gernails and the sides of his hand, including what he describes as the "karate-chop part."

"You get some results that you're like, 'Wow.' You don't even know how you did it," he says. "It's free art. It's expressionistic art at its most basic."

To date, he has completed about 30 original finger paintings and taught several classes. Among the finished works are *Sneaking Up on a Candy Tree*, *Reaching for Heaven While Clinging to Earth*, *The Catfish and I*, *Atom Dance* and *Uh Oh*.

Some are quite surreal, offering very little specific detail. Others have been carefully marked with fingernail precision. They were a hit at the 2009 National Folk Festival in Butte, where he was one of the only visual artists invited. He will return in 2010. He is also illustrating a three-part series in the *Big Sky Journal* with finger paintings.

The paintings, less expensive than his original acrylics and litho-graphs, are currently his gallery's top sellers. For both longtime follow-ers of his art and newcomers, the paintings represent something childish we can relate to, something accessible. And while they're fresh and fun for us, more importantly they're fresh and fun for him.

My dad would say that when art loses its fun, it loses some of its magic. And, for the artist, it simply becomes a job. Parks Reece is keen; he isn't about to be tricked into a job. In the past, he has been an art teacher on the Crow Indian Reservation and in Wales, a ranch hand, a muralist, a construction worker and a gallery curator. But it's been many years since he held a regular job, a testament to both his artistic accom-plishments and his stubbornness.

Last fall, he discovered a fan of his finger painting: Ronald Wallace, a well-known lighting design specialist who worked on Broadway for 25 years. In Wallace's retirement, more like a second career, he has gotten into photography. Using his lighting expertise, he has a vision to combine nude models, dancing, finger painting and photography into a distinctive art form.

When Wallace first told my dad about the project, he thought it was a joke. It's an uncommon proposition, for sure: "I would like to pay you to paint the bodies of beautiful nude models." It has made me question my career choice.

Months later, my dad found himself in a lighting studio, experimenting with different paints on models. Shunning the artificial intrusions of canvas, paper and brushstrokes, this kind of art relies on human-to-human contact, with natural anatomical contours influencing the painting's final form.

After a couple of practice sessions, just as they were figuring out appropriate paint types and lighting, Wallace suffered a stroke. But he is recovering and the project is continuing.

Novelist William Hjortsberg once said: "In the hands of Parks Reece, fine art becomes fun once again, and God bless him for that." As Hjortsberg noted, fine art is in a good place when in my father's hands. Now it's all over his hands, and God bless him for that. ◪

True Talker

By William Kittredge

Summer 2008

"She's gone, goddamn it! Gone!"

"Gone, by God, and naught to care but some of us who seen 'er new."

"Why'nt they leave it to us as they found it? By God, she's ours by rights."

"God, she was purty onc't. Purty and new, and not a man track, savin' Injuns, on the whole scoop of her."

WHO SPEAKS? It's the 1830s, up in the Teton River country at the foot of the Rockies, and the speaker is a mid-life mountain man who feels his beloved natural world has been utterly transmogrified. He sees the future.

"You'll be out on the prairie, hide hunting, chasin' buffler and skinning 'em, and seein' the end come to that, too."

IT'S *THE BIG SKY* AND WE HEAR BUD GUTHRIE. In 1991, shortly before his death, Bud was honored when the Western Literature Association picked *The Big Sky* as the best novel about the American West ever published. What did that mean—true to its times, heartbreaking, infuriating, compelling and defining? His readers have tended to rethink notions of heroism and never again see the shoot-'em-up story of the American West in the same ways after some hours with Boone Caudill and Teal Eye and Dick Summers and the decades they lived through. There were other first-rate literary novels about the West, like Willa Cather's *My Antonia* and Wallace Stegner's *The Big Rock Candy Mountain*, but *The Big Sky* was the overwhelming choice.

On a vivid autumn afternoon, Annick Smith and I spent some hours with Guthrie and his family at The Barn, his home west of Choteau on the Teton River. There were eight of us on a glassed-in sun-porch: Bud and Carol, his wife, and a stepdaughter, a stepson-in-law, a daughter-in-law, a grandchild, the family. The first winter storm had come over the Rockies the night before, and the snowy mountains were distinct against a white sky. Bud was good humored and bright though no doubt pushing back an abiding sense that these were last times. He told us jokes. Wish I could remember them.

The next day there was a celebration of Guthrie at the Montana Nature Conservancy headquarters near the Pine Butte Swamp. It was a mix of literary people like James and Lois Welch, Ripley Hugo, Mary Blew, Richard Ford, and locals like Alice Gleeson, who'd known Bud for decades.

After Bud showed up with his family, the most moving part of what followed, for me, was listening and watching while his neighbors, each by each, stood and told stories about Bud. Alice Gleeson, close to weeping, almost Bud's age, told a time when Bud asked her to pick up groceries for him and some pals since she was going to town anyway. His grocery list read, "Bread and bourbon."

That winter Bud was gone. But he'd carried on right out to the edge, staring down the devil, implying what he'd always told us: *Love what you love fiercely as you can, and never lose heart. Play your cards.*

MONTANA WAS A FAR-AWAY LAND WHERE GIANTS WALKED WHEN I WAS young. And the largest was Guthrie, the old man of the mountains as I imagined him, a king storyteller and a true talker. The summer I was 16, 1948, in a valley on the high deserts along the Oregon/Nevada border, I did a man's work, driving a home-built, power-driven buck rake (Buick chassis, the transmission reversed, engine in the rear), pushing one-ton loads of meadow hay across to a beaver-slide stacking crew. After dinner I'd shower and put on a fresh t-shirt and sit on a screened-in veranda, lights from other ranches flickering in the distance, and take up my reward, an hour with *The Big Sky*, reading slowly, maybe 15 pages at a sitting, making it last, loving it for reasons I didn't understand.

It was maybe the first time I'd been captured by a book. In that ranch-land world reading was seen as useless, like whittling. In high school I learned some Latin and to recite swatches of *Macbeth*. Both were like languages from another planet. Things you might learn as you read, by our priorities, were of no consequence alongside the urgencies of getting the work done.

So my hours with Guthrie were like a revelation. He was teaching me the worth of paying attention to invaluable natural and emotional intri-cacies and the degree to which they are interwoven. During that summer I spent more time thinking about early-day life along the Missouri River than I did about the hayfields where I worked every day, and I sensed the dimensions of my ignorance, and was shamed by a feeling I had so far lived wearing blinders. But I excused myself; I was young.

Guthrie showed me powerful personalities, how they conducted themselves in an untouched paradise and thus what they made of it along with what they did to themselves and those they loved in the work-ing out. He showed me the long results of conduct. *The Big Sky* was about the consequences of overweening ambition. Guthrie showed me men much like my father and grandfather, who were determined to make the world go their way, and the essential powerlessness of women and Native Americans in that world. He was showing me mistakes I might make if I wasn't careful and who I might become. He was showing me how easy it is to blunder into irrevocable lifetime sadness.

Guthrie helped me see that my people and our stories were part of history in the country where I lived. He lead me to the thought that the place where I lived even had a history, and that our history connect-ed to larger stories, like the one about the conquest and settlement of the West. He introduced me to the idea that actions generate strings of consequence and that consequences reverberate through generations. Guthrie helped me see that we are responsible for our actions and their impact on future generations.

Not that I, at 16, out on that porch reading *The Big Sky*, got those concepts to the exact forefront of my mind. It took decades for his mes-sage to settle into my head in an articulated way. We see our society still struggling with notions he dramatized long ago.

I N 1964, I was driven to try writing. Part of the impulse came from my admiration for Guthrie. I had it in mind to tell stories about people and places I revered just as Guthrie had written of Montana. It was a naive impulse—I didn't have a clear lineup of stories I wanted to tell, or any real notion of what they might mean to a reader—I just wanted to say we in the outback West were significant. I wanted stories about my homeland in southeastern Oregon to reverberate in the imaginations of far away people.

It's the writer's job to help readers see and deal with processes that drive their own lives. Useful stories help people see themselves. But at that time I didn't know such things. I was floundering along, sending out stories, getting them rejected and desperate for help.

That help came from Bud Guthrie's autobiographical book, *The Blue Hen's Chick*, which I checked out of the Lake County Public Library. In chapter seventeen, Guthrie tells of getting serious about writing *The Big Sky* while on a Nieman Fellowship at Harvard in 1944. He learned, he says, to quit "hamming" and show readers the story, not talk to them about it. He found his "identity with my characters—which meant I lost my own for the time. I was at Harvard but wasn't. I was in the young mountains trapping prime beaver."

It was instruction I needed. Chapter eighteen is a primer of the art of fiction writing as Bud understood it. I copied his maxims in my notebooks. *The Blue Hen's Chick* was the best and most useful teaching story a young writer lost in the deep sagebrush West could have encountered.

HE BIG SKY FLOORED ME THAT FIRST SUMMER AND STILL DOES. The story breaks and enrages my heart in ways that would be sentimental but for the fact that the explosions of pride, anger, violence and sorrow that Guthrie shows us can so easily become absolutely real in our own lives. Bud laughed when he said *The Big Sky* was about hugging a kitten to death, killing what we love, but he meant to be taken seriously.

The Big Sky is ruthlessly accurate about our impulse to conquer as we settle. It is a story about trying to possess what you love and in the process crushing the beloved. The beloved, Guthrie seems to say, can only be cherished, given the freedom to be what it is. Or it will wither. This song is at the heart of *The Big Sky* and all Guthrie's attempts to care for the world he so cherished. ◪

Saying Goodbye with a Song

By Maryanne Vollers

Winter 2013

YOU COULD PRETTY MUCH WRITE THE STORY OF LIVINGSTON, Montana, from a barstool at the Elks Club. The big room in the back is where folks hold their landmark events: wakes and receptions, reunions and fundraisers. So it's no surprise that, on a warm August night, twinkly lights and chiffon swags left over from a wedding adorn the stage—a festive counterpoint to the ghostly herd of mounted elk heads gazing down from the walls.

Ben Bullington, long and lean and craggy-handsome, settles into a chair with his vintage Gibson guitar and grins at the crowd. A couple hundred faces smile back, family and friends, mostly, and a lively contingent of nurses from the hospital in White Sulphur Springs, where Ben practiced family medicine for 12 years. Ben's second song, "Two Headlights." is about a man who's learned he has cancer. In plain, matter-of-fact verse, the song takes him through the medical procedures the doctor knows so well: *"First the x-ray, large lymph node, biopsy, then what it showed ..."*

Then the songwriter takes over, describing a lonesome drive back home, his headlights cutting a path to midnight, the man taking inventory of his life:

I stopped the car
Cut the engine
Stepped out in the night air sensin'
Things I didn't sense the day before.
It's all I want from life
And nothing more.

Ben finishes the last refrain and leans on his guitar. "That song, I actually wrote three years ago," he says, in a scratchy voice that's never lost the lilt of his native Virginia. "It's funny, I've got these premonition songs, or something." He chuckles, shaking his head. "Well, it's funny to me. Not in an entirely mirthful way, I guess. But some part of me knew what was happening ..."

What was happening, and what every member of this audience knows, is that 10 months earlier, at the age of 57, Ben was diagnosed with stage 4 pancreatic cancer. It's always fatal, and most patients don't live more than a year.

B EN BULLINGTON HAS BEEN ONE OF MY CLOSEST FRIENDS FOR THE BETTER part of a decade. My husband Bill Campbell and I have spent many an evening with Ben—and other fine musicians—trading songs and stories in the living room. I've seen a lot of him since his diagnosis, and watched in awe as he's navigated the tricky terrain of saying goodbye to the people he loves and the life he's known. When he's in pain, he tries not to show it. When the conversation turns to cancer treatments, he changes the subject. Like the man in the song, he wants to drink in every moment of what remains, and to spend as much time as he can with his friends, his family, and most of all his three grown sons, Samuel, Joseph, and Ben. That, and making as much music as he can for as long as he can.

My cousin went to Vietnam
And left the first six Dylan records with me
I was 15 then
Just a gangly kid
All heart and appetite and misery
—"Appalachian Mountain Delta Blues"

Ben grew up in Roanoke, Virginia, the middle of five children. His dad was a Naval officer who became a stockbroker; his mom was a beauty with deep local roots. Ben's older sister Mary showed me a report from Ben's preschool teacher, who observed that the five-year-old boy had an excellent attention span, was interested in stories, enjoyed music, and "sings often as he works or plays." She concluded, "Ben lives well in his world."

Ben didn't develop a real passion for music until he was a teenager. His first instrument was a Kent guitar he bought for $20 from a kid in the high school lunchroom. "To my surprise, I took to it," he says. He started taking lessons and trading for better and better guitars, which led him deep into the culture of Appalachian music that seemed to pour out of the hills around him. It touched something in him that he couldn't name. The first time he saw somebody flatpick a guitar was at the Union Grove fiddlers' festival. "When I asked about it, this guy said, 'Get a Doc Watson record.'" So he did, and within 30 seconds of putting it on his turntable, Ben started jumping up and down, he was so excited. "It went right through the middle of me," he says.

Before long, he was listening to Mississippi John Hurt, and then his cousin went to Vietnam and left him his Bob Dylan collection. (The cousin made it back; it's unclear what happened to the albums.) Ben started working out his own tunes and lyrics while he was still in high school, although none of them has seen the outside of his old orange notebook for decades.

He went to Vanderbilt University ("'cause it was in Nashville"), absorbing the music scene in the picking parlors as he studied for a geology degree.

After college, there was an oil boom in the West. Ben hired on to lead a seismograph crew that traveled all over the Rockies, packing dynamite to shake up the earth and sensors to see what oil it contained. He liked it fine and didn't mind the cheap motels in dusty corners of Montana and Wyoming. And he was gathering material. "Corby Bond" was based on an oil field driller he met in Douglas, Wyoming. In the song, the roughneck tries to articulate why the settled life isn't for him:

Red sky to the east on the northern plain,
Every day don't have to be the same.

Ben, too, couldn't stand the thought of a desk job. And he was falling in love with the wide-open country. Then he transferred to Brazil and came down with a bad case of hepatitis A, which meant a helicopter out of the jungle and a stint in a Roanoke hospital. Before long he decided his oil field days were over. The question was what to do next. "I was pretty good with science and liked working with people," he says. "So I figured I'd put the two together."

He was accepted at the University of Virginia medical school in Charlottesville. There was a vision in his head of becoming a country doctor, living outside of the big cities, seeing all kinds of patients with something new happening every day.

Ben met his future wife, Debra, a nurse at UVA hospital. After he got his license, he and Debra and their young son, Samuel, moved to Montana, where he took a job with the Indian Health Services on the Northern Cheyenne Reservation. Two more sons would follow, Joseph and Benjamin. The Bullingtons stayed in Lame Deer for a few years, then moved to a small coastal Alaska town and then to a clinic in the mountains of West Virginia. "I didn't go into medicine to make a lot of money, and I've been very successful in that way," he says. "But my boys grew up with a lot of elbow room."

Ben had always pictured settling down some day on a farm in southwestern Virginia, but the Rockies kept tugging at him. "There was something about the big space out West that I needed to feel free in life," he says.

Dreams don't come easy
On seven bucks an hour
Maybe it's a matter
Of what kind of dreams you have
There're trout streams and the air is clean
And money don't mean everything
In a place called White Sulphur Springs.
—"White Sulphur Springs"

The family ended up in central Montana, where Ben worked at the six-bed hospital in White Sulphur Springs, surrounded by mountains, ranches and miles of empty. When his youngest son was four, Ben started writing songs again in the quiet early morning hours. Those sessions provided most of the tunes on his first CD, *Two Lane Highway*, released in 2007.

The album was produced by Sean Devine, a singer-songwriter from Livingston, who met Ben by chance and discovered that the doctor was also a songwriter. By then Ben and Debra's marriage was ending. Devine encouraged Ben to start performing at local venues and introduced him around Livingston. Which is how Bill and I met him. And it was at dinner at our house that he met Joanne Gardner, his future manager.

Joanne was a recovering music industry executive who regained her senses and moved from Los Angeles to Montana.

"I had no idea he was a doctor; I honestly believed he was a traveling songwriter," she says with a laugh. "That was because he looked kind of homeless, and he was real hungry. Then he started playing music and I was sure he was a traveling songwriter because the songs were so damn good. But I remember being perplexed when he stood up and announced that he had to be on call the next morning. I was like, 'Uh, where would you be on call? Is there like a poetry hotline?'"

Ben and Joanne were fast friends from that day on. After a career in the big-time music industry, she was moved by his homespun lyricism, "the level of detail and nuance in his songs that make them completely come to life for me." He also inspired her to start singing again and she became a regular part of his act. Before long, she was managing his career, booking gigs, and introducing him to some of her influential friends in Nashville, including Rodney Crowell, the Grammy award-winner whom Joanne also co-managed at the time.

When Ben recorded his next album, *White Sulphur Springs*, Crowell stopped by the Nashville studio from time to time, and even traded verses on "Toe the Line," one of Ben's anthems to honesty in art and life, with the refrain, "Do you find your own truth, or do you toe the line?" But Rodney says he didn't realize the depth of Ben's talent until the two of them went for a ride in Crowell's car and listened to the album top to bottom.

"I said to him, 'This is poetry. You've really created something here.' And that's when I became a fan of Ben's," says Crowell.

White Sulphur Springs established Ben Bullington as a songwriter to be reckoned with. His artistry resonates in every song, from the title track, an homage to the simple but bountiful life of small-town Montana, to "Twangy Guitars," the story of a farm family dealing with the wife's cancer and finally getting some good news. His exquisite sense of detail puts you right at the kitchen table for breakfast, in the antiseptic waiting room, and then driving the pickup back from the hospital on a snowy, wind-whipped highway, a country western soundtrack pulsing hope over the radio.

N 2008 BEN LEFT WHITE SULPHUR TO TAKE A JOB AT THE SMALL HOSPITAL IN Big Timber. He put thousands of miles on his SUV, burning up highways between Big Timber and White Sulphur, where his two younger sons were still in high school.

Meanwhile, he was honing his chops as a performer, traveling around the country, sometimes opening for Crowell. He broke into radio, too, climbing the Americana charts, and new songs came in a torrent. He wrote them in his head while he was driving those long stretches; he jotted lyrics on the 3-by-5 notecards he always kept in his shirt pocket. Before long he was laying down tracks for his third album, *Satisfaction Garage*. By the time it was released in 2010 he already had all the songs lined up for *Lazy Moon*, an album that is Montana to the bone: recorded at Electric Peak Studios in Gardiner, and featuring a lineup of locally based musicians, including Bill Payne of Little Feat.

Payne, who co-wrote some of Little Feat's greatest hits, asked Ben to write a song with him about a dear friend, Stephen Bruton, a songwriter who had recently died of throat cancer. "Tapping Ben was kind of unusual because he didn't know Stephen," says Payne. "But they were very kindred spirits in a certain sense."

The result is "The Last Adios," a sweeping elegy, earthbound in its details, sublime in its reach. The subject matter was hauntingly prophetic.

Our hearts are thorns and roses
And you can't ever know
If it's the first step of a journey
Or the last adios ...

IN THE LATE FALL OF 2012, Ben noticed an ache in his gut that wouldn't go away. At first he thought it was an ulcer. But the pain got worse, and he finally checked in with a colleague who ordered a CT scan and then delivered the hard news: a tumor in the middle of his pancreas and spots on his liver.

By the time this kind of cancer produces symptoms, it's too late to cure it. Soon after the diagnosis, Ben took leave from the hospital. ("Nobody wants a sick doctor.") He decided on a mild course of chemotherapy that would hopefully hold back the disease without giving him terrible side effects, like neuropathy in his hands that would make it impossible to play guitar. He even delayed the start of treatment so he could fly to Nashville to record his fifth CD. Afterwards, he arranged chemo treatments early in the week, so that he could feel well enough to perform on the weekends.

Some of his friends worried that he should be doing more to fight the disease. He pointed out he'd spent a career trying to help people make good decisions, that he knew what he was doing.

"I just say to them, 'Don't worry. I've got this.'"

The self-titled album, *Ben Bullington*, came out the next spring. It's an elegant, stripped-down piece of work that flows like a musical memoir, from the story of his Virginia roots in "Appalachian Mountain Delta Blues," to the poignant refrain of "The Last Adios." Along the way he tweaks the rank commercialism that pervades Nashville in "Country Music (I'm Talking to You)," and connects climate change to the human heart in "Here's to Hopin'" (with harmonies by another good friend, Mary Chapin Carpenter).

To the astonishment of his friends, Ben kept up a solid schedule of touring all year. With Joanne by his side, he played music festivals from Florida to Texas to Tennessee, topping off the summer with his third appearance at Red Ants Pants, the White Sulphur Springs answer to Woodstock. He even went back into the studio to record a track for a compilation he's putting together called *Montana Jukebox Songs*.

The one thing he hasn't done much is write songs.

"It takes a lot of work to do something good," Ben says. "You have to go over it, and over it, and over it. It removes you from the world. I don't want to take what little part I have of the day and use it for that. I'd rather watch movies with the boys."

The one song he's written since he got sick is a farewell to his boys, called "Son, We're Good." It's the only song he has a hard time singing: "Things don't always work out the way you wish they would. Go on and do what you need to son, we're good ..."

"I've got plenty of stuff that I'm happy with," he says. "It's a fair body of work now. That can be enough."

Although it wasn't planned that way, the concert at the Elks Club in Livingston was Ben's last show. It just got too hard after that. But he's okay with it. That, too, was enough. "I looked out at the audience and everyone was a friend," he says. "Just what I'd always envisioned when I started out. It was the best concert I've ever done, a perfect night."

THESE DAYS BEN SPLITS HIS TIME BETWEEN THE HOUSE HE'S KEPT FOR HIS sons in White Sulphur and the couch in Joanne Gardner's living room in Livingston. His best time is the morning. Often he'll pick out a tune on his banjo while the sun lights up the Absarokas beyond the picture windows.

Ben's goal was to live long enough to see his eldest son get married to his hometown sweetheart in early October. He made it. It was a classic outdoor wedding in Montana, with folding chairs and cowboy boots sinking in the uneven grass. Sam Bullington and Lorinda Hunt said their vows beneath a wide blue sky anchored by snow-dusted mountains, the Yellowstone River running just behind the cottonwoods, like a welcome guest tying everything together. Young Ben, who postponed college to help out his dad, served as a groomsman, and Joseph, a promising young writer, officiated the ceremony. Their father sat in the front row, beaming from beneath his Stetson.

Ben has been spending his time making lists, getting his affairs in order, tying up loose ends. There have been lots of talks with his boys about finances, women, fate, politics, and joy, cramming a lifetime of advice into a few short months.

But he's already said it best in a song, of course. "I've Got to Leave You Now" is another one of those "premonition" songs, written a couple of years before he learned he had cancer.

Promise me you won't worry
It's probably like the time 'fore I was born
Make some waves out on the ocean
With all the best inside you, my sons.

Our souls might mingle in the after torch
Like four friends smokin' on a midnight porch
I always loved you the best I knew how
I've gotta leave you now ... ◼

Ben Bullington died November 18, 2013. He was 58 years old.

Cowboy Cool

By Scott McMillion

Fall 2010

ONSIDER THE COWBOY, he of the work-thickened fingers and the heart full of bruises. What smolders under that hat? What simmers beneath the pearly snaps on his shirt? What makes him sing, this creature of the West?

People have been trying to answer those questions, to give the cowboy definition, ever since somebody first downsized a sombrero and pointed a herd to the north. He is a national icon, after all.

Fiction writers and Hollywood productions both offer a schizophrenic view of the man in the big hat. Is he a nihilist or an altruist? Is he a clown like Howdy Doody, or a hero like John Wayne? What is his true story? Is it *The Wild Bunch* or is it *Brokeback Mountain*? Could both those movies have a point?

"We've gone from Sam Peckinpah's West to Ang Lee's *Brokeback Mountain*," notes Paul Zarzyski, whose poetry has been helping the West define itself for 35 years. "Boy, things are changing. And you've got to roll with it."

So he's rolling. So is singer/songwriter Wylie Gustafson, with whom he wrote seven songs on Gustafson's newest album, *Hang-n-Rattle*, a Western euphemism that means get tough, cowboy up, get real.

And Zarzyski and Gustafson are the real deal. Between them, they're making a kind of music they call "rock and rowel," (named for that jangly bit on the end of a spur). Listen to this music in a honkytonk and your feet want to go live. Listen during a long drive, when you can focus on the lyrics, and your life looks into itself. These are songs to make you dance and make you wonder.

"It was among the best work I've ever done," Gustafson said of the CD, and he's done a lot of them: 15 so far. "I felt we'd hit a home run."

Still, Gustafson said the new album has disappointed some of his many fans. He's been entertaining for so long—everywhere from the Conrad rodeo to the Kennedy Center—that people approach his music with certain expectations. For one thing, while the new songs don't skimp on the country themes of horses and heartache, there's not much yodeling—and Gustafson sure can yodel. He provided the famous trademark yodel for the internet service provider Yahoo and he's written a book on how to yodel. But his musical roots spread both deep and wide. When he rounded up cattle as a teenager, he often serenaded them with Rolling Stones songs.

And those roots pop up in the new album.

"We both think that cowboy poetry could use a good infusion of sex and energy," Zarzyski said.

So this album rocks more than it sashays.

The songwriting partners say they're just trying to move the ball forward, in an artistic sense, to recognize the West as it exists, with a nostalgic nod to its history. Accomplish that and you're looking at something that just might have a future.

"The imagination is synonymous with the future," Zarzyski said. "I'm not sure where this is going to go, but I'd sure like to keep pushing the envelope."

Here's an example: The song "Double Wild" tells the tale of a rodeo rider in love with a Mescalero Indian. He rides bitch on the back of her Harley, mescal in the saddlebag, and that's the way they both like it. Zarzyski wrote the words. Gustafson put the dance in them.

Leather jacket skinny-dippers
Fingers swimming through her zippers
Whiskers rubbing up against her tattooed neck
Suicide shifting, weaving and a-drifting
What he whispers in her ear could cause a wreck...
Ah, the West is still wild as she ever was

If there's a message here, it might be this: Hang-n-rattle, Roy Rogers, what's wrong with riding bitch? It's her bike, after all.

A changing West indeed.

And despite the tutting of some entrenched fans, the album is gaining traction with the arbiters of cowboy cool. Its title song won a Spur Award from the Western Writers of America and Zarzyski won another one for the poem "Bob Dylan's Bronc Song," which he recites on the album. True West Magazine named the team the "best living wild west troubadours." The Western Music Association named it the best cowboy/swing album of 2009.

"It's like Lennon and McCartney in cowboy hats," gushed *American Cowboy* magazine.

The duo has performed at the Library of Congress and the Kennedy Center in Washington D.C. and appeared with symphonies in Tennessee and Washington state. They've performed separately on National Public Radio's *A Prairie Home Companion*, and Gustafson has appeared more than 50 times at the Grand Ole Opry while Zarzyski won the Montana Governor's Arts Award for Literature in 2005, joining the likes of Norman Maclean, Thomas McGuane and A. B. Guthrie Jr.

And they met at Woodstock, the cowboy version.

GUSTAFSON, 49, grew up on a cattle ranch near Conrad and was playing in dance bands by the time he was in high school. He studied for a year at the University of Montana ("not enough to slow me down") and later put in his time in the honkytonks and studios in Los Angeles and Nashville before moving home to Conrad. With his band, The Wild West, he's created all those albums and when he's not performing (70 gigs or more a year, from London, England, to Australia to North Carolina, playing with everybody from Merle Haggard to Elvis Costello) or writing songs, he raises champion cutting horses and even keeps a small herd of crafty, agile bison that he uses to train his horses. "They're smarter than cattle," he said. As horsemen go, he's got plenty of chops.

"But I'm all hat and no cattle," said Zarzyski.

That's not entirely true.

Now 59, Zarzyski spent a lot of years living rodeo. He put the spurs to somewhere between 800 and 1,000 bareback broncs, won his share of paydays and buckles, while honing his own chops as a poet at UM under the tutelage of the renowned Richard Hugo. Though he grew up in northern Wisconsin and retains the round-voweled accent of his youth, (We all come from somewhere. Even Charlie Russell grew up in Missouri.) his is an authentic Western voice. He made his name as a rodeo poet, but with his eight published volumes of poetry, he reaches a lot wider. He's no rhyme slinger offering odes to flapjacks. Working on a Smith Corona typewriter at his home near Great Falls, he can write an ode to a bronc or a buckle bunny, but he can connect Auschwitz to Wounded Knee, look at a calloused palm and trace out the sorry heart of South African racism, rue the loss of love and youth, and still take some time to laugh at himself.

One critic called him a "rodeo Ferlinghetti," and the *New York Times Book Review* said "his verses bristle with audacity and whimsy. Mr Zarzyski alternates between bluster and lyricism."

He and Gustafson found each other in Elko, Nev., at the annual Cowboy Poetry Gathering. That's the Cowboy Woodstock and they're both there every year.

"Without Elko, Wylie and I wouldn't be sitting here together talking," Zarzyski said.

"The first time I saw Paul, I was excited because he represented what I thought cowboy poetry could be," Gustafson said.

A talented and successful songwriter himself, Gustafson said that in the past he often tried to make the words fit the music. Now, working with Zarzyski, he's learning how better to make lyrics and melody complement one another.

"Paul was the one who taught me how important the words were," he said. "He taught me to think about every word, every image."

"And I learned what makes a song tick," Zarzyski said. "It's exciting to see how the words come together musically."

They both had to make some adjustments in the approach to their labors but together they landed "in the zone," the place you've got to be to make songwriting work.

Hang 'n' Rattle was produced at the Cash Cabin Studios by John Carter Cash at a time when both men were pulling through a tough time in their personal lives. Gustafson's marriage was breaking up and Zarzyski's father was dying. But the creative process, building something real, working together, helped put the pains where they belonged.

Despite the grief, "we were surrounded by an aura of joy," Zarzyski said.

Music is a challenging business these days. Everything is digital and most people expect it to be free. But Zarzyski and Gustafson are committed to making a difference, to helping the West understand itself as it stands today.

"We're more a reflection of the contemporary West," Gustafson said. And while the West is not an easy place to define, it's one worth protecting.

"The more people we can get to celebrate the Western culture, the better the odds are that we can keep this country wide open," Zarzyski said. "And we could use some help."

Ride, boys.

Hang-n-rattle. ▉

Music Finds
Its Way Home

By Scott McMillion

Summer 2010

SOMETIMES, you can go home again.

You can win a music scholarship to Harvard. You can help make a bunch of hit records. You can tour with Elvin Bishop and Peter Gabriel, with all the fame and the fans and the accolades that go with a great big road show. You can write your own songs and make your own records and you can be nominated for a Grammy. You can master classical music, and rock and blues and jazz, and you can gather it all up in your head, blend it, and send it to your fingers, which is how you share the magic.

You can do all this, and you can still go home to Chester, Montana, add your small family to the 700 or so people who remain in that wind-battered burg on the prairie. You can move into the house where you were raised, make your music in a grain bin and when the work is done for the day, when the breeze comes up on a hot afternoon, you can relax in the shade of your grandfather's favorite tree and wait for your son, wait for him to come bouncing home from the same school where you studied music and math and basketball, the school where your mother took her lessons, too.

And you can listen to the wind and the quiet. You can stand and see the Sweetgrass Hills looming in the north. You can hear the approach of a train from the east and maybe smell the coming of a storm from the west and while you might or might not see antelope on that day, you will know they are around somewhere. And all of this – the wind and the weather and the animals, the sound and the smell and sights – combines in your ear, the inner part, where you make music.

This son of yours, this laughing boy, is the fourth generation of your family in this house and you have come home, where he can grow up much as you did, with sports and music and friends and elders in a place where almost everybody knows almost everybody. It can be done. You have proven this.

And that, in a nutshell, is the story of Phil Aaberg, a kid from Chester who became one of the nation's most accomplished pianists and composers.

"High, deep art," is the way George Winston, another Montanan who wows the world with a piano, described Aaberg's music. "He's just the greatest composer. He captures Montana as well or better than I've ever heard anybody capture anything."

Elvin Bishop was more succinct: "He's the best piano player I've ever heard," the rocker once wrote.

Aaberg was always something of a prodigy at the keyboard. He first demanded piano lessons when he was four years old, inspired by church music, and put on his first recital when he was eight.

After the show, people clapped and his piano teacher's mother gave him $10. Something clicked in Aaberg's young head. Applause and money? For doing something fun? What's not to like?

"I felt really lucky growing up the way I did," Aaberg said. "I got to do all the things the other kids did. I played basketball and baseball. But I had this other thing that the other kids couldn't do." He nodded at the nearby grand piano in the windowless studio, the grain bin attached to his home.

He credits his small town upbringing with giving him the confidence to succeed as a musician. It was easy to be the best in a tiny place, and nobody ever told him no, he couldn't aim even higher.

Rather, his mother, whose husband had left her to raise two small boys alone, had done so in an era when single parents stood out in a crowd, determined that her sons would be somebody. No questions. Period.

His talent was obvious, and his mother encouraged him, scraping together money for lessons and driving him to concerts in Havre, Great

Falls and Shelby, which seemed like the bigtime, compared to Chester. There were summer music camps, contests to win, and frequent trips to an acclaimed teacher in Spokane, too far to visit weekly but close enough for regular train trips.

Woven through all of it was practice and more practice, three or four hours a day at the keyboard, learning Beethoven and Bach and more. And it paid off. When it came time for college, he aimed high. Dartmouth, Yale, the University of Chicago and Harvard all offered scholarships. He chose Harvard, which is a lot farther from Chester than 2,000 miles of highway can explain.

"It was a little like being on the moon," Aaberg said. But he didn't know enough about the place to be nervous. He just set himself to his music. "I was blessed by naivete."

Boston offered concerts of all kinds, as many as three a week, and Aaberg played in lots of bands, from blues to bluegrass. He played rock. He played funk. He played New Orleans jazz.

"A lot of stuff was out of school, and my grades reflected that," he said.

After college, he joined a band and they all lived in the same house in New England and played in the same venues with people like Bonnie Raitt and the J. Giles Band. It was fun, but it didn't scratch the itch inside him.

"I wanted to play in a blues band and I wanted to study Beethoven," he said. So he moved to Iowa, and focused on sonatas in the daytime, the blues at night.

Then his first wife decided she wanted to try California.

"And I thought, oh, that's where they make records," he said.

Once in Oakland, word spread of his skills, and he lined up lots of work, mostly as a session player in recording studios, playing with Elvin Bishop, Henry Gross, the Pointer Sisters, Peter Gabriel and more.

"I played on a lot of top 10 records," he said, but being a sideman is a tough job. "I didn't want to go in there and have to sound like somebody else."

He went on a couple tours, but the road didn't appeal much. He wanted to stay home with his three young sons.

Living in Oakland, he picked up work closer to home. He composed jingles for Saturday morning cartoons, Peanuts specials, small movies, even the California Milk Board.

"I'd get $20,000 for a half hour's work," he said. "It was the kind of work musicians would kill for, but it was killing me. My stomach hurt. My shoulders hurt."

So, at the age of 32, he quit. And he came up with a plan, writing his goals on a couple sheets of paper.

He wanted to play chamber music and he wanted to compose and play his own music. And he wanted to support his family doing it.

"Nobody does that," he said.

But he knew he had to try. He gave himself a year.

"If it didn't work, I was going to take the civil service exam and be a mail man. And as soon as I made that decision, it was like a miracle cure."

The pain lifted from his shoulders and his guts and in short order he had a record contract with Wyndham Hill, a popular independent label.

"I toured the world, playing my own music, which I never thought was something I could do," he said.

And it lasted for years, until the company was purchased by a corporate giant that favored formulaic music and frowned on his politics, which favored letting nature be nature. So Aaberg found a way out of his contract and formed his own label, Sweetgrass Music, named for the hills north of his hometown.

His second album, *Live from Montana*, earned him the Grammy nomination in 2002. It was recorded in the Chester High School gymnasium, the place where Aaberg played basketball.

The Grammy nomination arose from the same place Aaberg did: Chester. Home.

Shortly afterward, he moved back to Chester for good. He cleaned out his grandparents' house, added the studio, and brought his new wife Patty and their son, Jake. Now 60, he wonders sometimes what took him so long. Throughout his career, he'd written songs with rural Montana in mind: the stretch of the prairies, the cleansing winds, the blessed abundance of quiet.

"I think I was always trying to get back here," he said. "Every time I crossed the pass and saw the prairie, my mind opened up and my lungs opened up. And I thought, 'why am I not doing this?'"

Work followed him: compositions, movie scores, albums, commissions and concerts. He stays as busy as ever, producing albums for friends in his grain bin and writing more music all the time, jotting it on napkins or the back of his hand, recording it on his cell phone or his computer, refining it later, putting Montana in your ears.

"I know I get a lot more done here than I ever could before."

But he's brought more than himself back to Chester. He's brought a message for kids a lot like himself.

Through a nonprofit foundation he calls Arts Without Boundaries, he stages seminars and free concerts in small venues around the state. Sometimes he performs, sometimes he brings in other top talent.

The message is a simple one.

"Here's what I do," he tells the kids. "This music comes from where you came from."

If you doubt that, pop one of his CDs in the stereo and drive the Hi-Line. Or Highway 191. Even I 90, in the quieter stretches. Then pull off on some high point, watch the horizon, and listen to Montana rendered as melody. You'll get the point.

Aaberg knows that few students will match his success. Doing so takes luck, talent and perseverance, especially perseverance.

But success in the arts is possible. He repeats this message, wanting it to stick.

"I go into a place and I say 'Art happens here. I want you to be a part of it.'"

He wants to see the evolution of a Montana musical tradition, something based not on the tastes of Los Angeles or New York or Nashville. And it's starting to happen.

"Montana is increasingly starting to have its own voice and style," said Erik Funk, a longtime friend of Aaberg's who composes classical music for musicians around the world from his home in Bozeman. "It's not just an American sound or a western American sound. It's a Montana sound. And it's as subtle and varied as the topography of the state."

What Aaberg wants is a musical version of something the lucky ones among us already understand.

A place called home. ◪

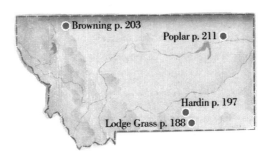

FIRST MONTANANS

They were here first. Their stories count.

War Hoops

By Jeff Welsch

Spring 2011

A VENERABLE CROW WOMAN SITS STOICALLY IN THE FIRST ROW OF BLEACHERS. Her back is hunched but the dark eyes behind her thick glasses are fierce as she watches 10 teenage boys race back and forth in a frenetic blur.

Around the woman, a thousand or so Indians—the Crows on one side of the glossy basketball court rallying for the five boys in Lodge Grass' home orange and white, the visiting Northern Cheyenne on the other side cheering the five from Lame Deer in black and teal—issue war cries as the boys pass.

Hours earlier, elders had prayed to The Maker Of Everything, asking the Creator to watch over the boys. Soon after, one elder spoke to the crowd, admonishing that the healing from shadowy recent incidents in the stands begins with them. And then the Crow Flag Song—"Hey-na-na-hey-hey-ha-no-hay-oh"—had reverberated through the bright gymnasium, where five state Class B basketball championship banners testify to the prowess of the tribe's rabidly competitive Mighty Few District.

Now the spotlight shines just on the current boys and their youthful innocence. Where were they in the hours before tonight's game? Where will they go after? "I worry about that," concedes Lodge Grass schools' superintendent Victoria Falls Down, mindful that coaches and teachers can do only so much against a tidal wave of drugs, alcohol, pregnancy, single-parent homes and the general aimlessness of a shattered culture's youth. "I hope they go home," she adds. "Sometimes it doesn't happen."

But for the next two hours, on a snowy bench above the Little Bighorn River just north of the Montana-Wyoming border, there will be no worries. The boys are running like the plains winds—just like the players who came before them and, in their fantasies perhaps, just like the great Elvis Old Bull, Jonathan Takes Enemy, Larry Pretty Weasel and the other legends on whose shoulders the tribe's esteem rose and fell. Their expressions are equal parts serious and toothy-grin, paradoxical reflections of both the importance of this night and the unbridled joy of shedding the reservation's shackles, however briefly, to run like the warriors of a noble past.

In this way, the Crow and Northern Cheyenne are kindred spirits. Both lost their land and freedom, forced onto tiny fractions of their historic territories, square red pegs pounded into round white holes, then abandoned. Broken spirits and tears littered trails to nowhere.

But tonight . . . tonight is like the old days. Over a century, since the Army banned intertribal warfare and banished traditional enemies to neighboring reservations, the lines between them have grown increasingly blurred. Traditions fade, barriers fall, animosities linger largely in the subconscious if at all. Today, the arenas where those lines remain clear—the arenas where it is especially meaningful to be either Crow or Northern Cheyenne—are few.

On this night, a last public bastion of tribal purity is on display. It's Lodge Grass vs. Lame Deer, Crow vs. Northern Cheyenne, on a different kind of battlefield.

The venerable Crow woman watches quietly, intently, for one quarter, two, then three as the boys' feet barely touch the hardwood. And then a Crow player slows for a split second, just long enough for a Northern Cheyenne to dribble past for two points. She straightens as if she were 25 again. "Come on!" she bristles, calling out the boy's name. "Remember—you're a Crow!"

BACK IN THE TIME OF THE GREAT CHIEFS AND WARRIORS—back when the *Apsáalooke* people freely roamed the coulees and ridges of eastern Montana, back when the sweet grass was plentiful and the buffalo darkened the horizon, back before the white soldiers and settlers came with their fences and plows and soulless pursuit of material wealth— they would paint their faces, mount their ponies and ride toward the distant eastern end of their lands.

They rode under the moon and the stars, until they reached the sacred Black Hills, where the Children of the Large-Beaked Bird, or Crow, came face-to-face with their Plains rivals the Isaapushe, or People of the Striped Fletching on their Arrows. The Northern Cheyenne appeared from the east and north, from as far as the great glacier-carved lakes. For days the Apsáalooke and Isaapushe fought, their war cries echoing across the piney boulders of an island mountain range. Then the Crow would ride toward the setting sun and their vast homeland, the Northern Cheyenne galloping the opposite direction to theirs.

Victors "counted coup" in stolen women, children and horses, and in scalps taken from warriors. The tribes mourned and celebrated their dead. And then they returned to their nomadic routines of hunting buffalo, singing, dancing, sweating, smoking sweet grass around teepee fires, and playing games. They adored competition—especially the Crow, whose greatest passions were reserved for a fast-paced contest where women raced back and forth in a chaotic blur on rocky fields, pursuing a ball with box elder branches hewn much like today's hockey sticks.

Buupchituua was the Crow term for what Anglos called "shinny stick."

For generations it was this way, the Crow and Northern Cheyenne meeting on battlefields in periodic displays of tribal pride that "had a lot more to do with the idea of gamesmanship," says Tim McCleary, head of the general studies department at Little Big Horn College in Crow Agency. "Certainly it was bloody and there was warfare, but until the pressures of the military it was more of a competition than outright warfare."

Neither the Crow nor the Northern Cheyenne thought much of the white man. But the tribes liked each other even less. Indeed, on June 25, 1876, the most famous day of the U.S. military's century-long Indian Wars, the Northern Cheyenne aligned with the Lakota Sioux at Little Bighorn against Gen. George Armstrong Custer's 7th Cavalry and six Crow scouts. Early on, the Crow had chosen a lesser of two evils, partly believing that the U.S. government would respond favorably—somewhat correctly, as it turned out; at 2.2 million acres, the Crow Reservation is easily the largest of seven in Montana—and partly because of Northern Cheyenne atrocities.

"They would steal Crow women and children," says Mina Seminole, a Northern Cheyenne historian at Chief Dull Knife College in Lame Deer. "Our prophets could never marry relatives, so they always had to bring in new blood. A lot of Crow captives were brought in for that purpose."

From archaeological accounts, it appears the Crow arrived in what is now eastern Montana around 1150, and their lives changed little until the white man came. The Cheyenne story is more complex. They were pushed southwest from the Great Lakes region, split into two bands in 1825 after sharp disagreement over signing a "friendship treaty" with the U.S. government and, in the case of the new Northern Cheyenne, were forced north into Crow country by white migration and the slaughter of buffalo.

After the massacre at Little Bighorn, the government intensified efforts to subdue the Northern Cheyenne, and Crow warriors eagerly hired on to help. What followed was consignment to the Southern Cheyenne reservation in Oklahoma, a subsequent escape, recapture in Nebraska, and finally a second escape three years after Custer's demise that took a small band of Northern Cheyenne back into eastern Montana.

Meanwhile, the Crows watched their reservation shrink from 38.8 million acres to 6 and finally to its current configuration in an 1884 treaty. *Annukaxuna*, the Crow called it: Living Within A Line Drawn On The Ground. That same year, President Chester A. Arthur signed a proclamation granting the Northern Cheyenne a much smaller reservation between Rosebud Creek and the Tongue River, in what had been the heart of Crow lands.

For ages, the Crow and Northern Cheyenne had been mortal enemies. Now they were dispirited neighbors, the Crow on 2.2 million acres and the Northern Cheyenne on 445,000, including a shared 50-mile border. The results were predictable.

"The Crow didn't want the Cheyenne there because they were uncivilized and aggressive, and the Cheyenne said they didn't want to move there anyway because they held the Crow tribe in contempt and as inferior," Seminole says. "The animosity was very, very prevalent."

Adds McCleary, an Irishman from Illinois who is married to a Crow: "The perception on the part of the Crows was the Cheyenne are backward, ignorant. The Cheyenne said the Crow are servants of the white man. And so on and so forth."

Their ancestral ways a distant memory, the tribes waged primal warfare in other ways. Anger and despair often reared their heads in drug- and alcohol-induced brawls at bars in Lodge Grass, Lame Deer, Crow Agency and Hardin. For a more civilized but no less intense outlet they played Hand Games, a guessing exercise involving elk teeth and bones. Teams from opposing tribes, and districts within tribes, converged on district halls across both reservations to chant, stomp, drink, bet and whip themselves into all-night lathers.

Among the many cultural Crow traditions lost was the spirited women's game played with a stick and ball. Jesuit priests, seeking converts, saw this void in the 1880s when they built missions at St. Xavier, on the Crow Reservation, and St. Labre amid the Northern Cheyenne. Eventually they began teaching a game invented on the East Coast in 1891. Like shinny stick, it involved a ball, hand-eye coordination, the ability to run from sunrise to moonrise, and intense competition. Success was measured by who could best shoot a large ball through a small hoop or basket nailed to a wall.

Indians across the West were drawn like ponies to water to this new form of warfare. So enamored were the Crow that they carried a reverential name forward to christen this new game: *Buupchituua.*

The whites called it basketball.

T HE BOYS HAVE HEARD THE STORIES. They know of the legends. Of Hardin's Pretty Weasel, perhaps the greatest player ever to lace up sneakers on a Montana high school basketball court. Of Takes Enemy, another Hardin product who was a whirling-dervish magician with a ball in his hands. And of Old Bull, the fading black-and-white photos of whom the Lodge Grass boys see in the trophy case every day on the way to practice. It has been 21 years since the greatest player in school history took his last jump shot and disappeared to . . . where? Where have all the legends gone?

Yes, the boys hear about the relentless cycle of dreams fading in a haze of drugs and alcohol, and they vow not to fall into the same trap. "I want to go away from here for awhile," says Lodge Grass senior Ashton Old Elk, who smells of sweet grass smoke and tucks a tightly braided waist-length ponytail into his jersey. He wants to go to college and major in mechanical engineering. "I was raised with one parent. I'm kind of used to living on my own. It'll be tough leaving my mother alone, but it'll be OK."

Those dreams are for another day, though. Tonight, it is all about The Game. "Like a sanctuary," says another Lodge Grass senior, Martin Stops, who dreams of playing basketball at the Haskell Indian Nations University in Lawrence, Kan. "I clean my thoughts." And not just any game. It is two Indian teams. "Pretty intense," says Lame Deer senior Micco Talawyma. "It's always that way against Lodge Grass."

Before tipoff, the boys stand in arrow-straight lines in front of their bench. "And now," the public-address announcer says, "the Crow Flag

Song!" The boys from Lodge Grass stand like statues at rapt attention, each with his right hand placed over his heart. Down the row, past the scorer's table, the boys from Lame Deer also stand respectfully. But this is not their song. Some fold their arms across their chests. Others clasp their hands behind their back. A few rock from one foot to the other as the speakers blare.

The National Anthem follows the Crow Flag Song, and the boys from Lodge Grass sprint across the floor to shake the hand of an elder who sits in a wheelchair. "Ladies and gentlemen," the announcer says emphatically as the crowd settles in, "it's basketball time!"

EVEN AS FAR BACK AS THE MID-1800s, the barriers between the Crow and Northern Cheyenne began to fade away. Some tried to make peace, realizing that after years of pillaging each other they were spilling their own blood as surely as they were spilling their enemies'. One of the Northern Cheyenne's great chiefs, Crazy Head, was a full-blooded Crow whose mother was pregnant when captured.

In later years, with distances shrinking with the automobile, paved roads and telephones, the tribes slowly, if suspiciously and often secretly, began to mingle. Lodge Grass High School principal John Small is half Crow, part Northern Cheyenne and carries the name of a white Texas cattle man who married a Cheyenne in the late 1800s. A burly rodeo enthusiast with silver hair, Small was the product of a mixed Indian marriage at a time when such relationships were no more accepted than whites marrying blacks in the deep South.

"A lot of times we went over there," Small recalls. "Sometimes we were well-liked and sometimes we were not because we were Crow. For me, I got to see both worlds. That enemy-tribe thing, even in the '50s and '60s it was still really prominent."

Slowly, though, more intertribal relationships were forged. Crows grudgingly acknowledged Northern Cheyenne blood in their veins, and vice-versa. Crow students took buses to St. Labre, and the Northern Cheyenne began venturing to Crow villages for jobs. Forays between the Northern Cheyenne communities of Busby, Lame Deer and Ashland and the Crow bastions of Crow Agency, Lodge Grass and Hardin gradually stopped routinely devolving into fistfights.

Meanwhile, the tribes have had more to worry about at home than happenings with their traditional enemy. Cultural genocide sent both down a path of Third World futility. Unemployment approaches 75 percent. Alcoholism is so rampant that surely every family has mourned a relative gone too soon to The Other Side Camp, the victim of cirrhosis of the liver or a plunge through a guardrail on an isolated country road. Homelessness ranks with the worst major U.S. cities; it isn't readily apparent because the indignity of sleeping under an Interstate 90 bridge or shivering next to a burning oil drum is unconscionable in the Indian culture. Often a dozen or more family members sleep on top of each other in weathered single-wide trailers or box homes with rusting vehicles cluttering scraggly yards.

"You have to realize the Northern Cheyenne were a really beaten people," McCleary says. "They weren't going to let up until they were totally defeated. So to this day they live in extreme poverty. The Crows have poverty, too, but it's a happy poverty—if there is such a thing."

Where to turn for dignity and a way out? For the Crows, Northern Cheyenne and other tribes across the West, nothing has equaled the unfettered freedom of basketball as a dream-catcher. Here, ironically within the black-line confines of 84-foot by 50-foot wood floors inside cramped gymnasiums, Indians play a breathless version of basketball unlike any seen even on the rat-ball playgrounds of the inner city. The chaotic scoring-fests stop, grudgingly, only when the final buzzer sounds.

"I know why—because we're nomads," explains Byron Bends, the Lodge Grass coach. Adds Lame Deer counterpart Ben Lonebear: "It takes the place of Plains warfare."

Basketball also has become the aloe for unconquerable pain. The players are today's great warriors, and the best are idolized like immortalized chiefs. Children begin bouncing a ball before they can walk. Indians of all ages play day and night, in the heat of summer and the howling cold of winter, taking thousands of shots at rusting iron rims nailed to rotting plywood backboards next to seemingly every dirt driveway. Tribal pride ebbs and flows with the success of the high school teams at Lodge Grass, Lame Deer, Plenty Coups, Busby, Hardin and Ashland—a scenario played out across Montana's reservations. Entire communities follow buses in lengthy caravans to state tournaments, often wearing traditional garb and chanting to implore the boys to run even faster.

"It's the euphoria of the game people like," says Falls Down, the first woman superintendent for the Lodge Grass School District and wife of another Crow basketball legend, Myron Falls Down, who once scored 80 points in a single game.

Indeed, basketball itself has become like a narcotic, and there are those who worry that it creates a false prosperity, citing the tragic stories of Pretty Weasel, Takes Enemy and Old Bull. The spotlight shone on them with excruciating glare, forcing upon them the dual burdens of expectation and resentment. To some, they were beacons of hope that would restore tribal dignity in the outside world; to others they were abandoning The People to be servants of the whites.

A few tried to leave for colleges, culture shock resulting in staggering dropout rates and a new trail of tears leading back to the reservation. Many once-great players now lurk in the shadows, emerging to play in sandlot pick-up games and in weekend Indian tournaments that are little more than an excuse to drink.

So toxic is the brew that three decades ago Myron Falls Down gathered most of his trophies, tossed them in a Lodge Grass dumpster and vowed never to take another drink. Now a pastor, Falls Down sees basketball not as a ticket out but merely an escape from a world that has no doors.

"I don't like to go here, but there has to be healing first," says Victoria Falls Down, the school superintendent. "Maybe we need to go back and find the root of the problem. It will be up to us to decide: We can go back 100 years and forgive the white man for the atrocities, or we can deal with what we have here."

Falls Down turns back to the game and the boys—to the future faces of the Crow and Northern Cheyenne, and to the men who by necessity are more father figures than coaches. She knows the odds against these boys are daunting.

For a few hours, at least, they will shed the burdens of a culture turned upside down. They are free, dignified and defending sacred turf in a snapshot of a lost past.

"You see the expressions on their faces," Falls Down says. "It's the pride of the community."

YES, time, geography and a shrinking world have muddied the distinctions between two enemies. But not here. Not tonight. "You don't ever want to lose to an Indian team," Old Elk says with a grin, "but because I'm Crow I really wouldn't want to lose to them."

In the end, it is Old Elk still grinning like a coyote. Both teams are young and the caliber of play does not equal the days of Old Bull and Takes Enemy, but the Lodge Grass boys simply have too much depth and strength for Lame Deer. The Indians defeat the Morning Stars for the third time this season. Almost as important, though, is how close they are to 100 points, the goal of every Indian team. For the losers, there is solace in looking like the warriors of old, in the counting coup of points on the scoreboard. On this night, there is satisfaction on both sides. The losing team will mourn the loss and celebrate the effort, then return to their daily routine, this one now fraught with uncertainty.

In the front row of the bleachers, a venerable woman watching with fierce dark eyes behind thick glasses stands, eases slowly through the crowd, and disappears into the darkness, just a little prouder to be Crow. ◪

Barney Old Coyote

By Gail Schontzler

Spring 2012

BARNEY OLD COYOTE WAS IN HIGH SCHOOL ON THE CROW INDIAN Reservation when World War II broke out. He enlisted in the Army Air Corps, and soon found himself flying combat missions, serving as a gunner and "windtalker."

Flying in squadrons of B-17 Flying Fortresses over France, North Africa, Italy, Norway and Berlin, his crews were under strict orders to maintain radio silence. But Old Coyote could radio messages in the Crow language back to his brother Henry's plane, following a half-hour behind, sharing information about targets and enemy strength while baffling German code-breakers.

As a tail gunner, waist gunner and engineer riding in the top turret, Barney Old Coyote's main job was shooting down German planes and attacking troops on the ground. He flew 72 combat missions.

"It was always terrifying," said Old Coyote, now 88 years old, sitting at the dining table of his family's home in Belgrade.

On raids, 500 planes might fly out, but only 200 would return. Surviving planes came back riddled with bullet holes. After a while, he said, they stopped counting all the holes.

"I gained a reputation for being a good marksman," he said simply.

In fact, for his prowess shooting down German planes and for bravery in combat, Old Coyote became the most decorated American Indian in

World War II, earning 17 awards, the U.S. Army reported last year. His decorations include the Distinguished Flying Cross, the Air Medal with 14 oak leaf clusters, and the Silver Star.

World War II was one chapter of Barney Old Coyote's remarkable life. It has taken him from the one-room log cabin where he was born on Montana's Crow Reservation, to a job as a presidential assistant in the White House. Back home in Montana, he worked as an advocate preserving traditional Crow language and culture, a leader of higher education for Indians, and a founder of Native American studies at Montana State University.

As civil rights movements swept the country, the Old Coyote brothers fought in court and lobbied in Washington, D.C., for legal recognition of the American Indian Religious Freedom Act, passed in 1978. He was the founding president in 1974 of the American Indian National Bank, an attempt to give Indian tribes more control over their assets and destinies.

His many honors range from an honorary doctorate received from MSU in 1968, to his induction this year into the Montana Cowboy Hall of Fame for trick roping and bronc riding he did as a young man. His history also illustrates how opportunities and attitudes have changed for Native Americans, from his grandfather's era to his grandchildren's.

Age and the deafening noise inside World War II planes have taken a toll on Barney Old Coyote's hearing. He has to use a walker to steady his 6-foot frame. Yet he remains an impressive figure.

"I think I've had an amazing life," he said, "a fortunate one."

HE WAS BORN APRIL 10, 1923, on the Crow reservation in St. Xavier on the Bighorn River, one of eight children born to Mae Takes the Gun and Barney Old Coyote Sr.

He grew up hearing stories about his grandfather, Old Coyote, who fought with the U.S. Army against the Crow's traditional Sioux enemy in the Battle of the Rosebud on June 17, 1876, just a week before the Battle of the Little Bighorn.

"My grandfather was wounded at the Battle of the Rosebud," he said. "He was the bravest one."

His father was a renowned rodeo trick rider and roper, who traveled with Buffalo Bill's Wild West show around the country. His mother appeared in movies, like "Before the White Man Came," in 1920. Having lived with whites, his parents taught him about the white world.

His father was one of the first Crow to go to college, attending Gonzaga University, training at one time to be a priest. He spoke English well, and went to Washington, D.C., with an Indian delegation in 1910, at a time when few Crow men spoke English. Growing up, young Barney learned both Crow and English. Knowing English made him unpopular with his playmates, but he said he's thankful he did because it gave him many opportunities in life.

Barney was raised by two sets of parents. His mother's sister had lost all her children, including a baby girl born about the same time as Barney.

"My mother handed me to her and said, 'Raise this one,'" he said.

So he was raised by his aunt and uncle, Susie Takes the Gun and Alphonse Childs, who renamed him Alphonse Childs Jr.

As a boy, he had chores milking cows and feeding chickens. He competed in rodeos.

"I was going to be a big cowboy," he said. "Those were my heroes."

The Japanese attacked Pearl Harbor on Dec. 7, 1941. The next day, Barney, 18, and four other young men from Hardin High School took the bus to Billings to join the Army.

But Barney needed his parents to sign the enlistment papers, and his adoptive parents refused. "We wanted a child," they said, "not a gold star in the window."

"My natural father said, 'I'll sign for you, keep you with the warrior tradition. You can go to war like we always did,'" Barney recalled.

So he enlisted under his original name, Barney Old Coyote Jr. His brother Henry, nine years older, promised to look out for him. His mother sent a letter to the secretary of war, asking that Barney and Henry not be separated, despite Army policy. The secretary of the Army sent a letter saying that they would make every effort to keep the brothers together.

The brothers trained as airplane mechanics in Long Beach, Calif., and went to gunnery school in Panama City, Fla., with movie star Clark Gable. Just before shipping over to England in 1942, the brothers participated in a sun dance ceremony at Crow Agency.

The recruits knew only two Crow men who had fought in the World War I trenches, he recalled. Asked for advice, "They said, 'Just do the best you can. And don't run away.'"

Thanks to their World War II service, the brothers earned a good reputation, both on the reservation and off.

"People had heard of the Old Coyote brothers, that helped a lot," he recalled. His brother Henry used to tell people, "When the [German] planes came at you, they didn't question if you were Indian or not. We were Americans."

AFTER WORLD WAR II, Barney Old Coyote came home and enrolled at Morningside College in Sioux City, Iowa, where he met his wife, Clara Teboe, a Winnebago Indian.

He attended several semesters of college, but left to work for the Bureau of Indian Affairs, starting as a clerk typist. Over the next two decades, he worked for the BIA, rising to the post of superintendent on the Rocky Boy Reservation.

Lyndon Johnson was president in 1964, when his wife, Lady Bird Johnson, visited Billings. Old Coyote was one of her Indian guides at the Custer battlefield. Interior Secretary Stewart Udall took notice of him, and asked Old Coyote to continue on the rest of the tour to Wyoming, Washington, Oregon and California, as his special assistant.

That led to a job in Washington as a presidential assistant organizing the Interior Department's Job Corps, part of LBJ's war on poverty.

"My office was in the White House," Old Coyote said. "It was an exciting time."

In 1968, MSU awarded Old Coyote an honorary doctorate. That, he said, "opened a lot of doors for me."

It was an era of great turmoil across the country, a time of marches, riots and the assassinations of Martin Luther King and Sen. Bobby Kennedy. The black civil rights movement inspired similar civil rights movements by women, Hispanics and Indians.

In 1969, a group of Indians seized Alcatraz Island in San Francisco Bay. Old Coyote, then working as BIA assistant director in Sacramento, Calif., visited the protesters. He issued a supportive statement: "What is happening on Alcatraz is in a sense a product of what we have been trying to develop, namely, the Indians' capability and desire for self-determination."

"That was the first time I made headlines," he said with a smile.

Old Coyote continued the fight for Indian self-determination, by working within the system to change it, rather than protesting from the outside.

IN 1970, Barney Old Coyote met MSU President Roland Renne, and the two hit it off.

"We became good friends," Old Coyote said.

Renne said MSU was going to start an Indian studies program and he asked Old Coyote to come to the Bozeman campus. Indian studies programs were then starting from New England to California, and Old Coyote and other Indian leaders wanted to do the same here.

"Because Indian people are part of Montana," Old Coyote said.

"We wanted college students to know about the most ignored minority in the state."

Old Coyote recalled going around Livingston, Belgrade, Three Forks and Bozeman to speak at club meetings and town halls, explaining what Indian studies was all about and dispelling rumors.

"Ranchers were really uptight about anything Indian," he said. "They brought up incidents over 100 years old. We would tell them about changes that occurred. It was literally an education process."

From 1974 to 1978, he returned to Washington to lead the American Indian National Bank as president and board chairman. "It did a lot for [Indians], to be more self-sufficient," he said.

In that period, Old Coyote also was a plaintiff in a legal case seeking recognition of the Native American Church as a legitimate religion, with tax-exempt status and legalization of its use of peyote.

And he won.

"They used to raid meetings and send people to jail," Old Coyote said. He had used peyote "ever since I was 7 years old." His parents had gone to a peyote meeting to pray for the boy when he was suffering from tonsillitis. "I got well," he said. "My parents decided the peyote cured me."

Back in Montana, he taught Crow history and language at Little Bighorn College. He also helped correctly identify Indian artifacts and photographs at the Museum of the Rockies, the Montana Historical Society, Peabody Museum and Smithsonian Institution.

Looking back over his lifetime, Old Coyote said, "Montana, it's changed so much it's not the same place." Discrimination was once open and blatant.

"There was a time, in public schools they'd assign non-Indian kids to open and shut doors so Indian kids would not touch the door knobs," he said. "Indians would sit in a different row [in class]. That didn't happen to me because I could speak English."

Walter Fleming, MSU professor and head of the Native American studies department, said Old Coyote personifies a famous saying by the Crow chief, Plenty Coups: "Education is your greatest weapon. With education you are the white man's equal, without education you are his victim and so shall remain all your lives."

"He was a real pioneer," Fleming said of Old Coyote. "I think it's fair to call him the father of Native American studies" at MSU. "He continues to be an inspiration to our students today."

Old Coyote started informal powwows in the SOB Barn on the Bozeman campus, so Indian students could keep up their own culture, before the MSU American Indian Council powwows began 36 years ago and grew into a large annual event.

Old Coyote was also important, Fleming said, "as a symbol of success in the non-Indian world, without giving up our traditional values."

Fleming said another contribution Old Coyote and his family made was to create an Indian presence in Bozeman, which was part of Crow territory a century and a half ago, but today has few Native American residents. His oldest daughter, Patricia Bauerle, has been a Bozeman schoolteacher for many years, and one of his 12 grandchildren, Phenocia Bauerle, today directs MSU's Diversity Awareness Office.

In 2004, a book of traditional Crow stories, *The Way of the Warrior*, edited by Phenocia, was published. Barney and Henry Old Coyote had collected and translated the stories from Crow elders after World War II, driving around the West and recording tales with an old reel-to-reel recorder plugged into a car cigarette lighter. It was an effort to dispel errors in white accounts and keep their culture alive.

Bill Yellowtail, MSU director of tribal partnerships, wrote that MSU's "terrific success in recruiting and serving record numbers of Native American students in 2011 is owing to his [Old Coyote's] pioneering work on our campus 40 years ago."

"Barney is a gentleman, through and through," Yellowtail added. "Always engaging and articulate, but self-effacing and humble.

"Barney Old Coyote is walking evidence that one person can confidently, comfortably thrive in this universe ... from his undisputable Crow identity to his proven ability to operate anywhere, in any culture on the planet.

"He is a powerful role model to all of us, Indian and not, who walk in his shadow." ◄

Barney Old Coyote died on August 5, 2012. He was 89 years old.

Good Medicine

By Daniel Person

Fall 2014

WHILE THE FIRST TOUR PUT SHRAPNEL IN HIS BACK AND SCALP, it was the second tour that left the scars.

In 2005, Jonas Rides At The Door, a Blackfeet Indian who grew up in Browning, returned to a Fallujah, Iraq, battlefield that had turned even bloodier since his first deployment. As a Marine gunner, Rides At The Door repeatedly raced down roads that could instantly erupt into blinding flashes of homemade explosives and scrap metal. Around his neck he wore a small pouch given to him during a medicine bundle ceremony prior to his first deployment.

But like the steel armor on his vehicle, the pouch's protection didn't feel complete.

"YOU KNOW HOW YOU GO TO THE FAIR AND SHOOT THOSE DUCKS? That was us, and the insurgents were the ones shooting," he said on a sunny June day in Browning.

He manned the lead vehicle on 230 combat patrols during that deployment, a position that left him exposed to the brutal punches thrown by improvised explosive devices. Worse, many of his friends, young Marines he helped train, did the same job on other patrols. Some of them didn't make it; Rides At The Door has a tattoo on his right forearm bearing the initials of five friends who died in combat.

When the tour was over, Rides At The Door was overcome with guilt just for being alive.

There's an old Blackfeet proverb, "Better to die young at war than grow old." At the time, Rides At The Door believed that. He thought his own survival somehow implicated him in the death of his friends.

Back on base in Twentynine Palms, California, others in his unit weren't doing much better than he was and the group began to self-medicate in a bad way. The nights would start out like a party, lots of beer and close buddies. But they would dissolve into a stew of misery and anguish.

"The group of us would drink every night. Every single night. At the end of the night people would be crying, pissed off, punching walls. It was all about the war," recalls Rides At The Door, now 30 and discharged, but still carrying the clipped hair and bulky body of a Marine. "I loved being a Marine, the reputation that went along with it. But then that all went away."

By that time, in 2006, the effects of post-traumatic stress disorder and combat stress were well documented. But Rides At The Door says that in his corner of the military, nobody ever talked about it. "It was all about killing."

Rides At The Door would be deployed a third time to Iraq, but a psychologist pulled him off the line once he recognized his severe PTSD. That got him out of combat, but didn't reverse the damage already done. When he was discharged from the Marines, he threw his combat boots over a telephone wire and returned to Browning to continue his heavy drinking, lest the horrors of combat drive him to insanity.

Were the story to end there, Rides At The Door's narrative would have followed the sad trajectory of countless other veterans of the Iraq and Afghanistan wars, into a wrenching whirlpool of anguish and substance abuse. The debilitating effects of combat-related PTSD have touched every segment of American society, blind to race and gender. But in rural Indian Country like the Blackfeet Reservation, health care is scarce and ill-prepared to handle the particulars of the disorder. Meanwhile, the kind of liquid therapy dispensed at stores like Ick's Place in downtown Browning is easy to find.

"IHS (Indian Health Service) has trouble meeting the needs. It's not really extensive counseling," says Clifford Whitegrass, Veteran's Alliance coordinator with the Blackfeet Tribe. "So what do they have to turn to, for ways to cope with it? From what I've heard, they turn to alcohol, drugs, which cause problems in themselves."

However, Rides At The Door's story does not end in Browning or with a bottle of booze; in fact his narrative hasn't reached its terminus. It's so far brought him through college and put him in boardrooms seated beside CEOs, senators and top military brass, advising them on what veterans like him—Indian or otherwise—need from our nation's leaders.

His transformation from blackout drinker to a voice for combat veterans cannot be tied to any one thing. There was certainly some luck involved, and a lot of growing up. But Rides At The Door also credits traditional Blackfeet warrior ceremonies, ancient songs and dances and sweat lodge rituals. And he found Blackfeet mentors who encouraged him to pursue higher education as a way both to process his own experiences and to help others around him.

In wars past, Native Americans have enlisted at rates that far outpace their overall population, only to be discharged into a civilian society that didn't understand the place of Indians in that society. As the United States concludes the longest war of its history, Rides At The Door's journey provides insight into both the dangers and hope awaiting the latest wave of Indian veterans.

FROM THE BEGINNING, America's military and its indigenous people have been deeply intertwined. In Montana, the particulars of those histories varied widely. The Crow Tribe in southeast Montana never took up arms against the United States, instead serving extensively as Army scouts. Other Montana tribes, including the Blackfeet, had a more antagonistic relationship with white men.

Beginning with the bombing of Pearl Harbor, however, a consistent narrative emerged from Indian Country: they were ready to serve. During WWII, the Defense Department estimated that 99 percent of eligible Indian men had signed up for the draft, though it was an almost insulting idea for the young men who wanted to fight for the Allies.

"Since when has it been necessary for Blackfeet to draw lots to fight?" one young man reportedly snorted as he registered for the draft.

WWII began a tradition of Indians enlisting in the military at rates higher than any other ethnicity. Ninety percent of the Native Americans who fought in Vietnam were volunteers. Today, while Native Americans make up less than 1 percent of the population, they account for 1.5 percent of military personnel. A 2012 report by the Department of Veterans Affairs showed that the percentage of Native veterans under age 65 was far higher than that of any other racial group.

These statistics are often attributed to a "warrior culture" among tribes, dating back to when young men earned status by displays of bravery in combat. However, this oversimplification ignores more immediate factors, such as the paucity of jobs on many reservations.

Many Vietnam-era veterans interviewed for this story noted that the Bureau of Indian Affairs long advised men that being a veteran would help them get a job with the agency.

Richard Rides At The Door, a cousin to Jonas, says he didn't really think much about Blackfeet warrior culture when he first enlisted in the Army six months after graduating from high school. Rather, he saw that his father had become a felon as a young man and his mom had gone into debt attending college.

"The army was a way to keep me out of trouble," he says.

But after he was away from Browning for 16 months and had served a tour in Mosul, Iraq, fellow veterans welcomed him home as a warrior, which opened his eyes to the cultural gravity of what he'd done. Today he is preparing to dance for a local warrior society which had danced and sung for him while he was at war.

"Every time I see [members of the society] they remind me that I owe them a dance," he says. "But I have to be ready first."

And the battles of his forefathers certainly played a role in Jonas Rides At The Door's decision to enlist in the Marines. In the Blackfeet tribal offices, a huge photo of his great-great grandfather—Chief Rides At The Door—hangs at the entryway. Chief Rides At The Door got his name after he stole a horse from an enemy's tepee entrance, a feat that spoke to his bravery. Jonas remembers visiting his great-grandmother's house and seeing nothing on the walls but pictures of service members. Before he'd even graduated high school, Jonas was speaking with the Marine recruiter. His course had been set generations before his birth.

THERE'S A PHOTO THAT WOODY KIPP CAN'T FORGET. It shows a Vietnamese woman up to her waist in water, crying in anguish after her village had just been bombed. The village was near the Da Nang Air Base, where Kipp loaded bombs for U.S. airstrikes during the Vietnam War in the late 1960s. He can't forget the photo because he can't rule out the possibility that he loaded the bombs that devastated that village.

"What if that was my mother?" he asks to this day. "What if that was my sister?"

This, as Kipp sees it, is the commonality of all war and all warriors: That no matter where the battle takes place—be it Iraq or Vietnam or the Great Plains—evil is done, and those who participate in it are saddled with a profound guilt.

"The locales, the geographic areas, are different, but the effect on the human mind is the same," Kipp says. "You begin to understand the depth of what you partake in. That sense of guilt. That sense of recrimination."

It's Kipp's belief—shared by Jonas Rides At The Door and many other tribal members—that many of the ceremonies practiced for centuries by the Blackfeet and other tribes were designed to address that guilt and heal the warrior when he returned home. In one ceremony, tribal members would paint their faces black after a battle "because they knew they'd participated in evil, in the dark part of the world," Kipp says.

However, for Kipp's generation, those practices had almost vanished, a result of both subtle and overt attempts by governmental and religious leaders to wipe out indigenous practices and assimilate Indians into white culture. Their parents had been beaten for speaking the Blackfeet language, and forced into Christianity.

"When I came home from the Marine Corps there were probably two sweat lodges on the entire reservation," Kipp recalls.

At first, that didn't concern Kipp, who gave himself to booze and partying after he was discharged.

Then, in the early 1970s, Kipp became involved in the American Indian Movement, or AIM, which wanted to bring back indigenous traditions and languages. The culmination of those efforts was the 1978 American Indian Religious Freedom Act, which acknowledged that the federal government had prevented Native Americans from conducting traditional practices in the past and guaranteed them the right to do so in the future. As a veteran, Kipp became a rare champion of the old ceremonies, and began facilitating sweats for himself and others, tribal members and not. He led a sweat for a cousin who kept dreaming about a man he killed in Iraq. He led a sweat for four Russian veterans of that country's war in Afghanistan.

"I do know the ceremonies have helped me," he says. "There's something out there. You rewind yourself spiritually. It has to be done spiritually."

Thanks to the resurgence of tribal practices ushered in by Vietnam-era veterans like Kipp, by the time Rides At The Door was preparing to deploy on his first of three tours, warrior ceremonies had returned to wide practice.

For Rides At The Door, many of his ceremonies centered on the Thunder Medicine Pipe Bundle, a medicine bundle that has been in his family for unknown generations. The contents of bundles are considered sacred and secret, but typically they contain items, often gathered during battle, believed to give a warrior strength and protection. Associated with the bundle are ancient songs and dances, which Rides At The Door performed before being deployed.

When he returned from war, he would dance and sing again, as well as participate in sweats. He was presented with an eagle feather by then-chairman of the Blackfeet, Earl Old Person. And he was given a new name in honor of his bravery in battle: Thunder Shield Warrior.

Each time he took part in a warrior ceremony, Rides At The Door meditated on what he'd done in war, and what it meant to be home.

"They know that you probably saw and did some terrible things," he says. "The warrior ceremony brings you back."

The ceremonies were not a perfect salve; Rides At The Door continued to drink heavily for a time after returning to Browning and going through the rituals. But on a fundamental level, he says, it began a healing process that continues to this day.

"There's your warrior mode—and you're not supposed to be that way in normal society," he says. "I did the bundle. I don't feel perfect. I don't feel like I am the way I was before. But I feel it gave me back my soul."

E XPERIENCES LIKE RIDES AT THE DOOR'S ARE GAINING THE ATTENTION OF mental health officials.

Despite the large number of veterans in Indian Country, Native Americans have historically shunned—or been shunned by—the Department of Veterans Affairs and its services.

The reasons for this are many: Indian reservations are typically deeply rural and many miles from VA hospitals; there is a culture of distrust between Native Americans and federal programs; and many tribal cultures continue to stigmatize the kinds of mental health problems that can afflict veterans. And new research suggests another factor: traditional VA treatment for issues like PTSD often don't work for Indians.

In June, researchers with Washington State University released a study showing that Native American veterans found typical, Western-medicine approaches to PTSD, such as individual counseling, had no impact or made symptoms worse for 49 percent of respondents.

Conversely, 72 percent of Native respondents said spiritual or religious guidance helped them with their PTSD symptoms.

"The traditional Native view of health and spirituality is intertwined," study leader Greg Urquhart, a Cherokee Indian, announced when the study was published. "Spirit, mind, and body are all one—you can't parcel one out from the other—so spiritually is a huge component of healing and one not often included in Western medicine."

The VA acknowledges how troubling the statistics are. According to the VA, battlefield research has suggested that not only do Indians enlist at higher rates than other ethnicities, they also serve in more dangerous positions—Rides At The Door leading convoys as a gunner, for example—putting them at greater risk for PTSD, traumatic brain injury and other harm. Indeed, Native American veterans suffer a higher than average rate of combat-related injuries, according to the VA.

In order to reverse the trend in post-combat treatment, in 2001 the VA began piloting a program in Montana that trained Native veterans to act as on-reservation representatives to help others navigate the VA system. Along with helping with paperwork and arranging transportation to medical appointments, the representatives are trained to connect interested veterans with local spiritual leaders.

"When we do it in the traditional ways, people feel more comfortable," says William "Buck" Richardson, a member of the Cherokee tribe who spearheaded the tribal program in 2001. "You can have Western medicine on one side and traditional medicine on the other side, but it's like a basket. Keep the sides separate and things will go right through it. Without the two sides together, you can't hold the whole veteran up."

The program has shown promise, and has since expanded nationwide.

However, Whitegrass, the Blackfeet veteran's coordinator, says the next few years will provide a crucial test.

"We know there's going to be a problem. We're downsizing our military. We know our troops are coming home and we also know they're going to have PTSD," he says. "Will we be prepared, or will we be reactive?"

IN THE YEARS TO COME, Jonas Rides At The Door will likely be in a unique position to answer that question.

He will graduate this fall from the University of Montana with a double major in political science and Native American studies. Over the course of his studies, he took classes at Blackfeet Community College from Kipp, who encouraged him to write and meditate on his time overseas. That kind of academic thought, as much as the traditional ceremonies, has helped Rides At The Door get past the worst of his emotional turmoil.

"A lot of it was just understanding who I am—self-actualization," he says.

He's already spent five months in Washington, D.C. as an aide to former Sen. Max Baucus on veterans' issues, as part of a fellowship program. While there, he advised the senator's office on issues ranging from college transition for veterans to the controversial National Defense Reauthorization Act.

In a particularly heady moment, he found himself surrounded by top military brass and the leaders of major corporations, discussing the impact that budget sequestration could have on the economy and the military.

"The CEOs were scared out of their minds by sequestration," he says with a laugh. "And I was basically the voice of Baucus."

At every step, he's emphasized that he suffers from PTSD, in hopes that he can ease the stigma associated with the disorder. Too often, he says, people consider combat veterans "damaged goods," rather than respecting them for their service and sacrifice.

After graduation, Rides At The Door hopes to continue working on issues at a state or national level, perhaps staying in Missoula or moving back to D.C., this time with his wife and 4-year-old daughter.

But eventually he wants to return to Browning, to give back to the community that raised him. He recalls the times in his deployment when he would think about the Rocky Mountain Front, the stunning alpine backdrop to life on the Blackfeet Reservation. Amidst those peaks the warriors who came before him found peace and solace, and sitting in the barren landscape around Fallujah he pined to be back among them.

"I hated looking at Iraqi horizons. I'd say, 'I come from a place that's beautiful and look at this,'" he says. "I missed these mountains. Each and every one of them." ◪

Little Newspaper that Could

By Jeff Welsch

Spring 2010

IT IS LATE AFTERNOON, and already weathered pickup trucks and cars are pulling up in front of the little white building on Second Avenue, just like they have every Thursday in tiny Poplar for nearly four years now.

A diminutive Sioux woman peers out one of the aging structure's two windows, squinting through the steel grate that serves as a barrier between the timeworn equipment inside and the occasional panhandler, alcoholic and indignant customer outside. Nearby, between puffs on a cigarette, the woman's older sister answers a phone that won't quit ringing.

"Are they here yet?" the callers wonder. "Are they here yet?" the drivers inquire as they poke their heads inside the door.

A similar scene has already unfolded to the east in Culbertson, in Brockton and in Sprote— all blips on U.S. Highway 2 between Williston, N.D., where the truck's journey began hours earlier, and Poplar, population 866 and the hardscrabble hub of the sprawling Fort Peck Indian Reservation, in Montana's largely vacant northeast corner. This weekly rite will recur several more times before the day is out, after the truck drops the bulk of 2,600 *Fort Peck Journal* copies at the office. At Poplar's Buckhorn Café, the lone sit-down eatery in a town with one stoplight and two gas stations, the phone rings. Owner Mertice "Mert"

Maroptek is calling from her nearby home to place an order for a copy of the *Journal* to be set aside.

"If I don't," she explains later, "I won't get one."

As such stories are recounted, Bonnie Red Elk flashes a smile that reveals a mix of humility, pride and wonder even though this weekly phenomenon is, well, old news. Indeed, she has actually witnessed it regularly since 1976, when she returned to the reservation three months before graduating from Kansas' Haskell Indian Junior College, was hired by the skimpy biweekly *Wotanin Wowapi* newsletter, and dropped into a Fort Peck Tribal Council meeting with a brief introduction and mirthful "good luck." And certainly these scenes have become even more meaningful since 2006, when she quickly rebounded from her controversial firing from the newsletter she had built into a real newspaper—and began publishing the weekly *Journal* in her kitchen using a basic computer program, glue sticks and 8 1/2 by 11 paper.

Yet to this day a wave of incredulity still washes over Red Elk when those people start lining up, all because their Thursday isn't complete without her Little Newspaper that Could. It is a striking anomaly. Newspapers everywhere are hemorrhaging circulation, and yet this old-school, black-and-white tabloid is growing steadily and its weekly arrival invariably, in newspaper parlance, stops the presses reservation-wide. Fort Peck suffers from 70 percent unemployment, alcohol abuse and social disaffection. Yet despite these stark realities, this unassuming and "simple" 57-year-old Dakota-Lakota woman who stands barely 5 feet tall, has carved a modest but secure living for her family.

Or perhaps it's because of all those heart-rending struggles. After all, for 34 years now she has given The People more than a weekly newspaper—she has connected them to their history, to their lands and to each other in ways nobody else, native or white, has for more than a century.

"Like a lifeline," marvels Richard Peterson, a Poplar native and current resident who contributes freelance pieces to the *Journal* after many years as a reporter for the *Great Falls Tribune*.

So every Thursday it is the same. Yes? Red Elk nods, and so do her co-workers in the little white building on Second Avenue—nephew Louis Montclair, the reporter and photographer whose recent graduation from the University of Montana is a family first; another nephew, Kristofer Boyd, the sole advertising salesperson; son Randy, the brand-new page designer; and sister Carol Boyd, the office manager and telephone gatekeeper who maintains contact with Bonnie's daughter Charley (distribution), son Vern (truck driver) and nephew Robin Youngman (flyer stuffer).

"You just can't believe it," Bonnie says.

JOHN LONEDOG WAS BONNIE CLINCHER'S GREAT-GRANDFATHER, one of the last of the great Sioux chiefs and leader of the proud tribe's final band of holdouts against the tidal wave of white settlers pushing across the northern prairies. As penance for their resistance, Lonedog and the "hostiles" were relegated to an inhospitable corner of the state 123 years ago.

Over lamplight, in a two-room log cabin without running water or electricity, young Bonnie listened as her parents talked of Lonedog. Each year, he would scrawl the family story on the hide of the sacred bison. The Sioux "Little Winter Count" tradition was a source of fascination for Bonnie, who often thought of her own ways to tell such stories.

Also intriguing were the many men who came all the way from Washington, D.C., to meet with her grandfather, Lonedog's son. He was a cattle rancher and land manager who knew every creek, cottonwood and coulee on the reservation, and he would strategize long into the night about how the Sioux might eke out a living from their stubborn new lands. Sometimes young Bonnie would even tag along to general councils with her grandparents.

Her mother, Mercy Lonedog, was Yankton Sioux from Fort Peck, and her father, Silas Clincher, was from Pine Ridge in South Dakota. They met in the U.S. Army. The Sioux custom was to live where the wife was from, and so they settled on the prairie not far from the mighty Missouri outside of Poplar. It was here that Bonnie Clincher was born on a summer day in 1952.

Though her youth was bereft of modern conveniences, Bonnie received a rare education. She graduated from Poplar schools and spent nearly two years at what was then Haskell Indian Junior College in Lawrence, Kan., the country's only all-Indian two-year school. Three months from graduation, she left school— "stupidly," she concedes now—and returned to Poplar in 1976 at age 23 to help raise her niece. She still doesn't have a college degree.

At the time, the *Wotanin Wowapi*—Dakota for "something to read"— was just that: something to read. Her brother-in-law, Terry Boyd, ran the newsletter and needed a reporter just as Bonnie returned. Though jobs were scarce, this one required special skills. She was the only applicant and got the job. A few days later, Boyd took her to tribal head-quarters in Poplar, informed the council that "Bonnie is going to come to the meeting," and disappeared.

"He just left me," she recalls. "I didn't know what to do, but it was so exciting."

Except, she did know what to do. She had John Lonedog's storytelling gift in her blood. She had memories of all those nights at council with her grandparents. And she knew enough raw basic newspaper principles from her lone journalism class at Haskell, though she left school before earning a grade.

Bonnie started writing, editing and designing the *Wotanin*, and as she slowly began to understand the business she also gradually went where no tribal reporter had gone before. She attended council meetings and took pictures. As the community's eyes and ears, she wrote down every-thing she saw and heard from the 12 council members and chairman. She informed readers of how their leaders were spending tribal money and time.

After a year, when Boyd retired to his farm, Bonnie took over as "act-ing" editor, pending approval of the council. As her stories grew more and more detailed, including publishing how councilors voted on every issue, the leaders grew nervous. Never had anybody made public what was happening in these meetings.

"What are you doing?" a specially formed committee of council members finally asked.

"I'm just writing the truth," she replied.

Reminding her that the tribe owned the paper, the council formed a board of directors for the *Wotanin* and told Bonnie they would dictate the news. She took a photo of the board and wrote a story about its intentions.

Readers enamored with her objectivity were incensed, and the notion of censorship lasted only until a television station in Williston and the national Indian newspaper *Wassaja* got wind of the tough woman who was standing up for her public's right to know.

"They backed down totally," she recalls.

That was 1977, and nobody on the council would threaten her in such a manner for nearly three decades. They didn't dare. Already, residents along U.S. 2 were queuing up for the weekly reports about life on the rez. Along the way, Bonnie married Herman Red Elk, and they had four children. Her life largely consisted of producing the *Wotanin* by day and raising a family by night.

Bonnie taught herself on the fly. She attended journalism workshops. She studied other newspapers. She quizzed other writers. By the early 2000s, she had built a small juggernaut, converting the *Wotanin* from a biweekly newsletter to a full-fledged tabloid newspaper. Locals read the paper for the uplifting Page 3 feature stories called "Our People" and for the unvarnished accounts of government wrongdoing. They read for the thorough arraignment and crime reports that played no favorites—"I was even in there," she says of an event that led to her first firing from the *Wotanin* in 2005—and for the coverage of all the K-12 school sports and activities. And they read for the "Man on the Street" interviews that always featured five Sioux and five Assiniboine.

Most of all, though, they turned to the weekly Red Elk editorial. One week she chastised the latest malfeasance by a tribal leader, the next she applauded one of the community's "young warriors" for taking the bold step of leaving for college. One week she poignantly lamented the waste of yet another teen's life snuffed out by alcohol, the next she fired up the Poplar Indians boys and girls hoops teams for another season of run-like-the-wind "rez ball."

Circulation grew. Advertisers noticed. Readers called from as far away as Williston and Glasgow with news tips. The Thursday lines grew. The so-called "moccasin grapevine" is always a potent source of rumor, gossip and speculation on a reservation, but in sparse Fort Peck country everyone knew where to turn for truth because, as Peterson puts it, "If it really did happen, they knew it would be in the paper."

"She'd been the only honest voice on the rez for years," Herman Red Elk adds.

The reservation's despair notwithstanding, it was a fulfilling and rewarding life in which Bonnie Red Elk and the paper were inextricably linked.

"It grew with me and I grew with it," she says. "It was like my baby."

EVERYTHING CHANGED WHEN JOHN MORALES WAS ELECTED TRIBAL CHAIRMAN in 2003. Two years earlier, a different makeup of the council began making news gathering more challenging. With increasing frequency the group went into executive session, excluding the media—which, at Fort Peck, meant the *Wotanin*.

Morales' authoritarian style led to his removal a year later and, naturally, Red Elk covered those proceedings, frustrating the chairman. And those hard feelings lingered when he successfully ran for chairman again in 2005.

"He just didn't like the paper," Peterson remembers.

Red Elk's council coverage regularly caused Morales grief. His child would come to meetings and run around or watch cartoons on a television playing loudly in the background. He would remove his shoes and put his feet up, "making a mockery of the council," Herman Red Elk recalls.

One day in 2005, not long after Morales' re-election, the tribe conducted random drug testing on all four employees at the paper. Red Elk failed and was fired. She doesn't deny smoking marijuana, and never even considered keeping her name out of the crime reports. But she quickly "cleaned myself up," passed a drug test and was rehired at the *Wotanin*. She was changed personally, but not professionally. She continued to cover the council and the chairman—including Morales' frequent trips to Florida on the tribe's dime.

In March 2006, Red Elk called him in Florida for a comment on tribal documents. Morales told her if she published a story there would be changes at the *Wotanin* upon his return. She wrote the story anyway. Soon after, the council "let the bomb drop," as she puts it. For his part, Morales said he fired Red Elk because she was confrontational and difficult, and didn't treat the council and others with respect.

And so, after more than three decades in the only job she could ever love, she was out. The *Wotanin*'s doors were barricaded. Notes, photos and other items of historical value belonging to Red Elk and the staff were destroyed. Herman Red Elk was arrested briefly for painting "The Chairman is a Dictator" on the side of his pickup truck. Cars gathered around her home and supporters brought food, a tribal mourning ritual.

The era of independent Indian journalism at Fort Peck apparently was over.

THE GRIEVING LASTED THREE DAYS, until a call between Red Elk and the former Great Falls reporter Peterson, who had returned to the reservation to tend to his ailing mother.

"Let's start over," he suggested.

Red Elk was already thinking the same. Reaction to her firing had been swift and irate, and the feelings intensified after the next few *Wotanin* issues, which had virtually become a mouthpiece for the council. Red Elk and Peterson knew they could succeed with a paper from scratch.

First, they needed a new name. They decided against an Indian moniker out of respect for the history of the *Wotanin*, and the first name that came to mind was *Fort Peck Journal*. Red Elk went back to the council meetings, this time as an independent and private voice that could not be squelched. While she began writing and designing the first *Journal* on an old desktop computer in the kitchen of her cozy, cluttered home on C Street, Peterson sold a half-dozen ads sight-unseen to the Buckhorn Café and other loyalists to cover the costs of the first printing.

"A lot of people in Poplar supported her," the Buckhorn's Maroptek recalls, explaining simply: "Freedom of press, freedom of speech."

Says Peterson: "We just kept going. We couldn't think of stopping; it just didn't enter our minds. I think we were just pissed off enough to want to keep going."

Red Elk gathered up her 16 sheets of 8 1/2 x 11 paper on a Friday morning and drove to the cheapest place she had found—A River Runs printing press in Nashua. They printed 2,000 copies. On the front page was a story about the tribe voting against publicizing a new code of ethics and a piece by Peterson on Red Elk's firing from the *Wotanin*; inside, her first editorial for the *Fort Peck Journal* was titled, "A new and independent voice for the Assiniboine and Sioux people of the Fort Peck Reservation."

Red Elk wondered what, if any, reception she'd receive. She didn't have to wait long.

When she arrived at the reservation's western edge at Frazer, people were awaiting her arrival and snatched up copies at 50 cents each. The scene repeated itself in the small towns all the way back to Poplar, where she left hundreds of copies at the Buckhorn, TJ's Quikstop and Tribal Express Casino. By the next morning, they were gone, and she had nothing to give pestering callers but the promise of a second edition the next week.

"Pretty epic," remembers Randy Red Elk, Bonnie's youngest son.

After the first issue, Peterson begged off to focus on his ailing mother, but Red Elk's sister, Marian Montclair, offered to sell ads. The next week she raised the price to $1. Soon she found a printer in Williston and began producing the 32-page tabloid she has now. And after six months her father gave her the keys to his graffiti-laced building on Second Avenue, which had had previous lives as a salon, tattoo parlor, bakery and pizzeria. Silas Clincher lived just long enough to see his daughter's new dream unfurl in newly scrubbed and painted offices festooned with a bright, hand-painted red-and-blue sign reading: *Fort Peck Journal*.

For a while, a full-scale newspaper war ensued. Morales ordered that no official tribal advertisements could be purchased in the *Journal*. But the *Wotanin* couldn't compete with 30 years of Red Elk's objectivity, trust and a commitment to the entire Fort Peck community, reflected in part by the dozen or so free issues sent to tribal soldiers in Iraq and Afghanistan. Readers left the *Wotanin* for the *Journal* and advertisers followed. By January 2008, its official paper awash in red ink despite a $59,000 bailout, the tribe closed the *Wotanin's* doors for good after 40-plus years of publishing.

"It was kind of a mixture of being joyous and also sad because the paper was the oldest Indian weekly paper in the country at the time," says Peterson, now an occasional contributor to the *Journal*. "It was recognized by the Native American Journalism Association and won a lot of national awards. We were glad we crushed it, but it was sad this big part of Fort Peck tribal history was down the tubes."

IT IS EARLY MORNING, and a half-dozen or so members of a tightly knit Sioux family have formed a circle and clasped hands in the center of the little white building on Second Avenue, just like they have every Thursday since 2006.

As they bow their heads, Bonnie Red Elk leads a Christian prayer of gratitude for the latest edition of one of America's few independent tribal newspapers. They offer thanks for all the office's donated items: computers and furniture from loyal supporters, a printer from a ministry in California, a scuffed camera for Louis from the *Missoulian* newspaper, the old refrigerator and older Pepsi machine from local businesses.

Life on the reservation can be discouraging, yet there seems no end in sight for the success of this newspaper anomaly. Circulation continues to rise even as many families and friends share the *Journal* until it is dog-eared and tattered. Advertisers come from as far as Williston and Glasgow. In 2006, the *Journal* won a Wassaja Award for fighting censorship, and two years later it was honored with the Montana Free Press award. The California ministry recently told Red Elk to start looking for a real newspaper office building, promising to pay for it.

"Everybody even gets a little money," Red Elk says proudly of paying a staff that once worked for free.

In the tribal offices, where so many had been nonplussed over the years by Red Elk's coverage, Thursdays stand out.

"It's pretty quiet because everybody has just gotten the paper," he explains. "It still blows me away to this day that people line up to get the *Journal*."

And yet in many ways it doesn't blow him away at all.

After all, the *Fort Peck Journal* and the diminutive Dakota-Lakota woman devoted to Jeremiah 50:2's admonition to "publish and conceal not" provides a lifeline—one that binds The People to their history, to their lands and, most importantly, to each other. ◼

Bonnie Red Elk died in June 2015 from complications of a stroke she suffered a year earlier.

PULLING TOGETHER

Nobody can fix everything.
But everybody can help. It's important.

Backbone of the World

By Jennifer Graf Groneberg

Spring 2011

OM POINTS TO THE TOPOGRAPHIC MAP SPREAD OPEN ACROSS THE KITCHEN counter and says, "Here, this is where the trail begins." He moves his fingers along a low, flat valley in the North Fork area of Glacier National Park. I peer at the map, repeating the names I read. Columbia Falls. Polebridge. Bowman Lake. Akokala. I look at the thin, dotted line that marks the trail. Our 18-month-old son, Carter, will be with us. I sigh at the weight of it all, both the decision, and what we'll be carrying if we go ahead with the trip.

Carter weighs 28 pounds, and the backpack to carry him weighs six. I could take that much, plus my sleeping bag, but Tom would have to carry everything else—the tent, our cooking gear, food, water.

"It's too much," I say aloud. "Isn't there any other trip we could try?"

Tom, as if he hasn't heard me, opens the hiker's guide and reads the description of the trail. "A moderate hike through pristine alpine forests with spectacular scenery." He's trying to tempt me. "Profusion of wild-flowers in late summer," he adds.

Not for the first time, I wonder why we do these sorts of things. When we were younger, I'd wanted the adventure. In fact, it was part of my pledge to Tom. I didn't care if our life together was easy; I just didn't want it to be boring. But since we'd become parents, adventure was less appealing to me, or rather, more complicated. We had a son to consider now.

Deciding the small details, such as what to bring on a camping trip, pulled me away from the broader uncertainty of our lives. Our home, a dryland wheat and cattle ranch in eastern Montana, wasn't ours anymore—it belonged to a neighboring family. It had been Tom's and my dream to move to the country and try to make a go of it, but four years of bitter winters and summers when the rain never came had turned the wheat into nothing more than grasshoppers and dust; the cows, thin and gaunt-eyed.

Still, the time we'd spent there felt more real and more alive to me than any other place I'd known. Despite the struggle, I'd begun to put down roots, and just as I realized this fact, life as we knew it was about to change. Our things would all be sold at a farm liquidation auction: my kitchen table, the quilts from the beds, the set of crystal we got as a wedding present, still in its gift box. I'd told Tom, "I can't bear the sight of those things anymore. Sell them all."

On the day of the auction, I was 600 miles away, in the region of Montana the Blackfeet call "The Backbone of the World." This was where Tom and I had gotten married in a morning ceremony on the eastern shore of Flathead Lake, and it felt right returning to our beginnings, as if we could go back and somehow retrace our steps and everything would become clear. We would see it and say, "Aha! This is where it all went wrong!"

I spent my time unpacking what we had saved into our new place, a house that didn't quite feel like ours. We had books, but no bookshelves. A computer, but no desk. A green couch and an overstuffed chair, but no end tables and not enough lamps. I settled Carter's room first, which was easiest. I put his crib against a wall near the window and organized the toys, mostly hand-me-downs from my aunt and uncle who live in Colorado. Even as I was pulling things out of boxes, miles away at the farm, other boxes were filling up. The image was too much for me to manage without tears, and I willed it out of my mind.

Instead, I thought about the camping trip. It was supposed to be a reward, a way to mark the end of the liquidation and the beginning of our new lives. So I spent my days caring for Carter and planning our hike, letting my mind drift to wild places, mountains with streams that run to lakes so clear they look as if they're made of glass.

My list included the Kelty pack for Carter, our sleeping bags, and two tents. Diapers, wipes, plastic baggies for the diapers and wipes. Instant coffee and Tang. Freeze-dried beef stew. Chicken-flavored Ramen noodles. Tortellini with a small packet of parmesan cheese. Plates that doubled as pot lids, cups that collapsed down into thin discs. I weighed and considered everything, which soothed me. The problems in our life that led us here—the drought, a summer range fire, a brutal winter—were so large and unmanageable, so far beyond my control. Packing these small things felt easy, free. A deck of cards. A lightweight set of plastic dominoes. Three matchbox cars, a small bag of crayons, and a tiny coloring book.

Bowman Lake was our first night's destination. We'd drive the three hours to the trailhead, set up a base camp, and stay the night. The next morning, we'd hike up to Akokala Lake with the little tent and enough supplies for one night. The next night, we'd hike back down to the base camp, spend another night, then head home. We'd talk about these plans over the phone, Tom in the eastern part of the state wrapping up the final details of our old life, me in the west, trying to begin anew.

When the day of the trip arrives, we head north, Carter asleep in his car seat, all our gear packed neatly in the back. We reach the park boundary, and pass through a ghost forest, burned gray and charred in a fire, but recovering slowly. I feel like the trees, light and scrubbed bare, but still standing. Soon after, the driving turns from peaceful to unpleasant. A washboard road wakes Carter. He's hungry, but there's no place to pull off, and there's no time to stop. We still have many more miles to go, and then we have to set up camp. Worry descends like night: What are we doing? What were we thinking?

I give Carter a few M&Ms and rub his leg, the only part of him I can reach from my seat. We drive into the night. At the campsite, I quickly set up the tent. Tom starts a fire and gets the water boiling. Nearby, I hear the nighttime sounds of other campers, the clang of pots and dishes, low talking, laughter. I toss a handful of tortellini in the pot of boiling water, and immediately it smells delicious. Tom sets another pot on to boil, for later. When the noodles are done, I drain them and add the cheese. Carter eats with his fingers, wearing the tortellini like rings. We share an apple for dessert, passing it back and forth. Carter sits in the cup of my lap and we watch the moon rise over the water.

I wake to the sound of rain hitting the tent in the darkness. Carter is curled into me in our shared sleeping bag. Tom is still asleep. I listen to the pit-pit-pit of the droplets, and the slow, easy breathing of my husband and child, and the whole world is reduced to the square footage of the tent, everything I care about contained in its small, manageable space.

Morning comes and the rain continues, a light mist. It's not uncommon.

It's not enough to deter Tom; I don't even ask. We begin our day dressing Carter in a rain suit. Tom makes a fire to boil water for our coffee, Tang, and the instant oatmeal with cinnamon and freeze-dried apples. After breakfast, we grab our hiking gear from the car, already packed. I strap Carter into the pack and hoist him onto my back. Tom carries everything else, our smaller tent, more food, extra supplies, and we head up the trail.

The mist hangs with us all morning, not-quite rain but too thick for fog. I'd hoped the sun would come out and burn off the clouds, but no. We hike past a patch of cow parsnip, bent and trampled. For a moment, I wonder what might have caused this; then I think elk, or deer, or even bear, bedded down for the night. We walk through fields of thimbleberries and wild strawberries. The trail descends, and we follow it. Down and down, lower and lower. Here, among the dampness and the ferns and mossy logs, the trees are so big you can't even see the sky.

The trail turns again, and we begin climbing. All the while, we've been singing silly made-up songs, or "Now I Know My ABCs," or a hopscotch chant I remember from childhood, "Miss Mary Mack-Mack-Mack, All Dressed in Black-Black-Black." When we've sung all the songs we know, Tom teaches me the words to a German beer drinking song, "*Lass Im Boot Tas Schaukeln Stein.*"

By now, my feet are sore and my legs ache. It doesn't bother me; it feels good to have a pain I understand. Still, I begin wondering how long until we reach our destination. We need to find a place to rest and have lunch, but the trees are thick on either side of the trail. Off to our left, deep in the darkest part of the woods, I think I hear the howl of a wolf. We stop singing. A shiver runs through my body.

We keep hiking.

The trail bends around a ridge, and I think surely we'll see something ahead, some flat, grassy spot. But the trail descends again, to a creek with a makeshift bridge crossing it. There is no bridge on our maps. Where are we?

There's no singing, no more happy banter. We are mostly quiet. The only sound is from our movement. The air is thick with mosquitoes. Carter is hungry and cross. We drop our packs and I pull out jerky and another apple and a little bar of granola. Just as I'm sitting down, it begins to rain hard. Tom and I scurry to put things away, to pack up Carter, to get moving again. But where are we going?

Tom takes the map from the Ziplock bag, the rain pelting it and us until we're soaked. I can't see anything; neither can Tom. It's impossible to know where we are. If I'd been a child and this were my family, the parents would have begun arguing. They'd take their frustration, their disappointment, their fear, and blame each other, erupting into a fight. If Tom were the child, our situation would have been seen as a chance to teach perseverance and determination, and they would have forged ahead, no matter what.

Tom and I look at each other. He's wearing a maroon baseball hat, water dripping from the brim. His parka is soaked through. The backpack is also sopping wet. All our plans, everything, is undone. We have a decision to make. Which way will we go?

"I'm sorry," Tom says, and the care with which he chooses his words lets me know he's talking about more than the hike.

"Me too," I say.

"I never meant for any of it to happen," he says.

"I know," I say. "It's not your fault."

"But it is," he says.

"It's not. It's just life. Sometimes things happen." I reach out to touch his face, his wet cheeks.

"I love you," he says.

"I love you too."

Without another word, we turn around and begin retracing our steps. The clouds have closed in, and the trail is hidden in mist. The large leaves of the cow parsnip hold water as if they were plates; as I brush past them, water dumps down my legs and into my shoes that squish when I walk. Carter falls asleep in the pack. I'm so tired, and my thighs have begun cramping up. Tom reaches back and takes my hand. "Just keep going. You can do it," he says. "We can make it. It's going to be okay." I appreciate his kindness and his gentleness. This is the man I will spend the rest of my life with. And Carter, our beautiful boy.

I can't see the path ahead. My shoes squish, squish, squish. I concentrate on simply putting one foot in front of the other. Eventually, the rain slows to a drizzle and then finally, it stops. The low-hanging clouds return, and as we continue walking, a sadness sets in. Despite all the trouble, I don't want to go back. The new house, with all its mismatched furniture, its strange creaks and groans in the night, its unfamiliar smell, doesn't feel like home yet, and we have no other place to go.

Out of the fog, I see the campsite in the distance. Wisps of smoke rise from the bright orange dots of campfires. There are tarps spread between trees, makeshift porches. The sight feels familiar and I'm overcome with happiness. Home is where we are now. Home is the three of us, together. ◆

The Small Things

By Craig Lancaster

Winter 2010

WE RODE THREE ACROSS IN THE BENCH SEAT OF MY FATHER'S FORD pickup. I was at the wheel, with my Uncle Bob wedged between Dad and me. We had ridden the interstate north and west about 15 miles out of Great Falls and now were following a winding, rutted two-lane road to the top of the Fairfield Bench, to a place my father hadn't visited in nearly 50 years.

"Slow it down, Craig," Dad said. "Let me see this stuff."

I pulled back my heavy foot, and Dad loosened his memories and, in time, his tongue.

FOR THE WHOLE OF MY LIFE, my taciturn father has been the embodiment of the West as I think of it. Born in Conrad, Montana, and reared in and around Great Falls, he overcame a childhood drenched in neglect and violence and made himself into a better man than any example he had known.

Conjure any well-worn description of frontier living—pulling oneself up by the bootstraps, muscling a living from the soil—and you can put it around his neck. You hear a lot about self-made men, but for Dad, it's not a throwaway line. Whatever he is, whatever he's accomplished, he's managed it largely on the strength of his own determination. He's not perfect; he was a poor husband and a lacking father in many ways, but even now, at 71 years old, he keeps showing up. He stays in the game.

I've spent much of my adulthood trying to piece together Dad's life in those years before he became my father. The details haven't come easily. Dad has rarely been inclined to part with them, and others who know the story have taken it to their graves. Over the years I managed to accumulate enough pieces to believe I had the outline. On our trip to the Fairfield Bench, I found out that I scarcely had even that.

The first indication of just how much I didn't know came when Bob said something about his wife—Delores, Dad's sister—and their older brother, Duaine, having spent time in an orphanage.

"I don't think you were there," Bob said to Dad.

Dad spoke quietly. "No, I was with my dad."

My head whipped around. I'd heard, or maybe I'd assumed, that my paternal grandfather, Fred, had walked out on the family when Dad was 2 or 3 years old. But here was Bob, telling me that it had been a proper divorce and that Dad's mother had rejected the children. So Fred, an uneducated day laborer, had taken them on, until it became obvious that he couldn't cope with three children and the demands of work. The two elder kids, Duaine and Delores, went to the orphanage, and Dad, the baby of the family, stayed with his father.

In the meantime, their mother, Della, had remarried. Her new husband, Dick Mader, owned a dairy farm up on the bench and saw in his wife's scattered children a source of cheap, controllable labor, so Duaine and Delores were whisked from the orphanage and ended up on the farm.

My mind reeled at these revelations casually dropped into conversation. Delores and Duaine are long since gone, so the story rests with Bob and Dad. It had taken a trip to the Fairfield Bench—something I had insisted on—to draw it out of them.

O N DAD'S COMMAND, we stopped along a fence line, and he pointed at a windbreak in the distance.

"That's it," he said.

"You sure?" Bob asked.

"That's it."

Dad is well into his long slide into dotage, and the steel trap of his mind doesn't close as hard or as fast as it once did. But he damn well knew the place where his childhood had been stolen from him.

I turned onto the muddy road and headed for the trees.

HERE IT IS, as Dad told it that day: When he was about 10 years old, he told his father that he would like to meet his brother and sister. Fred said he knew where they were and that he would take Dad to the farm for a weeklong visit.

Della and Dick had other ideas about the duration.

When Fred showed up to get Dad a week later, Dick locked the little boy in the basement and met Fred at the road. He carried a shotgun, all the better to send Fred on his way. Three children could accomplish a hell of a lot more work than two, and Dick aimed to keep Dad close, be it with a gun or a fist or a horse whip.

These memories got a full airing, and they became fodder for an odd bit of one-upmanship between Dad and Bob, whose own childhood had been marred by a father who found it easier to hit his kids than to talk to them.

"I've seen the business end of a belt," Bob said.

"A belt?" Dad said. "A two-by-four. A pitchfork. Dick would come at me with anything he could get his hands on."

NO ONE CAME OUT TO GREET US IN THE YARD AT THE FARM. Respectful of someone else's property, Dad sat in the cab of the pickup and took in the scene. I had seen the place before, in a crinkled black-and-white aerial photograph stashed away among the things Dad has given me over the years. In living color, the scene took my breath away. The milking parlor and the ramshackle chicken coops were still there, virtually unchanged. So was the sturdy little farmhouse, a simple white with dark green trim. The insulation around the foundation of the house had been chipped away by weather and the passage of time. The place was tiny, and my heart ached all over again for Dad. With a stepfather and a mother and two siblings sharing that small space, he had nowhere to escape and nothing that could belong only to him.

I watched Dad, and I tried to imagine what this place must have seemed like to the child he once was, stuck under the thumb of a brutal stepfather. I hoped he might find the words, sitting there and looking at it all through the lens of a half century, but those thoughts remained his alone. Revelations couldn't be found in his face or his voice.

Finally, he said, "Well, we'd better go."

BY HIS OWN ACCOUNT, Dad ran away a lot in those childhood years. He once showed up on the doorstep of his Uncle Ross' house, his back flayed open by Dick's whip. Ross was sympathetic, but he feared Dick, and ours was not the sort of family that told each other how to raise their kids. Ross gave Dad a place to sleep that night, and other nights Dad found other places, but for a long time, he always ended up back at the farm.

One day when he was 13 or 14 years old, he finally bolted for good, escaping to Great Falls. During the day, he would walk the streets, ducking into stores and stealing canned food. At night, he'd find shelter where he could, sometimes in an aunt or uncle's house. He would let himself in and sleep on the couch. The kin learned to let him be; if they woke him, he would run for fear of being turned over to Dick.

After a few weeks, he ended up on a farm in Three Forks, doing odd jobs and being attended to by a kind family that kept him shielded from Dick, who was still looking for him. After a year or two, Dad told the farmer that he would like to see his father again, and the man agreed to find Fred and take Dad to him. A few weeks later, word came: Fred was in Butte.

More than 50 years later, Dad's voice broke and his eyes floated in tears as he revealed what happened next. They were the only emotions he betrayed in telling the story.

"The farmer told me, 'I'll drive you to Butte and once you're there, I'll put you in a cab and follow you to your father's house. Once I see that he's come out to get you, I'm gone.' "

In a singular act, that Three Forks farmer, whose name has been lost to the intervening years, did for Dad what no one else could be troubled to do: He acted in the best interest of the child.

When Dad came of age, Fred saw him off to the Navy and then disappeared again, and life was finally Dad's to make of it what he could.

A T THE NEXT FARMHOUSE OVER, a retired gentleman came out and met us. He walked us around his place, and we stared out over fallow fields at Square Butte rising in the distance, far away and yet seemingly close enough to touch. The farmer remembered Dick. The old dairy farm, he said, was still owned by the family that had bought it from Dick in the early '60s. The farmer's wife, meanwhile, kept looking at Dad. When Dad finally introduced himself, her eyes lit up. She had been a little girl when Dad ran away for good, and her family had helped him make it off the bench and into Great Falls. She remembered.

I found it hard to tamp down the emotion. Dad wasn't just a piece of meat in those years. He had worth, and some people saw it and did the small things they could to recognize it. He mattered.

FOR YEARS, I wondered why my father held me at arm's length, never revealing too much, never letting me get too close. Knowing what I know now, I no longer harbor such questions. He neither raised a hand in anger toward me nor offered much affection, and the sum of that—keeping violence and tenderness away from me—was worth the cost, he must have figured.

I was 3 when he and my mother split in 1973, and I spent most of my growing-up years in a suburb of Fort Worth, Texas, held close by Mom and my stepfather, who showered me with love and support. I spent summers in the rural West with Dad, who worked as an itinerant well digger. I bore casual witness to hardscrabble lives that I never saw back home. I was there, I saw it, but I wasn't really part of it. At the end of the summer, there was always an airplane to take me back to Texas and the cocoon of suburbia.

Even so, I would sometimes close my eyes and try to imagine where Dad was and what he was doing, and I wondered if he wondered about me. Now I know that he did.

In 2008, a couple of years after his wife died, I coaxed Dad up to Billings, where I live. He bought a condominium upstairs from mine. We make up for the time we've missed with board games, errand-running around town and the occasional trip to some outpost of his past, where he makes peace with his memories and I fill in a little more of the picture.

The story of us and our people is wrapped up in Western lives, ones that are many years gone and ones that, God willing, have many years left. The sketches of these lives could be drawn almost anywhere, but it's the fine details of place and time that give them light and flavor.

Nowadays, the homes Dad and I live in are identical in structure and layout, with the walls set at the same angles. The differences lie in how they're furnished and who lives in them. My floors are filled with modern furniture, and impressionistic art adorns the vibrantly painted walls. I approach life by plumbing emotions and trying to draw out their deeper meanings. Dad's walls wallow in muted color, holding plaster birds and old pictures of cowboys, and he keeps a tight lid on his thoughts.

Like our houses, we're the same but different, he and I. Our West, finally, is a place where we watch the sun set from the same vantage point, realizing another day together, with the promise of more coming over the horizon. ◄

Ditching the Drug

By Scott McMillion

Winter 2007

SHAWN KESSLER SPENT A LOT OF YEARS BEING A BADASS. The history is in his skin, etched in ink.

On the fingers of his right hand, tattooed letters spell out "Evil." On his left hand, they say "Ways."

Evil Ways.

Then he lifts his shirt. A tattoo of a methamphetamine lab covers most of his back. Beakers and vials, with tubes connected to creepy skulls. There's a motto above it: "Only the Strong Survive." But alongside the most tortured of the skulls you see a pair of praying hands, with the words "In Memory of Jennie."

Jennie is Shawn's mother, a woman he never knew until he was 11, who died while he was in his early 20s. Ten years later, when he was in his 30s and after he'd already done time for running a meth lab, he got that tattoo, an homage to his mother and his life as a meth addict.

Death images and bad dope. Phantasmagoria along with hands folded in prayer, all of it beneath a defiant slogan.

Welcome to meth world, where nothing makes sense but you chase it anyway.

Now 36, Shawn's black hair carries a frosting of gray. He's on his second prison hitch, doing four years for cooking meth, a drug he's been smoking or sticking in his arm since he was 15 years old. He's off the dope now, says he wants to stay clean forever. He wants to get rid of those tattoos, too. They aren't who he is anymore. They tell you where he's been but say nothing about where he wants to go. And he's not happy about having his mother's name there, blended with images of death and dope.

"I got my mom's name up there with a meth lab," he says. "Man, that's not good."

Evil Ways.

"I'm not going to be living that way any more," he says, swearing this to himself, not to us.

So far, he's walking the talk, and he's leading others on the path.

The next morning, when we see him again, he stands up and sings for us, joins 80 other guys, all drug-addicted criminals, and belts out "You Are My Sunshine" for a couple of bald-headed reporters they've just met.

Later, another inmate, a former honkytonk crooner, sings "The Dance," a Garth Brooks song about taking chances, feeling the pain but risking the love. It's a sad song, the singer is good, and Shawn wipes away tears, unashamed.

"It's okay to cry," he'd told us earlier. "Before, I would hold my tears back. But now, I'm a big crybaby."

WELCOME TO NEXUS, a lockdown prison in Lewistown where no guard carries a gun or a billy club or even a can of mace. It's a place where guards and inmates are on a first-name basis and they all play kickball together, charging hard through the bases, diving for the ball, seeking victory. It's a place where the executive director— the closest thing this place has to a warden—steps onto a gymnasium floor and barks like a dog for the amusement of his charges. It's a place where an anger-management class takes a halt so everybody can sing "For He's a Jolly Good Fellow."

Sometimes these guys even do the hokey pokey.

It's prison. Have no doubt about that, but that's not the main point. Here at Nexus, on this windy bench out by the airport, where the prairie sweeps between the Snowy and Moccasin mountains, the focus is on kicking methamphetamine addiction. Meth, crank, ice, crystal, call it what you want. In here, most people just call it dope. It's addictive, destructive and dangerous. Prison officials say the lust for it is responsible for as much as half the crime in the state. Now, the state of Montana is intervening, spending money and sweat, trying to block the revolving door of addiction, crime and imprisonment.

Nobody's ever tried anything quite like this before: a state government lockdown dedicated to repairing the lives of meth addicts.

The treatment style is called "therapeutic community," where the inmates are called family members, the food is good and hardened cons hug each other with tears in their eyes. The therapy includes gathering every morning to sing those cornball songs, and the inmates are serious about it. They like it.

By 8:15 a.m., on a blustery Friday in September, they're ready to rumble. Everybody's hands and feet are working. Boomboom slap! Boomboom slap! Two stomps of the feet and a clap of the hands. Boomboom slap! It sounds like a pep rally, a hometown crowd eager to get on with the game. Exclamation marks crisscross the room at the end of every sentence.

That morning, the 81 men in attendance sang to photographer Thomas Lee and me. They ranged in age from 19 to 65. Some were largely illiterate. Others had master's degrees. They looked like shop owners or bikers, construction workers or truck drivers, guys you'd see on the street, which is what a lot of them used to be. Just guys. There were weightlifters and professional musicians, hip cats and rednecks. They were mostly white, but also Indian, Hispanic and black. Look them over and you see the octopus of meth addiction: Its heart is in blue collar America, but its tentacles reach everywhere. These guys all sang to us and then they sang for themselves. They sang "Old MacDonald," which is when Don Schroeder, the boss here, took center stage and barked like a dog, just for giggles. With a woof woof here and a woof woof there.

These childish songs boom out in deep male voices, a little off key but with full voice and throat. These guys are laughing and grinning, high-fiving and pumping their fists in the air. They're singing and hugging, and if you don't smile with them you might need a little therapy of your own.

Then it's time for "appreciations."

"I'm James and I'm an addict," says the first man. Everybody shouts "Hello, James." Shouts it.

A recent arrival, he thanks everybody in his orientation class.

Mike thanks all the guys who pulled him out of a slump.

Barb, the cook, looks like a ranch wife with hard and honest work written on her strong face and arms. She feeds these guys and wants to thank them all for keeping the place clean, making her job easier.

"I appreciate each and every one of you," she tells them, bringing the first of many standing ovations that morning.

Then it's time for "motivations." Steve reads a prayer for honesty, then Dan tells about talking on the phone to his wife, a woman he has wronged, committed crimes against.

"She's started to forgive me in her heart. It was the best conversation me and her ever had. It made me realize I've started to change. I'm gonna make it."

He tells his brothers they'll make it, too.

"People are gonna forgive you for what you've done."

There are wary smiles, now. They all have their own guilt and they know it. But there is hope, too. It's not on everybody's face, but it's there. You can see it.

"This program is a godsend," Nick Lignola told me. He's got a master's degree in psychology, even studied law for awhile. He was hooked on cocaine for 20 years, then spent 13 years on meth. Now 48, he tried many times to quit but could never do it. He's in here for stealing, to support his habit.

"Nothing has torn me apart more than meth," he said. "As bad as coke is, once I quit, I quit."

BOB LACROIX IS A BIG MAN. Six foot two and 250 pounds, with shoulders like luggage. At 40, his hair is jet black and he wears it pulled back into a tight ponytail. He looks like he's in the prime of his life.

"Let me show you something," he says, stepping to the locker in his sparse, dormitory-style room, where he sleeps on a bottom bunk. He pulls out a picture. It's Bob, but he's unrecognizable. Taken two years ago, just before he got busted for selling meth, he's incredibly gaunt and bony, with sunken cheeks and crazy eyes. It looks like he snapped the photo himself, holding a camera at arm's length to capture the miasma of some crank stupor that clutched him. He'd been shooting meth for two years when he took that picture and he'd lost 80 pounds, running for two weeks at a time without sleep, rarely eating, feeling his teeth rot away as the dope dried up the capillaries and saliva glands in his mouth.

"You wanna see some meth mouth?" he asks us, then fishhooks a finger into his right cheek and exposes the blackened stumps of his molars. "That's meth mouth."

He told us of tearing around the state, pulling off dope deals on his fast-as-a-rocket motorcycle. Sometimes, he'd fall asleep at 100 miles an hour, waking up just before he teetered over and smeared himself across the highway. Somehow, he survived. So did the girls who rode on the back of the bike, making dope runs with him.

Now he's working on an eight-year sentence for possessing and selling meth. He's lost his wife, his bike, his home and the 14-year-old son he now writes to every day, the one who watched his father twist into pieces. Bob moved a lot of meth, made himself popular with a lot of addicts, but he never even made any money at it. The meth took it all.

"I'd make a couple trips and all I'd have left is a little bit of dope," he says.

He worries about the son, now living in New Hampshire.

"It would kill me to have him go down this road."

A dozen years ago, living in Roundup, he messed around with meth for a couple of years. But then he and his wife moved to Florida and never touched it for nine years.

"There was some weed and coke, but we did pretty good," he said.

Then they came back to Montana, where meth had exploded into what some people call an epidemic.

"It just blew up in dope," he said of Montana. "It's everywhere."

One day, he had a weak moment.

And an excuse.

"What could a couple lines hurt?" he wondered. "We had to get a roof on the house."

LOTS OF PEOPLE START TAKING METH FOR WHAT SEEMS LIKE A LOGICAL PURPOSE, Schroeder told me: They want to work more.

At first, it does the trick. Methamphetamine has a similar chemical structure to cocaine, but it lasts much longer. People can work for 12 hours, 14 hours, rack up the overtime and still have energy for life, parties, whatever. It's all over the state, from the multimillion dollar homes rising at Big Sky to the oil rigs at Sidney to the verdant sweep of the Flathead Valley. Look around and you'll find it.

It's seductive, at first, but stick with it and it will screw you.

"You cross over that point where it's all about the meth," Schroeder said. "Your job is about getting more meth. I know guys who've sold their house to buy meth. They've sold their kids' toys."

You lose the rush, but you don't lose the need, the wanting.

Meth is expensive in all sorts of ways. It used to be a little cheaper than coke, but that isn't true anymore, according to Jeff Sweetin, special agent in charge of the Drug Enforcement Administration's Rocky Mountain Division. It now costs as much as $200 a gram, and some addicts consume an eightball (an eighth of an ounce, or 3.5 grams) every day, sometimes more. So people peddle dope to pay for their own habit. Or they steal. Family members usually are the first victims, Schroeder said, but everybody suffers. Coworkers and friends and anybody with a toolbox or a CD player in a car.

"It's the rural drug of choice," Schroeder said, much the way crack cocaine was the urban drug of choice in the 1980s.

Women often are seduced by promises of weight loss. Other people just want a rush. Then they want it again.

Steve Grant studies brains for the National Institute of Drug Abuse, which is part of the National Institutes for Health, in Bethesda, Maryland, where he is a neuroscientist.

For years, he's compared the effects of cocaine and meth. Both of them have the ability to soak the brain in dopamine, seratonin and other neurotransmitters that tell the brain it's happy.

But the response is not just pleasure, he told me.

"It's much deeper than simply the experience of pleasure," he said. The neurotransmitters tell the brain, "This is something important. This is something you should learn about."

He used a bathtub analogy. Imagine a hot soak on a cold day. You've had troubles. You want to escape. This is good. Problems are fading.

Cocaine puts a cork in the tub, so it fills with neurotransmitters radiating warmth. Methamphetamine uses the same plug, but it also opens the taps a lot wider and leaves it open until the hot water runs out, which means you've exhausted your dopamine supply, slopped it all over the floor.

Then the damage sets in. When the dopamine and other brain chemicals can't be reabsorbed, they convert into free radicals that pack some extra oxygen, chemicals that damage the cells that regulate the flow of dopamine.

"Think of it as rusting," Grant said. "Methamphetamine causes neurons to rust. That doesn't happen with cocaine and it doesn't seem to happen as much with other amphetamines."

And we're talking about your brain, not your fender wells.

Addicts know all this, though they use different language.

Eventually, you're still high as a kite, "tweaking" as they say, but you've lost the rush, the buzz. You're starting to rust and that's when users go into "spinderella" mode. They might take apart an engine, with every intention of putting it back together. At 3 a.m., they'll go to Wal-Mart, to wander the aisles, looking at things. Meth addicts often grow self-conscious, convinced everyone is staring at them. They hate this. So what do they do? Go to Wal-Mart.

Sometimes, in the addicted mind, the only option to this late night distress is more dope, but your brain has exhausted its dopamines. The tap offers only cold water. But you soak in it anyway, try more dope, hoping to warm it up. Otherwise, you have to face the comedown, which will smack you around.

"Thinking logically was right out the window," LaCroix explained. "You get lost in stuff."

There's a growing consensus among scientists that it takes at least two years of abstinence for your brain to heal from meth addiction, to scrape the rust off your neurons. While you're using, symptoms include rotting teeth, anxiety, psychosis, dramatic weight loss, violent outbursts and obsessive tendencies that can make you count and organize every screw and washer in your garage. Depending on the quality of your dope, you might hallucinate, see some "meth shadows." You might imagine bugs under your skin and scratch yourself raw. Your libido swells and you turn into a tomcat for awhile. But impotence often follows. Meanwhile, you've risked getting HIV, herpes, hepatitis. Women might swap sex for dope. You sweat hard, get filthy and don't wash. You talk and talk and talk. You bore most people, but you scare the ones who love you.

Kick the dope and you've got other problems. The aftermath can include depression, anxiety, memory loss, uncontrollable twitching or shaking akin to Parkinson's disease. The guy who only wanted to do more work suddenly isn't worth a shit for awhile.

The book is still open on whether recovery is ever "complete," which is a hard word to define, especially since most addicts started using when they were teenagers and don't try to quit until well into adulthood. They'll never be that teenager again, but can they ever be "whole?"

"It manifests itself in a whole host of ways," Grant said. "And we don't know the full extent."

Tests similar to computerized puzzles have shown that meth addicts have a hard time changing faulty responses, that they tend to keep repeating the same wrong answers, expecting different results.

For some people, that's the definition of crazy.

JAMES STREITZ HAS LIVED A CRAZY LIFE. He's the first to admit it. It got so crazy for awhile, that he even tattooed it on his face: three black dots, arranged in a triangle just under his left eye.

That tattoo derives from Latino street gangs. It means "mi vida loca."

"My crazy life," James said. "It used to be. I lived a violent life. The only way I was able to show emotion was through violence. Every time I cried, I got beat for it."

The 32-year-old Billings resident and father of three said he was eight years old the first time he took cocaine and he's wrestled with drug abuse most of his life.

Between 2001 and 2005, he was convicted of four drug felonies and an assault charge. Now he's doing a five-year sentence and it's not his first time behind bars. He's tried in the past to kick the dope, gone through outpatient treatment, done a 28-day rehab program and a 60-day program. None of it worked, he landed in prison again and now he's at Nexus, almost halfway through nine months of rehab. He says he likes it, feels confident it will work this time. "We're not skimming through it. We're looking at what our problems are."

I talked to him right after the first lunch serving, when 46 guys were lined up along the wall, waiting to file out for their afternoon sessions of group therapy, individual counseling, parenting classes, AA meetings. There's joking and laughter in the lines while the guards count noses, one of about 10 countoffs a day. Then everybody clams up. There's a moment of silence.

"It's respect," James tells me. It's for the addicts who won't get this treatment, for the ones who died.

He's changing, now, he says. He's learned to turn negatives into positives, how to do a "cognitive intervention," which means stepping back and analyzing your feelings when anger starts to boil, which beats lashing out with fist or weapon. He's learning about feelings. He wants to get back to his kids.

"In order to be a good dad, I've got to be a good person for myself," he says. "I'm honest with them. I told them I'm a drug addict. Kids. They forgive a lot."

His life has been crazy. He's working on sanity.

NEXUS ISN'T FOR EVERYBODY. Even so, you can't just walk in and sign up. There's a waiting list.

The 2005 Montana Legislature, faced with rising crime rates

and the connection to rampant methamphetamine abuse, decided that locking people up might provide some visceral satisfaction, but it wasn't solving many problems. So it decided to create two meth treatment centers, a 40-bed facility for women, in Boulder, and the one here in Lewistown.

Nexus is operated under contract by Community, Counseling and Correctional Service, Inc., a not-for-profit company from Butte that runs pre-release centers, juvenile detention facilities and addiction treatment centers in Montana, Washington and North Dakota. Montana has entered into a 20-year contract with CCCS, which has been treating people since 1983, so they've got a track record.

One of those facilities is the WATCH program in Warm Springs, where, since 2002, people convicted of four or more drunk driving charges spend six months in a therapeutic program. That program is working, according to Mike Ferriter, director of the Montana Department of Corrections.

"It's clear that that method of treatment was producing the kind of results we needed," Ferriter told me.

The contract calls for the state to pay Nexus $115 a day, per inmate. That's significantly more than the $76 a day it costs to house an inmate in the state prison, but Ferriter sees payoffs down the road.

About half the people entering the prison system have committed meth-related crimes, he said, and lots of them are back for a second or third hitch.

The immediate reward is in "restored lives for the offenders," Ferriter said. That translates into better safety and less crime for the general public, reduced prison time and expenses in the future, and the transformation of inmates, who are tax consumers, into tax payers, people with jobs or businesses who take care of themselves and their families instead of forcing the state to do it.

To get into this place, you must be convicted of at least two meth-related offenses, like possession, sales, or stealing stuff to buy dope. You must have a recommendation from somebody in the justice system: a prison official, a parole officer, a prosecutor, a judge or a public defender. You must pass muster with a screening committee that consists of Schroeder, the local sheriff and police chief, a parole officer and a community member in Lewistown. You provide all your records and rap sheets, submit to a variety of physical and psychological tests. If you've got a long history of violent offenses, you're out of luck. Sex offenders aren't welcome either.

If you're accepted, know that you'll spend nine months here. You'll be matched right away with a "mentor," an inmate who's been around awhile, and you're given some gray sweats to wear.

On your first day here, you're greeted with a goofy song and probably a hug.

"I had tears in my eyes the first 15 minutes I was here," Shawn Kessler told me.

"At first it was kind of weird. I didn't believe it," said Kevin Hyatt, from Bozeman. "But you're getting out of your comfort zone. It's worth it."

Then you get to work. You take classes in anger management. You learn how to be a better parent, how to find a relationship with a woman that maybe won't put you both in the gutter. You learn to read and write, if that's what you need. You polish your math. You learn how to write a resume. You develop a plan for how you're going to live when you finally get out of here, what you're going to do when somebody offers dope. You're going to think hard about the people you called friends and you're going to think even harder about yourself. You're going to pick some scabs. You're going to write a lifeline that spells out the big items in your past. And chances are, you're going to see you did a lot more harm than good. And you're going to figure out how to address that damage, fix some things. You're going to chip away at this every day for nine months, from 7 in the morning to 10 at night, and every morning you're going to join that whole family of 80 inmates and 40 staff members and sing goofy songs. You'll get some laughs and you might cry. People put on skits. You'll learn to like it. You'll clap your hands and stomp your feet, ready to get started. Boomboom slap. Boomboom slap. But this isn't a ball game. It could be your last chance at something resembling a normal life.

Cheat, or refuse to participate, and chances are you'll be back in the pen.

Stick with the program and after a couple weeks, you move to phase one, when you get some green scrubs to wear. Make it to phase two and you're issued jeans and a burgundy shirt. Make it to phase three and you can wear street clothes, but no shoes or jackets worth more than $100 and you always cover your tattoos as much as possible. It's still treatment: You're not here to make a fashion statement or to flash your ink. Along the way, you earn privileges, like telephone time and maybe a dollar a day, which you have to learn to budget.

Make it through nine months and you're still facing six months at one of six residential pre-release centers around the state, where you'll sleep every night. But you can work again, put away some money, see your family, your wife if she'll have you. You can ease into your recovery plan. Supervision's tight, but you're a long way from the pen. Stay clean and you can move even further.

So FAR, the program is working, though its first real test—keeping these guys sober on the streets—is still months in the future. But there hasn't been a single fight and everybody has passed all his piss tests and breath tests, showing that, unlike most of the prison system, dope is either unwanted or unattainable. Five people have been sent back to prison for refusing to cooperate, Schroeder said. The only major problem has been the two well-publicized escapes over the summer, but both inmates were captured within hours, nobody was injured and the chain-link fence has been beefed up with razor wire that blinks in the sun like a million polished knives.

Everybody I talked to said he's happy to be here, including Mac Watkins, who, at 30, is built like a badger with a shaved head.

He explained, while shoveling down a giant salad, how he got off the train in Shelby a couple years ago, trying to escape a bust that was coming down in Idaho, only to find the narcs waiting for him.

"I've been in prison in lots of states," he told me. "I was lucky to get busted in Montana. It gave me a chance to be here and learn something."

"These people have hope," Ferriter said. "They see blue sky."

He's spent 30 years working in prisons, spent a lot of time in a lot of lockups, talked to a lot of inmates. When he visited here, the guys sang for him, too.

That was something different.

"Usually," he said. "They don't sing."

KEVIN HYATT FIRST TRIED METH WHEN HE WAS 13 YEARS OLD AND LIVING IN Bozeman. By the time he was 16, he was a high school dropout with a $100 a day habit he couldn't afford no matter how many hours he spent scrubbing dishes at a local steak joint. So he stole. He broke into cars, taking tools, stereos, cash and credit cards if he got lucky.

"I'd just stay up and not eat. We'd run around and do the craziest things, drive around looking for dope, looking for things to steal."

He and his girlfriend got pregnant. The girlfriend laid off the booze and dope for awhile, but fell back into it after the baby was born. She's doing time for bad checks. Kevin, now 23, is doing six years for driving the getaway car in the robbery of a pizza joint. Deer Lodge is never easy, but it's especially hard for a 135-pound man, and Kevin found himself in lots of fights.

"In here, we're not treated like inmates," he told me. "We're treated like human beings."

He likes tools and engines and dreams of someday having a store that sells off-road vehicles.

He's young and personable and articulate, but he's never lived a sober life. He's been drunk or stoned or both ever since he hit puberty. Now, he has this chance, wants to make it work.

If he can't kick the dope, he doesn't like his odds.

"I'd either be dead or in prison for life," he said.

He misses that baby daughter. With both her parents in prison, she was taken away, then adopted.

That was the worst part, he said. Losing her.

"I hope to see my daughter again someday. If she ever comes to see me 20 years down the road, I won't be the same person: a criminal and a drug addict."

SCHROEDER IS OPTIMISTIC ABOUT THIS PROGRAM. Now 40 years old, he's worked in rehab for 15 years, mostly in Dixie, where he's seen horrors: newborn crack babies no bigger than the palm of his hand; 6 year olds hitting the pipe; abuse and theft and terrible violence. He's seen successes and failures. He likes the odds of the Nexus program, thinks he can hit a success rate of 70 percent, roughly double what traditional meth rehab programs have pulled off.

He likes the graphic TV ads and billboards the Montana Meth Project is putting out, likes the fact that they appear to be working. Meth use among teenagers has dropped by 50 percent since 2005, according to a September survey.

"First-time use is the key," he said. Clearly, not everybody who uses meth winds up with an addiction. But every addiction starts somewhere.

Still, he said he's not worried about working himself out of a job.

Nationwide, meth abuse continues to grow. Across the country, nearly half of all county sheriffs say meth is a growing problem. Mexican criminal syndicates do most of the manufacturing in "superlabs," the DEA's Sweetin told me, but people are still cooking it up in houses and trailers and campsites, using ingredients like battery innards, lye and Coleman fuel. (I Googled "meth recipes" and gave up after reading a dozen of them.) The dope is cleaner now, more pure, but just as toxic.

But Sweetin also said that Montana should be proud. In 2002, law enforcement busted 119 makeshift labs in the state. So far this year, they've only found seven, partly because of tighter controls on the key ingredients of ephedrine and pseudoephedrine, found in cold pills.

"The people of Montana hit the ball out of the park," he said. "There's a lot of great news in the meth story."

WHILE HE CALLS A 70 PERCENT RECOVERY TARGET "VERY OPTIMISTIC," he said treatment programs constitute the final piece of a three-legged stool. The others are prevention education, like the Montana Meth program, and good solid police work.

Still, as cops and teachers and rehab centers get smarter, so do the manufacturers and peddlers from Mexico. They import raw materials from Asia, cook them in sophisticated labs and have a vast distribution network.

"They've gotten incredibly good at being businessmen," Sweetin said. Street gangs and outlaw bikers used to own the meth trade. Now it's become too sophisticated for them.

"I think the business became bigger than them," Sweetin said.

Schroeder knows all this. The number of first-time users is down. Dirty piss tests on the job have declined. So has meth-related crime.

But it hasn't gone away.

He knows that three of 10 meth addicts will die, if not from an overdose, then from a car wreck, a fight, an untreated case of hepatitis C spread by a dirty needle. "The lifestyle," he calls it.

It's a lifestyle that embraces destruction, that accepts desperation and pain as inevitable outcomes. You see it in the tattoos here. Eight-balls. Prison bars. A meth lab. Evil Ways. La Vida Loca.

Schroeder and his staff understand the brain chemistry of meth addiction, the rusty neurons. They can't do much about that, except wait for things to heal or for the synapses to reroute themselves. So instead of the brain, they focus on the mind, which, as scientist Carl Sagan said, is what we use to understand our brains.

That's where the silly songs come in every morning. You start the day happy, then you get to work. It's a new concept for most of these guys.

"If we all started our day like that, we'd have a lot fewer problems," Schroeder said. "These guys have been yelled at and screamed at. They've been punished their whole lives and it hasn't worked."

At Nexus, the guys are treated like family members, a new thing for most of them. It means learning to ask for help when you need it, and offering it, too, without thought of reward.

"We know what works," Schroeder said. "We know what we have to do." ◪

Trash to Cash

By John Byorth

Winter 2014

ASYSTEM OF STREAMS RUNS THROUGH PARK COUNTY, but most people never see it. One stem parallels the Yellowstone River as it flows north from Gardiner. Another runs south along the Shields River. One drains Bozeman Pass in the west while another pushes uphill from Springdale in the east. Every household, ranch and outpost along the way adds potential to the flow, which doesn't contain much water.

Rather, the flow consists of discards and debris, the things people no longer want or use, or that are simply in the way. And it all pools up in Livingston, where a local woman's remarkable business converts unwanted items into community assets and cold cash for people who need it.

"The stream of donations coming in from every corner of the county tells us who has passed away, sold their home, or is going out of business," says Caron Cooper, founder and chief executive officer of the Community Closet Thrift Store. "The thrift store provides a wealth of information as to what is shaking in the greater community. We just took a donation that is clearly from a [Church Universal Triumphant] bomb shelter. We could tell, based on the books and videos."

Cooper uses the "stream" metaphor to describe the never-ending flow of used clothing, appliances and stuff that flows into the Community Closet's back door each day, undergoes sorting and processing, and then, hopefully, washes out the front door, where the cash flows in.

It's a tough job but Cooper makes it work. She, with a handful of staffers and volunteers, intercepts this river of stuff destined for the landfill, then figures out what people need and sells it to them at economical prices. The process has paid off well enough to generate $270,000 in grants to nonprofit groups in Park County since December 2005. That means some people can outfit themselves and their homes for a song, while others get help with everything from hot meals to gas money, mental health treatment to the senior party at the high school. And it all started from a stream of secondhand waste.

"THRIFT STORES ARE KIND OF CHAOTIC BY NATURE," Cooper says. "You have to rein it in because people don't like to shop in a cluttered store, yet we don't have control over the quality or quantity of materials and sources at any given time. The biggest threat is too much stuff."

A glut of items requires massive storage space and a large staff for processing, neither of which the Community Closet has. When things pool up and goods aren't sold or given away, the stream goes over the waterfall into the local garbage system, which isn't cheap. In 2006, the Community Closet's first full year of operation, garbage fees were negligible. Just two years later, after the Community Closet became the most popular place to donate used goods, waste disposal costs soared to $1,000 a month, and kept climbing.

"Not all donations are quality," Cooper explains. "Some have actually been recalled for safety reasons, or they are too old and beat up, stained, or simply don't work. Take bedding for example. We get sheets so thin that you can see through them. I can't sell those and consumers won't buy them. So what do you do? You have to throw them away."

Tossing junk is part of the thrift store business. But the cost was getting out of hand. Cooper projected that if disposal costs continued to rise, her garbage bills would approach $20,000 by 2013. That, she decided, wouldn't do. It threatened the store's mission of helping the whole community. When she started Community Closet, Cooper never imagined success could lead to failure. She knew what she had to do. She had to turn the trash into cash.

MARKET-DRIVEN EFFICIENCIES ARE NOT A NEW THING FOR COOPER, given her resume. She has a master's degree from Georgetown and a Ph.D. from Berkeley, both of which emphasized energy economics. She's published a long list of professional papers ("Economic Activity and Energy Demand in the USSR," for example) in scholarly journals, governmental publications and periodicals, and lectured at universities and international conferences on topics such as "Prospects for Energy Conservation: The Legacy of the Soviet System." She has worked in Washington, D.C., and Moscow, and spent enough time at London conferences to know a pub or two. She once created a database of the Russian coal industry for the World Bank and she examined pollution patterns in Central and Eastern Europe for the Congressional Office of Technology Assessment.

Even if all that brainy stuff was a lifetime ago—before she moved to Montana to start a family; before she found herself teetering in and out of poverty after a divorce; before she reinvented herself in the nonprofit world of thrift stores—Caron Cooper is a person you could bet on to figure out how to turn pollution into revenue.

"Our disposal costs clearly correlated with revenue," Cooper says, at once professorial and fashionable, gray hair battling for style with some fading punk-blue hair dye. Economist in cateye glasses or funky single mom? It's clear she is some of both.

As an economist, Cooper identified the need to keep the stream moving away from the dump and toward consumers. So the Community Closet held regular sales when everything was priced at 25 cents, which helped clear the floor for inventory heaping up in back. A quarter, apparently, was a threshold price for shoppers to pay for just about anything, plus it gave low-income consumers the dignity of paying instead of using a voucher for free items, a service the store provides if people have a recommendation from social service agencies. Still, donations flooded in and garbage fees kept climbing.

So Cooper wrote a new business plan. A little house across the alley behind the store was up for sale and she told her board of directors she wanted to buy it and make it the Alley Annex Quarter Store, a place that would sell overflow at the market-clearing price of 25 cents an item. Anything that didn't sell would go in bins in front of the East Park Street store on Sundays, and be left there, free for the taking.

The board approved the project, despite expected startup losses, because it supported waste reduction and provided significant economic support to poverty-level families—the primary mission of the organization. And Livingston has poverty, like much of Montana.

Once a thriving railroad town, Livingston's economy crashed in the

1980s when the Burlington Northern Railroad closed its local shops, eliminating hundreds of jobs. Many downtown stores shut down and stayed that way, until new businesses began to open with the recent "re-settling" of the New West. (Many of the clothes and donated items Cooper sees today are from those prosperous days: pearl button snap shirts, western sport jackets and formal wear, '70s-style bell-bottom jeans and name-brand dresses.)

Cooper can relate to the feeling of suddenly being underemployed and plunging toward poverty, and it seems to underpin every decision she makes. She and the board of directors work hard to provide a positive experience for low-income shoppers, fund programs that benefit and support them, and give away as much winter clothing as people need. Opening the Alley Annex chipped away at waste, too, creating a $2,000 reduction in disposal costs the first year. No-pay vouchers dropped by 70 percent as well, helping to boost overall sales by $3,000.

With low-income shoppers taken care of, and with fewer marginal goods going in the garbage, Cooper began looking for other ways to squeeze value from donations, many of which included once-expensive clothing.

"WE GET PLENTY OF PATAGONIA CLOTHING THROUGHOUT THE YEAR, but couldn't always get the highest value from regular shoppers," Cooper said. "So while I'm bound by our mission statement to give shoppers the opportunity to have high quality products like Patagonia, I'm also bound to get the most value out of a piece so that I can give that money back to the community. They are the two halves of our mission."

Cooper had held annual Patagonia sales before, but her new strategy took the show to the edge of town, where Livingston's largest private business—PrintingForLess.com—employs scores of people.

"It's the perfect market," Cooper says. "PFL employees are mostly young, outdoor types, with good incomes compared to the average in town. They'll drop 20 bucks on a nice jacket or ski pants, and it's half the price of secondhand stores in Bozeman but four times the price charged in our store."

Cooper noted that she would sell about 20 percent of her Patagonia stock at the PFL sale, and still have merchandise in the store for regular customers and sales.

"I call it 'squeezing value,'" Cooper says. "By segmenting the market,

I spread purchasing opportunities across a larger demographic while selling more pieces at a variety of prices. It raises far more revenue than it would if I just put them on the rack at the regular prices."

Despite Cooper's efforts with the Alley Annex and the special sales, both of which increased sales and reduced waste, disposal costs still peaked in 2010 at $13,000. The following spring, in 2011, the funky-single-mom side of Caron Cooper discovered another opportunity.

For the first time, the onetime world-traveling economist turned low-income single mom took her teenage son Bill on a big trip, to New York City, because she thought every teenage kid should experience the Big Apple. As it happened, one of the Community Closet's board members, Theresa Coleman, was also there on vacation. Coleman joined Cooper and Bill for a tour of Housing Works, an upscale thrift store benefiting homeless AIDS patients in Manhattan. The trip introduced Cooper and Coleman to a thrift store that was more like a boutique. Later, Caron and Bill dropped into a similar thrift store called Quality Mending.

"At the end of the tour," Cooper says, "I noticed this Union suit on the rack that had a $98 price tag. I was shocked! So I asked, 'How do you rationalize such a high cost for a thrift store?' The staffer said, 'Oh, we curate everything.'"

To "CURATE" CLOTHING MEANT LITTLE MORE THAN WHAT COMMUNITY CLOSET staffers already did: sort out similar pieces—just like the Patagonia stuff. But what Housing Works and Quality Mending did was put those curated pieces into one "fashionable" store. Upon returning to Livingston, Cooper wrote yet another business plan for what she would call the Curated Closet.

"It made sense," Cooper says, "because we were trying to increase sales, squeeze value from our goods, and expand our customer base. So we opened at a different downtown location because some people in the community will pay for used goods but are embarrassed to shop in a thrift store."

The boutique now occupies a downtown Livingston storefront, between an art gallery and a yoga studio, and features vintage and higher-end specialty clothing, such as those pearl-button western shirts or designer cowboy boots. Instead of $2.50 for a shirt or $5 for boots, the Curated Closet could fetch perhaps five times as much. And, by taking the top 2 percent of donated goods and selling them at a higher price, it kept the other 98 percent of items affordable in the flagship thrift store and the Alley Annex. Other curations followed, such as theme-sorting ugly Christmas sweaters, Halloween costumes and, most recently, the Deluxe Rural Wear line, branded goods popular with concert and festival goers, another funky mom idea that came to Cooper when she took her son to see the Decembrists in Missoula.

"I was looking around at all these kids dancing and they were wearing exactly the clothing that the Community Closet gets in by the carload every time one of our older residents passes away," Cooper said. "They were wearing vintage clothing from the '70s that only a specific segment of consumers will wear. It's retro fashion to them, but our average shopper will probably pass it over."

The DRW line, as Cooper branded it, needed to find its way to concerts around the region, necessitating yet another business plan. This time, Cooper found an old motor home, pitched her idea to her board, and hit the road in 2013. Her first event was Treefort, a three-day music festival in Boise, Idaho, with her son and some other teenage volunteers. They watched pieces fly off the racks as Indie artists played their tunes and hipsters danced about. In 2014, the DRW tour did 10 more local events—Red Ants Pants and the Wilsall Rodeo, for example—and paid off the mobile home in under a year. All the while, the trash was turning into cash.

The efforts have paid off. By 2011, Cooper was able to cut garbage fees by 50 percent, to about $5,400 a year. The Community Closet was making more money than ever, and the relationship between revenue and waste seemed stable. Then, in the summer of 2014, the Community Closet had its busiest season on record. Donations flooded in and sales shot up as much as 30 percent. The trash bill followed suit with a 20 percent bump. Having been through this before, Cooper knew it was a matter of simply moving more goods out to customers, so she expanded the scope of the Alley Annex to include a one day a week "dollar store," but instead of everything costing a buck, the dollar store sold multiple items per buck, as in five for a dollar. Cooper also made a deal with a recycler to sell bulk clothing and electronics to China. Between the two efforts, garbage bills have dropped back to 2013 levels.

That means money isn't being wasted on dump charges and instead is given back to the community. Elaine Kimbler, the executive director of Friends of the Community, Inc., recently wrote Cooper to thank her for a grant of $2,000. The money provided, among other things, help for a single dad working at a fast-food restaurant; end of the month food assistance for two families; a month's rent for a woman fresh out of the hospital; utilities for a family behind on its bills; and vehicle registration for a working mom.

"Thank you again for enabling us to help vulnerable people who just need a little help through a difficult situation," Kimbler wrote. "Every one of them was so grateful that there was a charity who not only cared about them, but actually helped in a real, concrete way. Your generosity made that possible."

And that generosity rose from a watershed of invisible streams that converged and pooled up at a thrift store. ◼

Double Life

By Jeff Welsch

Spring 2012

THIS IS WHERE A LIFE BEGINS. And this is where another ends.

In a modest home in tiny Conrad, a television flickers with frightful images of twin skyscrapers smoldering in a place far away from the wind-scoured wheat and barley prairies of the Rocky Mountain Front.

It is the morning of Sept. 11, 2001, and Shannen Rossmiller is staring with incredulity at the carnage. Her body trembles in a fusion of rage, fear and confusion. She can hear her heart pound. As she watches and re-watches the World Trade Center collapse, the Pentagon billowing with smoke, a Pennsylvania pasture burning, she is gripped by helplessness unlike any she has known or could imagine.

In this way, Rossmiller is not unlike 300 million other Americans; grieving for the more than 3,000 dead, frightened for her children's future, cursing a distant culture she knows little about. She eventually adorns her car with American flags and orders checks that read "9/11: We Will Never Forget." For months, she will wonder when or if normalcy will ever return to a way of life that seemed to change instantly, even in her lonely outpost off Interstate 15 north of Great Falls.

She was, she recalls now, an ordinary American farm gal living simply with her lifelong friend and husband and three kids, a Rockwell-meets-the-Rockies picture that might still exist today, she says with a hint of regret, if only ...

If only Randy hadn't suggested she soak away her range of emotions that night in their basement jacuzzi. If only she hadn't emerged clumsily and slipped on the wet tile and fractured her pelvis. If only she hadn't been confined to a couch or bed for six weeks, an already restless insomniac with little more for companionship than the TV, eight computers installed by her wireless-technician husband, and a 24/7 blur of burning buildings, gritty rescuers and terrorism alerts.

It's all conjecture now anyway, isn't it? For as she lay in intense pain the night of 9/11, Shannen Rossmiller became a dedicated channel surfer, and life as she knew it—thought she'd always know it—slowly began to erode, one click at a time, like a frog in tepid water on a burner set to boil. Who could do this to us? Why would anyone hate us this much? Aren't we good people? Her focus only intensified in the wee hours, after Randy and the kids went to bed, as she fixated on understanding the attacks and the people who masterminded them.

"Life was simple, predictable," she recalls. "And all of a sudden it wasn't."

Even then, it is possible that Rossmiller might have gradually moved on, much like the rest of us, once she was on her feet again. It's possible that she would have returned to her comfortable role as wife, mom, daughter, friend and—by the way—youngest municipal judge in American history. That, too, will always remain hindsight. For one day, during her convalescent channel hopping, Rossmiller happened upon a Cable News Network report about an especially active terrorist website where a Middle East jihadist group called al-Qaeda and its American-educated leader, Osama bin Laden, plotted ways to destroy the western lifestyle.

Rossmiller scribbled down the web address and turned to a computer. Undaunted after finding that the site was in Arabic, she clicked a few more keys and purchased translation software. Thus began an immersion into a right-to-left language that was as different from hers as her Christian faith was from Islam. In the following days and weeks she ordered *The Koran for Dummies* and signed up for an eight-week online Arabic class. She sent Randy to Great Falls to buy Arab novels and books about jihadists. She took copious notes and organized them in boxes.

Eventually she learned to create identities and online Internet Protocol addresses in places far from Conrad. She could pinpoint the locations of computers, often to within a block of the Internet cafes where much of the chatter originated. When she became mobile, she spent two weeks in Buffalo, N.Y., studying Arabic grammar.

And then late one night, about eight months after 9/11, with Randy and the children fast asleep, the former high school cheerleader and Miss Congeniality looked at her computer keyboard, took a deep breath and entered a chat room called The Arab Castle. This time, instead of merely monitoring the chatter she began typing, in Arabic, a message from an IP address set in the Middle East.

"*Al-mawt al-Amrika!*" Rossmiller wrote, the very words making her recoil and tingle with anticipation at the same time. "*Al-mawt al-Amrika!*"

THERE WOULD BE NO REVERSING COURSE NOW, neither for the start of this new life nor the end of the old. For a time, Rossmiller tried to be both—tried to be Superwoman, as she calls it. By day, she ebbed and flowed with her kids' schedules, the fickle Rocky Mountain Front weather, and crowded court dockets. By night, she waded ever deeper into a landscape of anger, intrigue and fear, a world in which she moved so adeptly that this seemingly ordinary woman from an ordinary Montana town would become, on her own time and her own dime, America's No. 1 civilian terrorist hunter.

Over the next 11 years, operating under as many as 32 Arabic aliases, Rossmiller built trust with tightly wound Muslim men who sold Stinger missiles, detonated bombs with cell phones, and sought to acquire nuclear weapons. She helped the Federal Bureau of Investigation and U.S. Army on their path to widely publicized terrorist prosecutions—most notably a soldier at Fort Lewis, Wash., who was sharing military secrets with al-Qaeda and a Pennsylvania man plotting to plunge America into economic ruin by blowing up oil and gas pipelines. Over time, she would be credited with creating the current template for the U.S. government's cyber-counterintelligence efforts.

In those same 11 years, Rossmiller watched her marriage, lifelong friendships and health unravel. Randy and the kids would require 24-hour protections. Her Pontiac Grand Prix would be stolen, trashed and riddled with bullets, and her family later spared tragedy only when four armed Muslim men driving a rented truck toward the Rossmiller home careened into a ditch near Valier. By 2006, she would feel compelled to leave her familiar surroundings in Conrad for relative anonymity in Helena. Eventually outed as an unlikely wife-mother-judge spy, she would be dogged by reporters.

Most days she ran on adrenaline and the deeply anchored motives that pushed her to continue even as conventional wisdom told her to stop. And occasionally, as her new life absorbed more of her time and thoughts, she would find a quiet place to think about an old life that was slipping away, and cry.

E LEVEN YEARS LATER, Rossmiller, now 42, sits in a restaurant in southwest Montana's Ruby Valley. She eats mashed potatoes with a fork and nurses a chocolate shake—typical fare these days for a woman whose ulcers could erupt at the slightest provoking.

"You couldn't write a script for how this happened," she says. "If it hadn't happened to me I wouldn't believe it myself."

However a terrorist hunter is supposed to look, surely this isn't it. Blonde with tired but friendly green eyes, her figure country sturdy but trim, and wearing snug jeans, she looks as if she just stepped from a combine or a Wrangler commercial. She has come to the Ruby because she cherishes its simple pleasures; fishing its trout-rich waters, riding ATVs in the surrounding mountains, and walking along quiet rural roads.

Nor can her motives be cast in one neat psychological profile. Yes, she attached American flags to her car and pinned them on her clothes. She avows Christian and conservative values, calls herself "more patriotic an American than ever," and talks fervently about "understanding the enemy." At the same time, she has acquired an abiding affection for Islam, a faith she describes as "beautiful" and "wonderful." She bristles at the counterproductive ignorance of talking-head terrorism "experts" on right- and left-wing news networks, chastises her own culture for being too insular in an increasingly global arena, and often fantasizes about visiting or even living in Lahore, Pakistan, one of the Middle East's cultural and religious centers.

How did she get to this place? It is a question she has asked herself daily for 11 years.

One life can't entirely begin and another end on the same day, of course. Rossmiller's complex journey harkens back four decades, to those same wheat and barley fields of northern Montana. Bright, inquisitive and just, well, different, Rossmiller at age 3½ was enrolled in a Montessori school; she quickly learned to speak fluent French and converse in Spanish and Russian. Tedious stretches sitting side-by-side with her college-educated father on the seat of their combine stirred her imagination. Long summer days revealed limitless storybook possibilities in the lands stretching to the Rocky Mountains. Unable to sleep more than three or four hours a night even as a small child, she'd slip out of the house in the wee-hour darkness to build theme forts across the farm. Once, her parents found her asleep in a garden at dawn and locked her in the house. At such times, she would read voraciously, often about the macabre.

For her end-of-year fifth-grade project she chose serial killers, and asked to be the final presenter. When the class wasn't nearly as impressed as she'd dreamt, and the principal criticized the report as "disturbing," she spent the entire summer as a devastated outcast.

"I've always been kind of a weird, twisted person," she concedes.

After high school, Rossmiller left Conrad long enough to take a few law-related courses in college, first criminal law at the University of Montana in Missoula and then paralegal at the College of Great Falls. Both schools were a comfortable fit—and so was Randy, a family friend from nearby Dutton whom she wed soon after a brief first marriage; partly, she says, "because it was just easy." In 2000, the couple sold their farm and moved into Conrad proper, where she was asked, as a 32-year-old paralegal, to become the municipal judge—Montana doesn't require a law degree for the position—after the sitting judge stepped down.

Then came the attacks and her immediate immersion into an intoxicating, invigorating, paradoxical world.

"I don't know if I just wanted the thrill or the challenge or to tell people this view of America is wrong," she recalls. "I didn't have a plan. It just started as an interest."

Within seven months, Rossmiller had created her first Arabic identity: Abu Khadija, an Algerian extremist. With a gift for what one friend describes as "cyber-theatrics," she began a deft dance requiring a credible blend of emotion, imprecise language and compelling themes. It was an art she mastered. Especially convincing for authenticity: the routine sharing of videos showing westerners being beheaded.

Soon after creating her first Arabic identity, Rossmiller convinced a Pakistani man that she was an Islamic arms dealer wanting to purchase his stolen U.S. Stinger missiles. Using a Persian Gulf dialect, she coaxed him to provide identification numbers for the arms. She put the information on a CD and drove to an FBI office in Great Falls. She remembers the faces of the four men sitting across the table listening to a Montana farm girl talk about a Stinger missile cache in the Middle East. She was sure they thought she was a kook.

"I think they did at first," she says, chuckling at the memory. "I had to pull out my Supreme Court card. Hey, I'm no dumb blonde—I'm actually kind of smart."

A few weeks later, the FBI called. The military found the stolen arms. It was Rossmiller's first chat-room sting.

She next learned that al-Qaeda planned to use cell phones to detonate bombs in western neighborhoods in Saudi Arabia, along with hotels frequented by Americans and Europeans. This time, she wasn't heeded. Four days after providing the FBI with a tip, three bombs rocked Riyadh, killing 34 westerners; a few days after that, five explosions rattled Casablanca, Morocco, killing 20 and injuring more than 100.

These episodes occurred within 20 months of the attacks, and Rossmiller was still living a double life. Yet neither Randy, the kids nor the residents of Conrad had any inkling of the extent of Rossmiller's subterfuge.

All that began to change in October 2003, when Rossmiller saw a chat-room message in English from a man in the Seattle area identifying himself as Amir Abdul Rashid. Through a series of 30 emails over four months, Spec. Ryan G. Anderson began sharing military secrets. He exposed the vulnerabilities of American tanks and revealed locations of U.S. troops in Iraq. In February 2004, eight days before he was to be deployed, Anderson was arrested.

Rossmiller says she initially was promised anonymity to protect her Arabic identity and her family's safety. But then she was told Anderson had the right to face his accuser. Now her name, her family, her hometown, her job and her online identity were public. Anderson was convicted of five counts of treason and sent to prison for life, but for Rossmiller the price of patriotism was high.

"It was over," she says. "They said my name, my three kids and that I was from Montana, but once they said I was a judge it was chaos. Nothing was in my control."

Media swarmed her after the verdict. A military escort provided a shield, but images of her pushing through the hordes were beamed worldwide. Finally in her car and driving alone back to her hotel, she tearfully replayed the unreal events of the past two years. She called Randy hoping for empathy; instead she was met with rage over the magnitude of her wee-hour endeavors and for the dramatic life changes ahead. Her cell phone rang and rang—nearly 50 times from reporters alone.

Equally disheartening for Rossmiller was the outing of Abu Khadija, the Algerian extremist that had served her so well as her Arabic alter ego. Abu Khadija had been her late-night companion, a best friend. Now she had to bury him.

"I was devastated," she says.

Suddenly everything was so different. Jihadists who had been chatting with Abu Khadija threatened to kill her, their ire inflamed by the revelation they had been fooled by a woman. In December 2005, Rossmiller's car was stolen from the family garage and dumped in a Teton County reservoir. A security system was installed in their home. Stunned friends and neighbors kept a wary distance. Local law enforcement had a new and heady task to add to the mundane that filled most of their days. Rossmiller bought her own .38 and kept it at her side.

Quit? No. Rossmiller couldn't forget. She couldn't ignore her hunger to understand the hatred for America. Above all, she couldn't abandon the thrill of the chase. Every night until midnight and every morning at 3, like clockwork, she was at her computer.

"I couldn't stay up late enough or get up early enough," she says.

In October 2005, Rossmiller had an online meeting with Pennsylvania native Michael C. Reynolds, who thought he was chatting with a fellow jihadist named Hani. They talked about how to blow up the Alaska pipeline. Within two months, Rossmiller's online sleuthing led to Reynolds' arrest in Pocatello, Idaho, where he had materials for making explosives that he had purchased at Walmart; he is serving a 30-year prison sentence. Unlike her emotional reaction to the Anderson verdict, though, Rossmiller felt as if she'd just shampooed the living-room carpet.

"I certainly had the passion that he gets justice," she says. "But when the verdict was read, I was like, 'Oh good.' "

This media circus, too, came with a price. In July 2006, amid the Reynolds trial, four Muslim men—from Bahrain, Eritrea and Suriname—drove through an unmanned U.S.-Canada border crossing in a Ryder truck, using gravel backroads to avoid detection. Their destination: Conrad. Twenty miles from the Rossmiller home, they miscalculated a corner near Valier and crashed, injuring one enough to require medical treatment. Local authorities found Qurans, GPS mapping equipment with Rossmiller's address programmed into it, and disassembled weapons. Her husband was ordered to round up the kids and leave the house.

By now, Rossmiller realized she could no longer stay in Conrad. She took a job with the attorney general's office in Helena.

THIS IS WHERE YET ANOTHER LIFE BEGINS, long after the first one has ended. At the restaurant in the Ruby Valley, Rossmiller ponders 11 years of twists and turns. She and Randy are divorced and aren't speaking. Her children are grown and living in Missoula. She is a grandmother. Another man shares her daily world.

She is trying to recapture a sense of "priceless peace" in her new home, especially after her health wake-up call in 2007. She began spitting up blood and learned she had life-threatening ulcers. Her doctor told her she had the body of a 60-year-old.

In 2009, she left Helena to become a cyber-intelligence consultant; she travels the country giving talks and seminars for law enforcement. The public fervor over her work has subsided, and despite her continued espionage she says she no longer worries about her safety, though she still carries her "beautiful .38." She carefully watches her diet. For therapy, she has written a book about her journey, with Sue Carswell, titled *The Unexpected Patriot.*

Yet the forces deep within beckon as powerfully as ever. She fights a war against an unseen enemy, one she believes is more dangerous than ever in part because of the missteps of her own country.

"I'm as patriotic as they come, but I think the biggest mistake we make is not trying to understand them," she says of Muslims. "They are extremely different from what we know, and as in our world there are good and bad. I have always been fascinated by how different we are and how we are perceived. How can we all be so human and be so polar opposite? Our hearts all pump the same."

What if she could turn back the clock? Knowing what she knows now, would she have spent those six weeks in bed watching sitcom reruns? Her answer is as dichotomous as the dueling cultures that fascinate her and the parallel lifestyles she once tried to live.

On the one hand, Rossmiller's service to her country is unquestioned. In 2007, James K. Hellwig, director of the U.S. Department of Commerce, wrote to Rossmiller: "You really deserve both a Congressional and a Presidential medal for your valor and outstanding efforts." Said *The Investigative Project* author Steven Emerson in 2009: "Our entire country owes her an immeasurable debt of gratitude." She has received words of appreciation from the Central Intelligence Agency, government counterterrorism officials, and branches of the military. Relatives of 9/11 victims call or write to express heartfelt thanks.

She refuses to let go of Sept. 11, her persistent desire to further understand the ideology fueling the attacks, and the love of a chase birthed somewhere on the bountiful prairies of northern Montana.

And yet ...

"IN HINDSIGHT I WONDER IF I WAS SELFISH. I know the reason why I did it, but look at what it cost my personal life," she says. Then she waves her hand, as if to dismiss the notion. "I know I'd do it again," she says. "I'd definitely do it again."

Admittedly, Rossmiller sometimes wonders if she'll ever shake the ghosts of choices she's made. That's when she daydreams of Lahore, a bustling cultural center of six million, a place that calls to her from Pakistan's Punjab Province. She could move there, immerse herself in the culture and, she says half-jokingly, "become a Super-burqa-woman."

She quickly eschews that idea, too. She will, she is certain, always be in Montana, where on a September day in 2001, one life ended and another began. ◄

Girls with Guns

By Alan Kesselheim

Winter 2014

I F YOU'VE BEEN AROUND MONTANA A WHILE, you know the Kari Swenson saga. How in July of 1984, Swenson, a promising biathlete earning respect on the world stage, was out on a training run near Big Sky and was abducted by two faux "mountain men" with a bizarre plan to turn her into a wilderness bride. How Alan Goldstein, stumbling onto the scene, was tragically shot to death by Don Nichols. How Swenson was shot in the chest by Dan Nichols and left chained to a tree, where she spent hours waiting for rescue near Goldstein's lifeless body.

Sadly, for many people, that story is the only way they know anything at all about the sport of biathlon. Also, sadly, that sensational news spasm is the sum total of their acquaintance with Kari Swenson.

Most people don't know or remember that after her ordeal Swenson spent two years rehabilitating from her injuries and came back to compete in the top echelon of her sport. Nor that Swenson went on to become a respected veterinarian. They don't know that Swenson, now in her early 50s, is part of the energy infusing a heady resurgence of biathlon in Montana, serving on the board of directors for the Bridger Biathlon Club and mentoring young athletes. Or that late last summer, Swenson suffered an appalling horseback riding accident and survived a battery of life-threatening injuries, including a bunch of broken ribs and vertebrae and two brain bleeds, that required a flight-for-life evacuation from the Montana backcountry.

Swenson got into the sport of biathlon for much the same reason young people are signing up today. She was already skiing, training and competing with the local Bridger Ski Foundation, but when she heard about this quirky tangential sport, which involved shooting at tiny distant targets, she was intrigued.

"I'd never shot a gun before," Swenson admits. "It was a huge challenge and responsibility, mental as well as physical. To ski as hard as you can, and then still yourself and shoot. It caught my imagination.

"Also," Swenson adds, "It was a sport that hadn't accepted women. That was part of what provoked me, too. We were pioneers."

"My brother, Paul, got into the sport," Swenson remembers. "My parents volunteered. Dad built a range in the backyard with railroad ties for a backstop. Our house was a revolving door of skiers and coaches coming and going. It was like a youth hostel."

"The whole family skied together," says Bob Swenson, Kari's father. "It never mattered to me whether our kids won. It was about participating. If you participate, you win. That's what it's still about."

Thirty years after her abduction, Swenson remains fit and athletic, and she is still participating. She skis every winter, preferring lonely backcountry tours with her dogs to groomed trails and race events. She is engaged with the budding local resurgence of biathlon. And she remains as outspoken as ever.

"People say I'm stubborn," she says, a little ruefully.

But then, when you think of the things she's overcome, maybe that's what got her where she is.

At first glance, biathlon seems like a strange, conflicted sport, something contrived by sadistic organizers to focus on extremes. Skiers race as fast as they can using a skate-ski technique on a groomed course, then come into a shooting range where they have to calm their bodies enough to shoot five tiny targets 50 meters away from both standing and prone positions. Then they sling the 22-caliber rifle over their shoulder and ski like hell again. Plus, they are assessed penalty laps for every missed target. The crux of the challenge centers on pacing energy output and finding the balance between all-out skiing effort and the focus and accuracy it takes to hit a target.

"It is all about strategy and overcoming problems," says Stuart Jennings, a Bozeman biathlete who trained and competed with Swenson 30 years ago. "It's always something—the wind, your scope steaming up, a rifle that jams. It's often not the best athlete who wins, but the person who makes the best decisions and manages the obstacles."

Contrived as it seems, there are practical roots to biathlon that go back thousands of years. In fact, 4,000-year-old cave art in Norway depicts two ancient hunters on skis, doing more or less what modern biathletes do—ski hard in pursuit of prey, then settle down enough to make an accurate shot, but with more primitive weapons.

"It probably happened in the Montana mountains as well," says Jennings. "There are sites that go back thousands of years within a few miles of Bohart Ranch, where we train and compete today. Those people had to get around in winter conditions, presumably on crude skis or snowshoes, and they hunted to survive."

Prehistoric biathletes, perhaps . . .

More recently, skiing and shooting has been featured as a military discipline, especially in Scandinavian countries. The rest of the world took note when, in the 1939 Winter War, the Finnish Army, on skis, held off an invading Russian force that outnumbered them 10 to 1. Notably, in the Battle of Suomussalmi, 11,000 Finnish soldiers annihilated a force of 45,000 Russian troops. Nimble soldiers on skis could match the speed of light cavalry, and were able to outmaneuver and decimate Russian troops and tanks for months. After that, ski troops sprouted up around the world, including in the United States, with the famed 10th Mountain Division. Early biathlon competitions grew out of military training events.

"A lot of the first push for biathlon in the U.S. came from the National Guard," Swenson says. "I had friends join the Guard not because they wanted to be in the military, but because they could continue to train and get paid."

"Back then, there was also a lot of chauvinism to overcome," says Swenson. "It took a long time for women to be accepted in the sport." In fact, women's biathlon didn't become an Olympic event until 1992.

"I remember training in Italy in the '80s," Swenson says. "We were in the rural countryside and local people were watching. The men started yelling at us. We didn't understand what they were saying, so we asked an interpreter. They were shouting at us to go home and cook and raise children, saying that women had no place shooting guns or ski racing. As if giving birth is so easy!" she says with a laugh. "Of course, now there are dozens of countries competing, including Italy, which has a proud tradition of women biathletes. It is a hugely popular sport there."

It turns out that women are often better all-around biathletes than men.

"Boys' sports go all-out, all the time," says Eric Love, one of the cofounders of Bridger Biathlon Club. "The idea of holding back doesn't come naturally. Girls are more coachable, better listeners, and they have that ability to pace themselves and focus when they need to."

"When I was competing, it was common for women to outscore men on the range," agrees Swenson.

"If you give me 10 girls and 10 boys to train in an hour, the girls will be better every time," says Jennings, now one of the local biathlon coaches.

The season before her 1984 abduction, Swenson competed in the first women's World Championship races in Chamonix, France. Swenson skied one leg of the women's relay team, where her team surprised the world by capturing bronze. Then she finished fifth, behind four Russians, in the 10-kilometer individual final.

"I've had two perfect races in my career," Swenson says. "That was one of them. Everything was perfect—the weather, my skis, the gun, my focus. Totally in the zone. I realized, part way through that race, that the crowd was chanting my name. I was leading at the time, but I'd never had that happen before. 'Swenson! Swenson!' I'd come into the range and after every shot I made they roared. Everyone else was shooting, too, but they were yelling for me. They'd be really polite and quiet while I took aim, then they'd erupt every time I hit the target. Thank God I shot clean."

For Swenson, regaining her form after her abduction and injuries took two excruciating years. Even then, she was plagued by lingering nerve damage that crippled her with pain, and by reduced lung capacity. Despite all of that, she skied solidly in the World Cup in Norway in 1986.

After a lot of soul-searching at the end of the 1986 season, in her mid-20s Swenson decided to leave competitive skiing and biathlon.

"My coach was really angry," she remembers. "But I was still dealing with debilitating nerve pain, and honestly, I looked ahead at the years of training and the prospects as a professional skier, and it didn't add up. I knew people who stayed too long in the sport and never really blossomed. Then they had to regroup and figure out what to do with themselves. As it turned out, it would have been another six years before a chance at the Olympics would have come up. I couldn't wait that long.

"In Europe skiers are on billboards and advertisements, they can actually make money and have a career in the sport. In America, even an Olympic medal in skiing doesn't get you much."

Swenson came back to enroll in veterinary school in Fort Collins, Colorado. She graduated in 1990, but her ties to biathlon kept tugging at her.

"I did a stint as an assistant coach with the United States biathlon team after I got out of school, but I didn't stay very long," Swenson says. "I think I might have been a little too outspoken," she says with a laugh.

She returned to Colorado to start practicing veterinary medicine, and, on the side, helped build a biathlon program in Winter Park.

The biathlon theme followed her back to Bozeman, where she relocated in 1995, and has now found an outlet in the budding biathlon club. No matter that Swenson's life has many chapters unrelated to skiing, her story, her triumph over adversity, and her inspiration remain undimmed within the biathlon community, especially in southwest Montana.

"When Kari is around, or at a meet, you can just see the young girls idolizing her," says Love. "The fact that Kari is willing to give back to our kids in this sport, especially our daughters, it makes me want to cry."

"I wish I could have started when I was 10," Swenson says. "Biathlon has done so much for me, handling emotions, overcoming hardships, building confidence, managing crisis situations, keeping that mental focus.

"I love to feel I'm helping to make kids better skiers, shooters, people."

And it isn't only Swenson. "Biathlon DNA has been floating around this part of Montana for a long time," stresses Jennings. "People like Brian Wadsworth, Clarissa Werre, Mark Shepard. There are communities of biathletes in West Yellowstone, and Casper and Cody, Wyoming. It goes deep. I keep running into people who say, 'Oh yeah, I still have my old rifle sitting in a closet.'"

Love and Bridger Biathlon Club cofounder Jim Sites both blame Clarissa Werre for pulling their kids into the biathlon orbit. Werre competed and trained with the U.S. National Biathlon Team in the 1990s and now teaches at Longfellow Elementary School in Bozeman, which both Love's and Sites' kids attended.

"One day my son Alex came home and announced that he wanted to be a biathlete," says Love. "He was 7. I didn't take it very seriously and I didn't know anything about the sport. Half-jokingly I told him that if he kept up training for a couple of years, I'd get him a gun. Ever since, there's been no stopping him and I had to make good on the promise with an Anschutz rifle."

Ben Sites also caught the bug, and the two friends have been training together for years now. Moreover, their fathers were drawn into the sport, and eventually had to do something to give the enthusiasm an outlet.

"We got our nonprofit status in 2013," says Love. "We've been raising money and organizing ever since. Already we have 200 to 300 members and some 45 skiers enrolled. We've bought rifles and targets. We're using Bohart Ranch for training and races."

"Look, what could be more Montana than guns and skis?" asks Katie Smith, who handles marketing for the club.

Jim Sites' daughter, Abby, started training at age 12, following her brother's lead. Abby is a shy kid who typically avoids competition and admits to test anxiety at school. Little by little, she has taken on more racing, and she serves as an example of a kid for whom participation is the magic.

"I get this great warm feeling whenever I hit a target," she says. "It's intimidating at first. I mean you're holding something that can kill.

"I don't usually like people watching me, but I just tell myself that it's another day of practice. And it's really nice to be around people like Kari and Miss Werre. It's made me better with tests at school too."

"The point is to promote healthy living," stresses Love. "It is about having fun, gaining a lifelong skill, becoming confident and fit, better human beings."

"If these kids still love skiing when they're 30, we've succeeded," adds Jennings.

In a milestone event in September of 2014, Bridger Biathlon Club built a state-of-the-art shooting range at Bohart Ranch so they can hold sanctioned events. "We have two races scheduled for the 2014–15 season," reports Love.

"Biathlon is a huge spectator sport in Europe," Love continues. "It is second only to soccer in terms of viewers. In America it has a ways to go. People don't really even know what it is. They say things like, 'Is that the Ironman thing?' when you talk about it."

As for Swenson, the resilience and fortitude she gained as a biathlete keep resonating. Late last summer, she went on a horse-packing trip with friends into the Cabin Creek drainage, north of West Yellowstone.

"We were spending the night at the Forest Service cabin," she remembers. "Very late, someone noticed that the horses had gotten loose. A couple of us headed out after them. Usually I wear a helmet and flak jacket when I ride, but that night, I went out with just jeans and a T-shirt.

"We caught the horses a couple of miles down the trail. I hopped on my horse to ride back, but he spooked and bucked me off."

It was a terrifying, violent moment, miles down the trail in the pitch dark. Lying on the ground, Swenson knew she was seriously hurt. She also knew she had to get help. "You do what you gotta do," she says. "Life is like that."

Swenson walked two miles over rough trail back to the cabin. "I think when you're used to training and competing until you puke, you develop a different threshold for pain," Swenson says. "It sets you up for a life of overcoming things, a mental and physical strength."

Turned out that Swenson had nine fractured ribs, serious lung injuries, a slew of broken vertebrae, a pelvic fracture, a concussion and two brain bleeds.

"If I had known that," she mulls, "I don't know . . ."

When she got to the cabin, her friends didn't fully appreciate the extent of her injuries until Swenson instructed them to send an SOS with their emergency beacon. Really, they asked, you think that's necessary?

Within hours, a helicopter managed to land near the cabin. For Swenson, the harrowing scene must have been reminiscent of her rescue three decades earlier, chained to a tree and bleeding from a gunshot wound, her world reeling. The fact that she has again recovered, and that, no doubt, she will be riding horses once more, is also an echo of her past.

"She's an extraordinary, tough woman," says Love. "When I talked to her later, still in her hospital room, the first thing she said was how bummed she was that she missed the Biathlon Club board meeting." ◪

FICTION

*Sometimes, the truth is bigger
than the facts.*

Twilight on the Little Bighorn

By Allen Morris Jones

Fall 2014

THE MORNING BEFORE OUR SLAUGHTER, I fretted: What if it happens that I'm a coward? What if I have to take a shit? In fact, there was little opportunity for cowardice, and I finally clenched up tighter'n a cork in a bottle. We needed to pee, we were thirsty. Poles, bohunks, Irishmen, Dutchmen, we died looking only to make a living. We did not consider ourselves historical. We were not remarkable. God, I was thirsty. That first charge? I went dry as sandstone. We feared nothing so much as embarrassment. Indians flowed up the hill in defiance of gravity, expectation, reason. I prayed, and when prayers fell short, I thought, *Damn you*, aiming the curse not at the heathens who would shortly be gutting us to the man but rather toward the incompetent who had put us in this fix. Custer, I mean.

IT AIN'T SO BAD. At first, there's that sloshy, seasick, jet-lag kind of feeling—a painful decoupling, a sense of simultaneously standing and falling—but after that, yeah, it ain't so bad at all. Absent ambition, hunger, thirst, you can sit at your ease and watch the world ratchet on past. I will admit that I'm the odd man out, though. Others are less pleased.

Take the General, for instance. Or the "general," as some folks like to put it. Courtesy calls for the use of his wartime rank, but there are those among us who are recently running short of courtesy. The man is one hundred and sixty pounds of conceit in a ten-pound bag. One of those who found virtue in scorn, derision, belittlement. It's about such men that history is written. Not me, not us. Rather, those who insist that the story should be about them, and by their insistence, make it so. We always said he was nothing but hot air and now he ain't even that. What keeps him around? It can't be our company. You'll sometimes see him with Lieutenant Cooke or his brother, Tom, but otherwise he keeps to himself, mumbling. Squinting at the horizon. Pretending to scribble notes into his palm. Still trying to piece it all together. His epic ass-kicking. How'd it all go wrong? It's clear to everyone but him.

Bad scouting reports, he says. That's his line. I'm heartily sick of those words. Bad scouting reports. There are days he'll take his Remington rifle—a noble piece of weaponry—and swing it from the stock like a saber, cut at the grasses, clang sparks against the corners of the monument, chop at the dirt itself. *Scouting reports!* he'll shout. Meadowlarks flush, gophers chirp and duck. When he's in a good mood, he'll present himself unbloodied. White buckskin and red scarf, wide-brimmed hat. "Sergeant," he's said to me, "I'll have breakfast in my tent this morning." He'll take off his hat to run a hand over his shorn scalp, a man still adjusting to his haircut. Other days, he don't speak to nobody. You'll see his face curtained in dried blood, bullet holes in temple and breast, naked from the waist down and one thigh slashed to the bone, the wooden shaft of an arrow tick-tocking out of his private parts. He'll stare about, wide-eyed. How'd I get *here?*

I NEVER SAID A WORD TO MITCH BOUYER IN LIFE—the scouts kept to themselves, by and large—but we fell on the same patch of grass. His arm over my knees, my blood in his trousers. I knew him by his piebald vest. In the early years, when the battle still raged around us—before the most ardent of us were the first to fade—back when you'd glance up to see a charge of Indians galloping bareback down the ridge, whooping, heels kicking hard, back when the Garryowen boys were still shooting their own horses to make bulwarks, again and again, Mitch and me would sit with ankles crossed, take in the show.

That first time, he spat tobacco, eyed my stripes. "We're dead, ain't we, Sarge. *Nous sommes mort?*"

I buried a finger in my bullet hole. "*Mort* as hell."

"Them others don't know it yet."

"I don't believe they do."

"*Pauvres bougres.*"

Bullets whined, arrows thunked into flesh, horses screamed. Somewhere in the haze, a man sobbed for his mother. The smells of gunpowder and dust, sweat and the tang of fresh blood. I said, "Where'd you come by tobacco?"

He cocked up on one hip for his twist. "Help yourself."

"Obliged. Where'd you get it?"

"Always had it, is all."

I arrived with my clothes, my Springfield, a letter from Nancy. Three pages of uncertain, blocky hand describing how William was just a few days from crawling. "He kan role over," she wrote, "grab a kob doll if I put it out afore him." She signed her letters with her full name. "My love, Nancy de Rasqaille." Our shared surname a fiction, changed after that mess down in Alabama. Nancy took to it willingly, bless her heart. I did love her. Heavy-nostriled and thick-lipped though she was, she was good hearted. She lived with a misery in her teeth but never let the pain show. I keep her memory like a candle you protect room to room. I cannot consider how she must have taken my death. The thought hobbles me.

VEN AS I WAS SHOT, I locked eyes with my killer, a red heathen crouched not fifty yards away, his ancient muzzleloader still smoking from barrel and breach. Blood pulsed warm over my fingers. I coughed up iron. A ragged hole bubbled air, and bone grated against bone. *Why?* Why me and not some other? I saw no justice in it.

He wore turkey feathers and black grease paint up the left half of his face, red on the right. For the Lakota, the colors of a brave man. A breach clout and a quill breastplate. His name, as I learned, was Counts Enemies, and he met his own reward not long after introducing me to mine. Catch him at a distracted moment, he'll let you see the ropes of intestine swinging out through the hole in his stomach.

Indians are standoffish. You'll hear them more than see them. They're fond of their dirges. The low, keening, vowel-heavy laments. Is it the wind or an eagle or what? Took me sixty or seventy years, but I finally reached out. It's harder to get to know people these days: Everybody's got their own afterlives, everybody's so busy. I come up to Counts Enemies and said, "Charlie de Rasqaille. They call me Rascal. Company B.

I do believe you're the one what kilt me."

Would he show resentment or anger? Maybe an aw-shucks kind of grin, maybe some of that *bonhomie*? No. Only skepticism. He squinted at me like I was a page he was trying to decipher.

"You speak English?"

He pushed out his lips. Finally said, "English ain't what none of us been speaking here white bread."

"Ohhkay…"

He pointed his lips toward Custer, toward where the General was putting on one of his shows, taking the high ground, declaiming, gesturing, ordering troops into position. "Any chance you could get him to shut the hell up?"

"Well, he's my commanding officer. My … you'd say chief, I reckon."

He spat dryly. "You think I don't know what a commanding officer is?"

"I, uh …"

"Jesus, you *wašíču*, all alike. Nobody knows shit but you."

"Sorry. I'm sorry."

Custer was reeling now between clumps of sagebrush, stumbling, fading in and out. Singing, "Old Susannah, don't you cry for me."

Counts Enemies watched him resentfully. "That guy creeps me out, man."

FLORETS GREW TO THISTLE, flowers ballooned into seeds. Tourists scrolled through like shadows thrown by a magic lantern. We picked up the news of the day in faint echoes, gossip, snippets of radio through open car windows. Sheets of newsprint catching on the grass. The fall of the Hapsburgs and the rise of the Bushes. Wars and assassinations, genetic engineering, cameras on phones. A moon landing, a Mars Rover. We saw biplanes growl low, then, in an instant, the sloppy stitchery of passing jets. Bouyer described again how it was to first take the full measure of Sitting Bull's village. The heat-wave mirage of tepees across the river bottom. "We seen that herd of ponies, and we told the General, even before we seen the tepees, we said, *big ass* village. We *told* him. So then what's he go and do? Hell, he divides his troops. I mean, *shrewd*, right?"

Counts Enemies appeared above us, ignoring Bouyer. "I been thinking, white bread."

"Oh?"

"I been thinking, I do believe you may be the first white man who ever said sorry to me. Ever apologized. For ... *any*thing."

"Huh."

"Think about that for a minute."

"Yeah, I mean, wow."

He grabbed my shoulder, used it to ease himself to the ground. "You ain't so bad. Rascal, you said?"

"Yeah."

"Maybe you can answer me a question, there, Rascal."

"Shoot."

Counts Enemies found this funny. He bared his teeth and cocked a finger, dropped the trigger. Bouyer snorted, let a breeze roll him on down Greasy Grass Ridge. A Lakota breed married into the Crow, Bouyer's had it rough. *Pauvre* Mitch. Lonelier than me.

"Why ain't you moved on?"

I hid my ignorance. "Why ain't *you*?"

"The battle." He showed his teeth again, a grin or a snarl.

"Eh?"

An Indian strode by with a fresh scalp held high, dripping; bashful with his success. Counts Enemies watched him fondly. "Who'd *want* to leave?"

"Me? I don't know."

"We are made to fight." He thumped his chest. "Our blood was so hot, our bodies couldn't hold it in."

"My wife was pregnant when I left."

"Regret's a hungry little mouse in your chest. It gnaws, white bread."

"His name was William."

"What do you want, an apology?"

"We did what we had to do."

He accepted this somberly, in the manner of a great truth. "We *did*, man."

WHAT COMES NEXT? We become birds, is one hopeful theory. Or, less happily, ghosts to ghosts. Or we simply disperse into grass, wind. I don't mind that thought. Is it regret that keeps us here? Fear? We all have our ideas.

Counts Enemies and Bouyer became friends the way tree bark grows around barbed wire. Animosity degrades first to tolerance then to fondness. Counts Enemies sat combing through his long black hair, picking out grass seeds. Bouyer sucked on his teeth and told us about Custer. They were a stove I held my hands to. I talked about Nancy, our boy. "Did he ever live to his manhood? I think about it." I told them about how my pap died at First Manassas, how my older brother, Clyde, finished the raising of me. "Nancy was cousin to my cousins." I did not share, will never share, how Nancy had begged me to stay. "We'll start over with my people down in Georgia." Leaving the yard, I'd pried her fingers off my ankle. This choice rather than that, left rather than right, guilt like a boot on my throat. Who the hell did Custer think he was, to take all this from me?

WE WAVERED, we flickered. Cheatgrass twisted up through crumbs of dirt, unfurled, flourished, wilted. Snow blew. Butterflies scratched out of cocoons only to be snagged at first flap by robins. We cheered for the birds. A mule deer doe, ribs showing, picked at grass grown through my bones. I felt her teeth. The tourists gained weight and became fond of tattoos, left their air-conditioned cars only reluctantly. A Catholic priest, florid above his clerical collar, tipped over by the monument. He arrived with one corner of his mouth pulled down by his stroke, smelling of piss and Dentyne. Hiking boots and a black blouse tucked into his Wranglers. "Ish that really Cusshter?"

We assured him it was. "What's in your fanny pack there, Father?" Turns out, a flask; a good Scotch. We toasted the priest's health, and passed his booze along, and along, and along.

The priest was a Custer enthusiast. "This wash my sixth trip to the battlefield."

"You don't say."

"He wash a schoolteacher, you know. Seventeen yearsh old, he taught school."

"I might have heard something."

"Monaseeta? Raped her, gave her an illegitimate child. Randy old basshtard, your general."

"Ain't *my* general," Bouyer mumbled.

I said to the priest, "You'll fit right in. Ain't a one of us can stop talking about the man."

The priest wore a sardonic half-smile. Sardonic or his stroke. He stared sidelong at our Seventh blues and blood. The Lakota in his feathers. Bouyer the breed, his face broad as a baseball glove. Custer, at a distance. "Bad scouting!" the General cried, pointing at Bouyer, glanc-

275

ing about for affirmation. His eyes found the priest. Eh now? A fresh audience. He drew close, squatting. I'd forgotten how the man could wound with his gaze. How you tilted toward his judgment. He touched his mustache, stroking it flat, and stared at Bouyer. Something vibrated between them. Bouyer was the weaker, and looked away first.

"Incompetence," Custer said. "Killed us all."

I must've made a noise, for his gaze fell on me. "Sergeant. I'm still your commanding officer. You ever want to leave this rat hole, you need to think about that. Think about loyalty. *Rascal.*"

I had grown accustomed to my resentment. Learned to let it slumber. But it awakened again, hissing up from its coil. "Yessir."

The General snorted, left us to find his horse. We watched him lead Vic down toward the water. The slow, echoing clop of hooves. Bouyer said, "He needs to quit talking to me like that."

"He does, he *does*." I reached back for the flask. "But I got no ideas."

The flask was gone, and the priest with it. Loss is the water in which we swim.

Counts Enemies scratched at his belly. "Me, I been thinking about it."

Bouyer fixed on him.

"Yeah," Counts Enemies inspected his fingernails for blood, fat, fascia. "I got ideas."

WE SPENT OUR WINTER AMONG THE HEADSTONES, drifting. Gift shop to Entrenchment Trail, riverbank to ridgeline. We looked for agreement, and found not one dissenting soul, not one who refused our invitation. Even the General's own brother, Tom—that sad man sitting with a dismembered testicle in each hand, a feminine absence where his manhood used to be—even Tom was nodding before we were finished. "Sure. Yeah. I'll do it."

WE FRETTED THAT WE MIGHT FINALLY LOSE OUR COLLECTIVE WILL. Bouyer said, "What if I don't have the guts? *Les couilles.* It's the *General*, man." I was sympathetic. "You'll be fine." Counts Enemies, the opaque slab of his face oddly vulnerable, shorn of just enough skin to show uncertainty, repeated it. "We'll be fine."

We found Custer at twilight, posed on the slight knoll he'd come to claim as his own, an unremarkable wrinkle in the long slope of grass. Just the same as all the other grass, save for the fact that it had received the blood of a man who'd felt himself worthy of ordering other men to their deaths. Flurries, and the sky dully aglow with snow and setting sun. Custer stood, hat in hand, taking the measure of the wind.

Bouyer drew himself up from the grass.

"You!" Custer said, offended by the incursion. He squared his hat on his head. "You miserable, incompetent. ..."

The rest of us rose behind Bouyer, flanking him.

Counts Enemies' notion? Nothing wounds an ego so much as scorn; there's no greater fear for a bully than being set apart. The only civilized response to arrogance is laughter. We were Lakota and Cheyenne, warriors and women, a handful of desolate children. And the men of the Seventh Cavalry, elbow to elbow with the cousins of Sitting Bull, the nephews of Crazy Horse. The scalped and the dismembered united in common cause with the men and women who had gleefully taken their fingers, ears, nuts.

Bouyer raised one heavy arm. Pointed a finger, and, with a visible wrench, began to laugh. Simply laugh. A grating parody of a giggle, a chortle filled with gravel. Within a few breaths, however, it had warmed to genuine mirth. Perhaps Bouyer was considering, as I had, our own absurd predicament, how we'd spent our small eternities held hostage to this self-important popinjay.

I tried out my own laughter. How long had it been? A century and more. It was rust in my throat. Rust. Then the dam let go. Behind me, around us, the dead of the Little Bighorn laughed, God we laughed. We held our knees, we fell on each other, we pointed, we cried.

In the face of this onslaught, Custer's arrogance wavered. He turned to each of us, faster and faster, bouncing within the circle, frantic. Brothers to lieutenants to confidants, he sought some measure of accommodation. Anything, please. But it wasn't there. His scorn segued to panic. He beseeched us with open palms. What's funny, what's the joke?

Finally, he bent at the waist, dropped to the ground; held his ears, hugged his knees. Rocked. Around him? The mutilated, manifest works of his ambition. Look at us. See us.

God, that was a fine moment. Custer, humbled.

WE CONSIDERED EACH OTHER. Compatriots. Within the crowd, a few unfamiliar faces, uninvited strangers. The priest, for instance. He produced an iPhone and snapped a selfie. I noted uniforms from wars separated by generations. It took Custer to draw us together. A private in digital camo from Afghanistan stared out from the ruined landscape of his skull. A young lieutenant in the tigerstripes of Vietnam held one of his own arms over his shoulder. Then I saw, I saw ...

I saw my son. His mother's nostrils, my own flat cheeks. I'd have known him in a riot. Late forties, and dressed in the sour brown wool of WWI infantry. Heavy pockets on his chest, a flattened steel helmet. Worn sergeant stripes on his shoulder. A careerist, then. Had I influenced him? His father, the fighter. I flinched at the notion.

My son.

His left cheek, flickering in and out, was swollen with the heavy yellow blisters of mustard gas. His eyes were black specks lost in the folds of drooping skin. There were twenty yards between us. Twenty yards, plus or minus an age. His father, me. Father and son, slain by the frustrated impulse of men trying to impose their wills on other men. Stepping toward him, I saw the sweat beaded on his face, noted the labor it took him to stay fixed in this place, so far from his own patch of French mud. He raised a hand heavy with blisters. He smiled, and even as he smiled he faded to sepia, blurred at the edges, crumbled flat in the manner of a suit falling from a hanger. Where he had stood, only a more complicated swirl of snow.

Counts Enemies, at my shoulder, said, "He looked like you."

"That was my boy. Pretty sure that was my boy."

"Lucky."

I considered the word. "I think he was tired. Didn't he seem tired?"

WE DID NOT FINALLY FEEL LUCKY, nor historical, nor vindicated. We simply were. We considered the grass, we watched Custer regain his swagger. Bouyer was no longer a ready mark, and so, like every frustrated bully, Custer sought easier prey. At one point, he fell on the Arikaras, pointed to the small group of them hunkered by the Indian memorial. "Scouting reports!" he cried. To a man they showed him their fists, then raised their middle fingers.

Counts Enemies said, "Everybody's got to feel good about themselves."

"True, true ..."

"That's why wars are fought, man. Everybody's working their asses off, trying to feel good about themselves."

I put a blade of grass in my teeth. "Should we get on with it, then?" ◢

A Mother Writes a Letter to Her Son

By Glen Chamberlain

Winter 2009

14th June

Steen—

I'm sitting with one of the photo albums, looking at a snap of you and your dad. You're no more than two, mud-coated like some bog child, and you're grinning and staring straight ahead, your arm stretched to the camera, your little fist offering me a soggy twig that dangles between your fingers, as if exchanges were easy, as if you don't even have to care very much, as if all your barters will be accepted.

YOUR DAD PRESSES YOU TIGHTLY TO HIS SIDE, muddying the front and arms of his coat, despite his hatred of dirt. He does not look at the camera but studies you, his face close to yours, studies you with your curly brown hair and apple cheeks, he with his straight, thin, blonde hair; his straight, thin face; his pale skin. Though he is in profile and looks down, you can see that he smiles with the delight he always has when he watches you. He still does, even now that you're a grown man. Behind the two of you, the hills that stretch to the Buckle Summit are green and velvety, and above them, clouds drift like small, remaining floes of winter across the blue sky.

"Look at you," I like to remember saying. "You little philistine!" And I snapped the picture and then changed the phrase just slightly: "Phil's steen!"

Your dad looked up at me then, so pleased that I had called you his, that you were named after him and that your relationship was secure enough that you could be teased about your name, and that, finally, you were so eager to immerse yourself in the nitty gritty of the world. Your dad seldom laughs out loud, but that spring day he did when he said, "He looks more chocolate than mud-coated." What he meant, of course, was that to him you were exquisite and sweet and beautiful.

Since that day 24 years ago, we've called you Steen instead of Phil. It has been a better name.

Other than the story about Phillip morphing to Philistine morphing to Phil's steen, then to Steen, other than the story of some wordplay on a pretty spring day, you've never heard the context that day fits into. I suppose that's why we like snapshots. They're pared down and made simple; nothing but white space surrounds them, and when we look back on these incremental images of our lives, our lives seem simple, too. And happy. The context we've forgotten or chosen to forget. But sometimes the white space between snapshots—between then and now—begins to fill in, and we're shocked, because we haven't expected it. I know I haven't. And Phillip hasn't expected it, either. And but for you, we might have been able to keep it that way.

Perhaps we still can, but I am frightened that when you encounter him on your rounds at the nursing home in the next week, you will sense his importance to you, and, because you are like your mother—left-handed and right-brained, paying attention to intuition—you will wonder at this feeling you have, and you will honor it; and because you are like your father, with his accountant's belief that the truth can be found in data, that one has only to be aware of the need to find it and record it and examine it, you will search for data to explain your feeling.

We have always been so proud of you, Steen, for balancing in yourself so well our warring personalities. It is no wonder that you have become a physician, a healer, for you intuit the discomfort of people and then diagnose its cause.

How ironic that what thrilled us—your return to Buckle to do a residency and reduce your med school debt by doing duty in a rural community—might undo what your father and I have worked so hard to protect you from. Might undo you. Might undo us all.

I wondered about returning to Buckle when Phil and I graduated from college and you were 3, because, as in any small town, gossip abounds, and gossip never revolves around people's secret virtues. Even though we had been married for almost three years by then, I felt coming home might once again start people talking about what an odd match your dad and I were, might start them talking again about our shotgun wedding, about how Phil didn't seem the type to get a girl—let alone me—pregnant. On this we have always been honest with you; you know that we married when I was six months pregnant, and we have always told you that you were wanted by both of us. So wanted.

And this seemed enough—that you were wanted. Your dad convinced me that if we kept the context secret and our countenances open, we would live securely in the world of Buckle. And we have.

But yesterday we heard that Fergus Meagher has come home. "He's back," your dad said, in as nonchalant a way as he could, and he didn't have to give his name; I would know because, even though we have pretended otherwise, Fergus Meagher has never left. He has always been here.

And now, because he will live at the nursing home, you will meet him. I don't know what he will look like. I don't know if, as stroke victims often do, he will have deadened, twisted features. All I know is that people who have had brainstem strokes maintain their ability to receive information; they just struggle disseminating what it is they know. And I don't know what he knows, or if he will be able to tell you anything.

At first I prayed that he is terribly deformed, that you will look on him and see nothing resembling . . . what shall I say . . . a man? A human being? What a terrible thing to wish on another, but I did. I thought that if he had been afflicted by a terrible twist of fate and face, then there would be a chance that you would never see this letter. Sometime next week, you would drop by and tell us that there is a new patient at the facility, the youngest son of the Meagher family, the one Phil and I went to school with, the one who has been living in California, the one about whom gossip abounds. You coyly ask me if I, like every other woman in Buckle, have seen one of his films, and I tell you no, even as I blush, but not for the reason you think.

But if he is not transformed into some lost creature, you may look at him and feel a resonance in you, because the face pinning you with its gaze reveals a chastening secret.

How you might hate us should that happen. And, so, ironically, I will assure your hatred by telling you the secret now. It is, after all, only fair.

I think I've always known I should tell you, but I've been so thankful to your father, and he has never wanted this divulged. While I've loved your father, like any mother I've loved you more, and with each year that you have grown, so has my love. It would be remiss of me not to forewarn one I love so dearly of danger, which Fergus Meagher clearly represents.

Your father and I have always had what you doctors call unremarkable histories. And for years, you have assumed that you have inherited this genetic encoding that allows you to be, in this one area alone, unremarkable. And I'm sure you've looked at both sides of the family and been grateful for such normalcy. I pray, of course, that this failure to excel at illness remains. But this stroke of a man you've never met could suggest otherwise.

I LOOK BACK AT WHAT I STRUGGLE TO WRITE, Steen. Four pages. Do you remember that old joke you used to tell over and over about the young man who calls home from college to see how everyone is, and his little sister tells him his cat died? He gets angry at her for being so blunt and tells her she should have broken this news to him gently by first explaining how the cat was up a tree and they couldn't get it down. When he called again, he should have been told the cat was still in the tree and weakening, and when he called again, expecting dire straits, he could have been told that the cat had died. The little sister apologizes for her insensitivity. A week later, when the young man calls home and gets his sister, he asks how everyone is. "Mom's up a tree, and we can't get her down," the sister tells him. This is what I'm doing. Stalling the truth. And you, no doubt, have already surmised what that is.

YOU KNOW THE MEAGHERS; both men and women are handsome. They are tall and well proportioned, ruddy in complexion, blue of eye, and topped with auburn curls. Even the men, with their angular features and muscular bodies, are softened by ringlets. To a degree, they have been distrusted by the town; it's not because they seldom come to Buckle—many ranch families come in just once a week; and it's not because most of them still live on the old homestead—a quality of feudalism still functions on many of the ranches in the Buckle Valley, if the holdings are large enough; and it's not because they're Mormon—half the valley is that, and why should we distrust them anymore than the Catholics or Methodists? I suspect it is their steadfast handsomeness, which makes most of Buckle, when they look at the Meaghers, seem unfinished, as if God was still experimenting on features and body shapes, as if He'd been shaping their clay forms with the hands of an amateur till he got to the Meaghers. And only then was He pleased. So pleased that He forgot to squash the imperfect experiments and start anew, to make each creation as perfect. And so the people of the Buckle Valley limp and shuffle around, too pudgy and too thin, bow-legged and knock-kneed, splay-footed and pigeon-toed, all the while envying the Meaghers.

What's more, the Meaghers' physical perfection doesn't fade. You know this because Reba Meagher is one of your patients at the home; though she hasn't a thought left in her head, she's still stunning. It doesn't fade through the generations, either. The Meaghers seem incapable of throwing an ugly child.

After all, look at you.

And there you have it. The truth.

I KNOW WHAT YOU ARE DOING NOW; I used to watch how you read—intently, with your nose not more than 12 inches from the page, even though there is no flaw in your ability to see; and after a few pages you stop and stare into space, the blue of your eyes stormy with words and then calming as they become moored in the fine harbor of your mind. Only when all the words are anchored do you return to reading, and your eyes storm again. And perhaps I should be quiet now and just let you settle this idea. But I am so frightened of losing you that I will keep writing, trying to hold onto you.

WE ARE SO OPTIMISTIC, we humans. No, let me rephrase that: we try so hard to be optimistic. Drunks believe a new day is a new beginning; most of us pretend that a new year erases the old, that new habits will write themselves into new calendars we receive as Christmas presents; all of us embrace a baby as a new life with its own story to make. I know I certainly did.

But what I now understand is that babies are merely new characters in a plot already unwinding, a plot that began with Adam and Eve; I think they were the only two people ever allowed to start a story. What would they have done differently had they had the foresight to understand this? What would any of us do? And perhaps that, more than our mortality, is our punishment: it is only after we have lost our youth, our impetuosity, only after we have lived a while and garnered, if not wisdom then at least consequences, that we understand how fully, and sometimes how terribly, we have affected the plot.

I MET FERGUS MEAGHER IN EIGHTH GRADE, when he couldn't go to the school at Smelt anymore. I think that one-room school has stayed open because of the Meaghers—there are always so many brothers and sisters, and so many cousins! He was the youngest of Reba's and Lem's kids. When he came to Buckle High, I was a moon-eyed girl, in love with poetry, in love with love, and when I saw Fergus, who was so beautiful, I was sure he had been named for the mythic king of Yeats' poetry. In truth, as they had for all their children, Reba and Lem had turned to the state map and chosen a county name. But for Fergus, you've met them all at the nursing home when they come to visit their mother: Lewis, Carter, Clark, Judith, Bonner and Dawson. All counties. Every last one of them.

I remember studying Fergus from my desk the first day he came in, and Lila Breathwaite—Miss Breathwaite to me then—who was our homeroom teacher, introduced him to us. He stood there still as a statue, except for his hands which twirled an old felt hat round and round, and the pointy, duct-taped toe of one cowboy boot which tapped the floor. He was an odd combination of vulnerability and impatience—like a caged animal, I thought. That day, every girl in the class fell in love with him. I think even Miss Breathwaite—who was indomitable then— fell. While we girls sat and stared transfixed, the boys—even your kind dad—turned away from him; they excluded him for the next four years.

Not long after he arrived, Fergus and I became best friends. Perhaps it was because the boys would have nothing to do with him and most of the girls were too shy to approach him. Oh, just like everyone else, I thought he was beautiful, but I liked him more for his connection to the poetry I loved, the poetry I've read to you through the years. You know it all, Steen. And some he fit so perfectly! Remember "a king and proud! and that is my despair" from "Fergus and the Druid?" Of course it was only high school in a small western town, but when I thought of how Fergus was treated by everyone, of how he kept his pride in the solitude the students forced upon him, he became in my imagination that Irish king, and all I wanted was to befriend him.

And that's really all it was, a friendship, a great friendship, in which we did everything together. We snuck our first cigarettes together, drank our first illegal beer together, smoked our first weed together, necked and fondled together. We committed these acts in haystacks on various ranches surrounding Buckle; everyone still used the old beaverslide method of stacking, and we would scurry up the big green loaves with a blanket in the evenings and lie in the heady blue blossoms of alfalfa and stars. Truly, Steen, it had not been any kind of emotion which drove us but the lasered curiosity of inexperience coupled with a spacious comfort made of both landscape and familiarity, the same kind of curiosity I suspect you shared with Abigail your senior year of high school. We would trace the outlines of each other's bodies with a studiousness, more biologists than lovers.

I remember once sitting with him on top of a haystack watching the sun melt into the warm September horizon and waiting for the sigh of the finished day that would cool the world. "You know that Keats poem we're doing in English, about the Grecian urn?"

"You mean the one that doesn't make any sense?" Fergus asked. I think he was angry because he'd wanted to study my anatomy further than I would allow, and he was trying to provoke me. "Beauty is truth and truth beauty, and that's all I need to know? I need to know a lot more than that. I hate that poem. I've seen things that are true, and they sure aren't pretty."

I wasn't thinking about that part of the poem at all, but I was impressed that Fergus, who was straightforward and direct—not one to remember lines of poetry—knew them, so I asked, "Like what?"

"Like watching cows have sex. Like chopping chicken heads off. Like cracking an egg open and having a bloody chick fall out. Like having to shoot a horse that's broke its leg. Like like like. You want me to go on?"

You're probably wondering how I can so exactly remember this, but, in this case, I do, because I was using "Ode to a Grecian Urn" to keep my virginity, and the part of the poem I meant was where Keats says that the figures on the urn will never catch each other, and that makes life better. And I, shaped by the ambition that a scholarship would be my ticket out of Buckle, recited, "'Bold Lover, never, never canst thou kiss, Though winning near the goal—yet do not grieve; She cannot fade, though thou hast not thy bliss, Forever wilt thou love, and she be fair."

What I was trying to tell Fergus was that he and I could never love fully. You must understand that I was 17, and I thought having sex was tantamount to loving fully, and I couldn't do that because I so desperately wanted out of Buckle, and I knew if I loved Fergus fully, I might get pregnant, and then I'd never be able to leave. My life, which in my sweet youth I thought should be informed by poetry, would end up being prosaic.

The irony, of course, is that, as you know, I did get a scholarship. And because I did and had escaped Buckle, I believed myself immune to everything prosaic. When Fergus stopped on his way to Los Angeles to become a stuntman in the movies, then, I let him in. The figures kissed, and more. Just that once, Steen.

NOW THIS SOUNDS LIKE A LETTER OF APOLOGY TO THE CHILD OF THAT BRIEF union. I don't mean it to. How could I ever be sorry for you!

But understand that at the beginning of my college education which I believed would take me to all the places I had imagined, I rued the pregnancy. At Christmas of my freshman year, I went home, saying nothing to your grandparents or aunt, watching the days during which I could get an abortion—if only I knew how and where—wind down. That new year, when I returned for my second semester, I realized what I have earlier told you: that there are no new beginnings. The story was in play, and there would be no stopping it.

What I didn't yet accept was that I was the story's author. And this is where I let your father—not Fergus, but your father, your real one, the one who has adored you all these years—enter the plot.

Just as I loved Fergus through high school, Phillip loved me. Though he was too shy to act on his affection, I could tell. I remember one snowy day complaining to your grandmother that he loved me, and I knew it, and everyone else knew it, too, and it was embarrassing. Everything about him was thin and pale—the back pockets of his Levis drooped around his buttocks, his shoulders rounded over a chest that seemed concave, his hair had a see-through blondness to it, and it was not thick so that when he failed to wash it, you could see his white scalp, and his face was long and pulled on his lips, giving him a constant look of be-reavement. He was not the kind of boy girls wanted to be loved by.

"Phillip likes me," I told Mama. "Too much." She and your aunt Alice and I were sitting around the old kitchen table, the one Mama and Daddy still use, the one scarred by previous owners. You know the story, how along with that table and some other old furniture, the ranch came with anecdotes, and when we moved onto it, we cozied into them—both the furniture and the stories. The table, from the cook house, had been signed by Lyle. Do you remember how you used to trace his name with your fork whenever Mama made you macaroni and cheese and broc-coli? Then you'd try to divert our attention by asking to hear his story again—how long before even I was born, he had blown his hands off with dynamite and so wore two silver hooks, and how he scratched away with whatever hook he wrote with until, eventually, "Lyle" appeared. His name, deepened by your tracing, still floats on the table like a soul on a ouija board.

I remember Mama glancing at me as she slid a piece of lodgepole into the woodstove. "How could anyone like you too much? You're worthy of all the affection you receive." She dropped the iron latch on the firebox. "You should be flattered that such a nice boy likes you."

Alice and I looked at each other and rolled our eyes when Mama said, "He's good to have in a crowd of kids. He's like the piece of green cottonwood you throw into the cookstove to calm the fire." Neither of us was interested in boys who cooled. We were after boys of willow or aspen, boys of fast and fierce heat.

Despite my dismay over Phillip's constant crush on me, I used him in my math and science classes because he was so smart. Without him, my grades, though strong in the humanities, wouldn't have been well-rounded enough to get my scholarship. And I like to think that without my help in his essays, Phillip wouldn't have received his. At any rate, we were habituated to each other's company, and at college, though less often, we still met to help one another.

It was during one of those meetings in February. We were sitting in the library, and I had just pointed out a sentence in an essay he was working on for a philosophy class—problems of good and evil. There was nothing wrong with the sentence except for what it said—at least for me. Phillip had written, "Our culture panders to a morbid interest in our misdeeds; we create trouble just for the pleasure of wallowing in it."

"That's not true," I said. I was, of course, thinking of myself, of my own troubles, and how there was no pleasure in them, and because I knew he loved me, it was easy to take it out on Phillip. I crossed his lines out, pressing so hard that the pencil ripped his paper in half. Then I pushed it back to him, crumpling it.

Calmly he straightened it out and wrote for just a moment before handing it to me again. "Are you pregnant?" it asked.

In embarrassment that I must be showing and in relief that I could finally talk to someone about my state, I leaned into his shoulder, my eyes pressed against his thin shoulder, and sobbed. I will always remember the firmness and the gentleness of his hand as it stroked the back of my head. I will always remember how mature it felt, and how even as I welcomed its touch, it was not the kind of touch I longed for. But I would learn.

You, of course, have heard part of this story, and while we never lied, we let you assume that that evening in the library, a young man was being informed of his own potency instead of someone else's.

A month later, we were married at the courthouse and went home to announce our marriage and your impending birth. Both of our families were disappointed.

Of course, when they saw you, their disappointment disappeared. You were beautiful, and everyone talked with amazement at the nicking of two average looking people, dumbfounded that our ho-hum genes—at least as far as looks go—would come together to create such perfection.

DO YOU REMEMBER HOW YOU USED TO ASK ME WHY WE DIDN'T HAVE A brother or sister for you to play with?

As I grew fond of your father's touch, I wanted to have more children—not for you but for us—but so proud was he of you, and of the fiction that you were his, that he refused to consider it. "What if the baby looks like me?" he'd ask.

It has been a deep disappointment to me that you were an only child; but more than that, it has been a deep sadness to me that your father has so doubted the kind of beauty he has that when we have made love, it has never been complete. Always separating us has been .05 millimeter of latex. Only when my fecundity has ended will your father fully love me.

The deepest sadness of all, however, my beloved Steen, is that with this letter, you will never look on us again with the love we have come to expect on your face.

I don't know if I can bear that loss. I don't know if I can bear to change the myth of your life that we have created. I don't know if I can give you this. I don't know. I don't know. ◾

Cruelty to Animals

By Craig Lancaster

Spring 2011

WE WERE DONE FOR WHEN I BOUGHT THE DOG.
That's what I'm thinking somewhere over Idaho, on a twin-prop sputtering toward Seattle, where I'm going to hunker down and try to figure out what to do next, now that my last next thing has fallen apart.

Look, we had problems. Who doesn't? I might even be willing to concede that we had more problems than most people do, although you'd have to satisfy me that such a thing can be quantified before I'll cop to it. In any case, I'm not going to fight the basic premise: We were a mess. We were two people living in two cities in two states in two houses, and we kept pretending that maybe someday those circumstances would change and we'd be together. You know what? I'm going to say now that maybe that was a lie. I don't know. It didn't feel like a lie, at least not always. I do know that we were making it work, even if it was dysfunctional as all hell.

Then I bought the dog, and now nothing works anymore.

But, look, I'm leaving a bunch of stuff out.

IF I'M GOING TO BE TRUTHFUL, and now seems about as good a time as any to start, I knew what I was doing when I sent her that first e-mail. My marriage was skidding off the runway, and if you think that I should have been in a counselor's chair working on a solution to my troubles at home, I'm not going to disagree with you. But I didn't do that. No, I wrote a note to the kid sister of the first girl I ever loved. I hadn't seen her in nearly 20 years, when she was a 14-year-old, all arms and legs and orthodontia. I had added her as a Facebook friend the previous spring, along with a good chunk of the 400 or so people I'd graduated with back at Billings West High, a few co-workers and a handful of people I didn't even know but who seemed to know me. The more the merrier, as they say.

Most of those people quickly receded into the background. Facebook, like so many things these days, is all surface and no depth. You see somebody you once knew, say hello, exchange a few pleasantries, realize you can't possibly bridge 20 years, and you move on.

But Diane, she was different. For one thing, she wasn't a gangly little girl anymore. She was 34 years old, 100 percent woman if her online pictures were to be believed, and beautiful in a way that moved me in all the right places. Her sister, Rachel, lurked somewhere in my little online universe, but I rarely heard from her and spoke with her even less. But Diane. Oh, man, Diane. I took advantage of any chance I had to swap notes with her, stay up late chatting online or whatever. I even played that stupid farm game, just because she did. Even if I grant you that online communication is two-dimensional in a way that makes it a poor substitute and a dangerous stand-in for genuine human interaction, I couldn't help myself from falling in deep with Diane. She got me. She could tell when I wasn't eating well or sleeping well, just from my demeanor in the little electronic box where we talked. I began sharing my frustrations about work, and she helped me there, too. When I told my creative partner, Jonathan, that his big-footing of me during pitches was damaging to our relationship, he was properly chastened. "I owe you an apology, Doug," he said. "It was weird to hear you say it so directly. I don't know. Usually, you just go into your office and break something when you're frustrated." That was a gift from Diane, the ability to confront Jonathan. She was changing me.

Anyway, a few months later, I'm heading for D-I-V-O-R-C-E, and beyond my most immediate thought, which is that I'm glad we don't have any kids, I'm thinking this: Who do I know who can tell me what I'm getting into here? And just as quickly, I'm thinking: Diane. Diane. If she can't do it, nobody can. Diane's been married and divorced twice. Now, you're probably thinking that someone who's 34 and has been divorced twice maybe knows more about the subject than is healthy. I might have thought of that, too, if I hadn't been thinking about what Diane would look like with her clothes off.

So I shoot Diane an e-mail: "Hey, looks like I'm getting divorced. You have any advice?"

I'm sitting there browsing through some fantasy-football website when the reply comes not three minutes later: "I have tons of advice, but the best thing I can do is pray for you. Would that be OK?"

I'm thinking, well, it's not really what I had in mind, babe, but yeah. Pray for me. It can't hurt.

CAME TO FIND OUT THAT DIANE PROBABLY ISN'T THE PRAYING TYPE, which is just as well, because neither am I. What she was, though, was a text-messaging fiend. I started getting them by the score—when I woke up in the morning; on my commute to work, when I was fighting half of Seattle up I-5; in the middle of brainstorm meetings, where I was trying to figure out another way to sell cat food. ("Your cat will die if you don't feed it. Buy Little Friskies!") I was digging the attention. The messages came so fast that I eventually turned my BlackBerry to vibrate only so my co-workers didn't kill me, and in time, I came to associate that little double-buzz in my pants—no double entendre intended— with the pure pleasure of seeing her words.

Diane wanted me to come home to Billings, to spend some time with her, to make love to her. She started sending me pictures to let me know exactly what was waiting for me, pictures that didn't leave anything to my imagination, which was in hyperdrive anyway. It's all yours if you come, she said.

I blocked out a week's vacation, booked a flight and hoped that people could keep their cats alive until I got back to Seattle.

(I'm going to say this for the benefit of anybody who thinks I've got a good thing going to this point: When you buy that snazzy new phone—and you will, my friend, or I'm not doing my job correctly—and you sign up for that unlimited data plan, it's important to note that data and text messaging are not the same thing. Had I known this, I'd have not come home to a woman who still lived in my house, who stood in the living room quaking with fury, holding a 13-page-thick cell phone bill and screaming, "Who in the hell do you know in Billings, Montana, who you sent 5,314 text messages to in a month?" What can you say to that? I said, "Well, we weren't talking about the weather, that's for sure." I want you to learn from my mis-

takes. Paying the unexpected $800 bill is the least of the indignities. That night, I was living in a pay-by-the-week motel and my friends—Facebook and otherwise—had begun to flee the Good Ship Moron.)

AFTER A FEW MONTHS, things had begun settling out, at least a little. The divorce decree came in and Bree, my ex-wife, moved on nicely, as I knew she would. She got the house and the better car. I got the goldfish, which died the first week I was in my new condo in downtown Tacoma. Everything else, we split.

I saw Bree in February at the Experience Music Whatchamacallit—you know, that thing over by the Space Needle that looks like a giant loogie. She was holding hands with someone, a guy taller and thinner than me, and that socked me in the gut in a way that I couldn't have anticipated. I don't think she saw me; I started working backward through the exhibits and left. I don't think I could have taken actually speaking to her.

Funny thing about seeing someone I know in a metro area of 3.3 million people: When I was in much-smaller Billings—I flew there once a month, and once a month Diane came out to see me—I never saw anybody I knew, except Diane. That's odd, right? I mean, I grew up there, in a little house on Lyndale, next to a stretch of pasture that's now jammed between a McDonald's and a strip mall. Man, if that's not quintessential Billings, I don't know what is. "Welcome to Billings. Oil Changes and Unwanted Lip Hair Removal in the Same Building."

It's not like I was going to see my people; my folks are dead, and my brother and sister scattered with the wind. Jeff was in Concord, N.H., the last I heard, some kind of professor or something. We don't talk much. Laura, she's an Army wife down in Tennessee. But Diane's connections were still strong. Her parents lived there. So did Rachel and her family. Diane and I hit our fifth month of being an item, whatever that is, and I hadn't seen any of these people. It started to bug me, and I told her so.

"Don't pressure me about this," Diane said.

"I don't mean for it to be pressure. I'm just asking what the deal is. We've been together a while. Do they even know about us?"

"I'm not sure what together means."

"Well, look, we're something, aren't we? I don't normally make a dozen trips a year to Billings. Something's going on."

"Yeah, well, you're not here. Once you're here, we'll be together. Otherwise, I don't really see the point in getting them involved. You know that's going to be awkward, especially with Rachel."

I spilled the Coke I was pouring into my Jack Daniels. "I stopped dating Rachel in 1990. I think we can move past that pretty quickly, don't you?"

She didn't say anything to that, but she moved in close and she kissed me, and soon enough, I was chasing her down the hall into the bedroom. I knew she was trying to divert my attention. It worked.

B Y MIDSUMMER, doubt hadn't just crept in; it was sleeping on my couch and eating me out of house and home. It wasn't just the hiding me from her family. In retrospect, I should have confronted the "once you're here, we'll be together" bit the first time it flared up; I'm convinced now that a pro-active course would have stopped things before they got out of hand.

Why should I have been expected to move? I was the creative director at one of the best ad agencies on the West Coast, in a city that fed us as much work as we could handle. Damned if I could find something similar in Billings, the 169th-ranked media market in the United States. Advantage: Seattle.

And Diane, she was a nurse. Billings has fine hospitals, some of the best in the region, but they can't really compare with Harborview or Swedish or Virginia Mason or Seattle Children's. Advantage: Seattle.

I'd put these things in front of her, implore her to come join me, and she would say, every time, "If you loved me, you'd come here, where I need you."

I LOVED HER, OK? I still do, when you get right down to it. A million pop songs can be wrong, because I'm here to tell you: Love isn't enough.

On a mid-July evening, after Jonathan and I had sold a concept to a chain of coffee kiosks, we sat on the roof of my condo building and watched the setting sun glittering off Commencement Bay.

"How's it going with Diane?" he asked.

"Stuck in neutral."

"How so?"

"There's the whole won't-move-to-Seattle thing, for starters."

"Yeah, I don't get that at all."

"That's just the tip of it. You know, that way she could see through me and my problems when we first started out, I loved that. But now it's like she's turned that power against me."

"What do you mean?"

"Conversations are full of land mines. She seizes on individual words and beats me over the head with them. The other day, I'm fumbling my words pretty badly as we're going around and around again on being a couple publicly. And I say, 'Look, I'm trying to articulate something here.' And she says, 'No, you're trying to formulate it. If you were articulating it, you'd be saying it.' Who says something like that?"

Jonathan chuckled. "That's actually pretty funny."

"In isolation, yeah. It gets old when it comes at you continually. And I'll tell you something else: There's a lack of empathy there. Last night, she asked how I was doing, and I told her, well, I'm nervous about this pitch tomorrow. I'm not sleeping well. I feel like crap. And she said, 'Well, I have to go to bed.'"

"That's cold."

"Yeah, and it happens all the time. I don't know, man. In many ways, she's everything I ever wanted. Drop-dead gorgeous, smart, funny. But more and more, I feel like garbage when I talk to her."

Jonathan took a long sip off his beer. "Sounds like she's 90 percent perfect and 10 percent battery acid."

"Apt description."

"And it's the 10 percent that will eat you alive."

AS RECENTLY AS LAST MONTH, I was hanging in there with Diane. We'd had a few good visits, and I was thinking that maybe we still had a shot. One day, she sent me an e-mail with a picture of a Chihuahua, one of those little yappy, chalupa-defending dogs.

"I want him," she wrote.

This smacked of opportunity. I set aside my work, figuring I'd just stay late to catch up, and I started searching for breeders in Billings. It didn't take long; I found one out in Shepherd, called the lady up, found out that she had a litter born four weeks earlier that would be ready to go in the next month or so. That was cool by me. I agreed to send her a $500 check, and then I hung up and called Diane and told her the news, and I could hear her jumping and clapping like a little girl. She said she would name him "Guido," because little dogs with gangster names are genius, and I was thinking that this was the best $500 I'd ever spent.

A FEW DAYS AGO, I landed in Billings. David Sedaris was playing the Alberta Bair, and while there's a limit to how much oh-so-cleverness I can take, Diane really likes him, and I was on a Greatest

Boyfriend in the World roll because I bought the tickets without her asking me to. We got a room in the Crowne Plaza and made a reservation for steaks at Jake's. After that, the plan called for hitting the show and then coming back to the room and wearing out the bed and anything else we could scale without clothes on. A good plan it was.

We were dressing for dinner when Diane said, "I wish I didn't have to wait for Guido."

I fumbled with the buttons on my sleeve. "It's just a couple more weeks. He's going to have a great home with you. Way better than that cage in the closet."

She stopped. "What?"

"You know, the closet. I saw her take him out of it when we visited him yesterday."

"He lives in a closet?"

"You didn't know that?"

"How could I know that? I was sitting on the couch. I didn't see where he was. How could you let him live in a closet?"

"I'm sorry. I didn't think anything of it."

"That's terrible."

"I don't know. I guess it didn't seem like a big deal."

"Didn't seem like a big deal? Of course it's a big deal. That's animal abuse. You call that woman. You call her right now and tell her we're coming to get him."

"Come on. That's silly. He's not ready yet. And we have plans."

She stamped her foot. "Call her now."

WE DIDN'T HAVE STEAKS AT JAKE'S. We didn't see oh-so-clever David Sedaris. We damn sure didn't have sex. We sat in our hotel room and played nursemaid to a quivering, big-eared, long-legged rat. Diane talked to Guido in a sing-song motherly voice that amused me for about 10 minutes and then had me wishing the windows could be opened from the inside so I could leap to my death. Guido sat on my chest and peed on my shirt. Daddy was not pleased.

This morning, Diane took me to the airport. I rode up the Rims in the passenger seat, rigidly holding Guido away from me, because if he started to evacuate his little bladder again, down to the floorboard he was going to go.

"Idn't he da tweetest widdle ting," said Diane, channeling Tweety Bird.

"Oh, yeah. He's the best."

She looked at me and grinned wide. "We're a happy widdle famiwy."

A S WE SAID OUR GOODBYES, I got a quick peck from Diane and was told to kiss Guido on the mouth. I didn't want to do it, but in the interest of famiwy harmony, I acquiesced. Neither Guido nor I seemed pleased with the encounter.

At the TSA counter, I turned back and Diane was holding the little guy up and waving one of his paws at me. I waved back and felt a flush of stupidity for doing so.

After I'd run my shoes and my belt and my carry-on through the X-ray and suffered the indignity of the wand, I turned around again for my customary blown kiss from Diane, but she was gone.

T HE CAPTAIN JUST SAID THAT WE'RE MAKING OUR FINAL DESCENT INTO Seattle, and here's what I'm thinking: When I bought that dog, I punched my own ticket out of Diane's life. She doesn't want me, not really. She wants a companion who won't challenge her, who won't make her deal with his moods or feelings, and she wants someone who thinks everything that tumbles out of her mouth is golden. She wants someone who's cool with living in Billings. Guido's her man, on all counts. I can't possibly compare.

I'm going to miss her. I'm going to miss those moments, increasingly rare, when she makes me laugh uncontrollably, like the story she told about a patient who was carping to go home. She told him that soon enough he'd be playing footsie with his wife, remembering a moment too late that he was a double amputee. I'm going to miss sidling up to her on a cold night and sleeping in a warm embrace till morning. I'm going to miss the way she could make me feel like the sexiest man on earth, which I most assuredly am not.

It's going to be lonely for a while. Maybe for longer than that.

I think I'll get a cat. ◀

Gray Ghost

By Malcolm Brooks

Summer 2005

THIRTY PEOPLE PILED OFF THE COMMUTER PLANE IN BUTTE, but only one family fit the description of my charges: two adults, late-thirties, well-heeled, one disenfranchised adolescent dragged along on the old man's fishing trip.

Bart, Toni and Teddy, from Mountain View, Calif. I think I saw The Dead there once but wasn't sure I should bring it up—despite youthful vitality this outfit looked more Nob Hill than Haight Street. Bart held the patent on some modem gizmo which allowed him to fish, as he put it, "two-hundred and twenty-one days last year," in locations as nifty as Tanzania and Tasmania.

"Well," I said, "Sounds like you ought to be guiding me," which got a flash of instant recognition from Toni.

Bart rode shotgun and bombarded me with questions about the local water—current hatches, stream flow data, and so on. He'd fished the Yellowstone and the Missouri before, but never this corner of the state. He was hoping, he said, for less of a mob scene. The last time he'd fished the "Mo," you could "about do cartwheels from boat to boat, all the live-long day."

I couldn't take any real stock of the kid until we hit the truck stop in Rocker for a late breakfast. Teddy was 12, and no early bloomer—arms like tired shoestrings, trunk a contrasting sag of baby fat. He stood a full head shorter than his mother, and lacked totally the hyper-athletic yuppie sheen of his parents. It didn't seem possible that he could be the product of such perfect Golden State archetypes.

Except that he had Toni's eyes, flashing like the middle stretch of the Wise River on a moonlit night—flat and deceptively calm on the surface, but hissing nonetheless with speed and volume. Though enormous plastic eyeglasses all but engulfed his face, these eyes unmistakably knew something.

Teddy packed a laptop under one skinny arm. He fired the computer up to check the weather once we were seated, ignoring altogether the actual weather as it existed just beyond the plate-glass window. Sky a faultless powder blue, high white cumuli over the Pintlers. Rain doubtful at best.

"He's been obsessed with weather ever since he got wireless Web access," Toni told me. She pushed a menu to Teddy, jarring the laptop. "Get obsessed with this, weatherboy."

Teddy didn't budge. "I already know I want waffles."

"Carbohydrates," said Toni, as though this was merely the latest round in an ongoing bout, and she was coming out swinging. "You've got to eat something besides carbohydrates. You need protein."

"I want waffles."

"Waffles are carbohydrates."

"What's a carbohydrate?"

"Don't give me that. Bread, pasta, cereal…"

Bart snapped to attention from his own menu. "Check it out, dude, there's a cowboy, without a gun. He's got his name on his belt, though—it's Wayne."

Outside the window the cowboy in question climbed into a flatbed Dodge containing three stock dogs, a sign that he had in fact been identified correctly.

"Don't give me that. Things that aren't, you know, protein."

"Pickup's got a gun rack. Lots of gun racks in these parts."

"French toast?" Teddy feinted.

"Carbo."

"English muffin?"

"Carbo," said Bart, on a withering prompt from Toni. "I should put a gun rack in the Hummer. That would drive 'em crazy down in the City."

"Yogurt?"

"CARBOHYDRATES," Toni yelped. Then she frowned. "Isn't it?"

Teddy went back to his weather.

WE GOT TO THE LODGE BY EARLY AFTERNOON, Bart already raring to wet a line. He asked how the river was this far up, winding through the willows below the lodge.

"Depends on what you want to catch."

"Brown trout, one as long as my leg."

But of course. "You need to go down river, to some bigger water." I hesitated, then admonished myself to go above and beyond. "We could do an evening float, if you're up for it. Stays light until ten, but most of the boats leave the water by six."

Bart lit up like a kid at Christmas. "Ready when you are."

Toni and Teddy were across the lobby, looking at arrowheads fanned in a display case on the wall. Teddy clutched his laptop to his chest like a thing with the power to deflect bullets. "We can probably squeeze everybody into the boat, if they don't mind skipping dinner."

Bart winced, screwing one eye totally closed. "Not tonight, man...I need to unwind. I need to focus."

"Fair enough," I said.

Down near the junction of the river's forks I spotted a rancher uncorking his diversion gate, set to flood a timothy meadow with a good mass of Big Hole stream flow. Ever a melancholy sight—once irrigating season started, the river dropped as rapidly as its temperature climbed.

"I'm as guilty as anyone," I said aloud. Bart looked at me quizzically. "The other night I went all the way to Dillon for prime rib." I gave the rancher a wave, and he let off the bull-wheel just long enough to flash a wave back. Bart still didn't seem to get it.

I put the boat in at Powerhouse. Bart talked about Teddy. "All he does is fool around on that computer, which I realize is an ironic thing for me of all people to complain about, but hey...life is not one giant mega-pixel. Kid needs to live a little. What is that?"

I looked up. A huge stone fly hovered upriver, wings flashing like chrome blades. "Salmon fly."

"Are they still coming off in these parts?"

"Prime time was maybe 10 days ago, and even then there weren't many bugs. A few bad drought years seem to do that."

Bart gestured with his chin at the water line on the rocks, at the dark wet stain an inch or more above the surface. "Looks like it's dropping fast right now."

I squinted at him. "There is no free prime rib."

"So can I catch something on a salmon fly?"

"Might. You object to foam?"

"Not if it catches fish."

I unzipped my fly box and pulled out a pink stone fly with a Prince dropper already trailing from the eye. Bart took the flies and attached them to his tippet with a Harvey dry fly knot, the first time I'd ever seen a client use that particular connection. Many of my bookings could barely tie their shoes.

"Anyway," said Bart, "Teddy. I'm getting to where I don't know what to do with him. What kind of kid wants to sit at a computer desk all the time? What kind of kid doesn't want to catch big fish?"

He started to cast, testing the specific gravity of this particular combination, then finding a rhythm and feeding line off the reel and into infinity. "My kid, that's who."

I steered toward a sweep of current along the opposite bank, where green grass danced in the water like a million lapping tongues. The water may have been dropping, but it wasn't yet what you'd call low. Bart cast his line about eleven-thirty off the bow, placing the flies a foot from the bank, without a word of instruction from me.

"Get set for the strike," I said.

A little later the salmon fly plunged forcibly under and Bart brought his rod forcibly back, tight to something that mustered a short, sharp run before relaxing to mere submissive weight in the water. Whitefish, of middling size. Bart dragged it in and tweezed the Prince from a puckered, admittedly unglamorous mouth.

"Trouble with nymphs," he said.

A half-hour later we'd had no attempt on the salmon fly. Bart pulled in a second fish on the Prince, a 12-inch cutt that didn't seem to make him any happier than the whitefish. "Beginner's trout," he called it.

"Plan B." I flipped open the rod locker in the gunwale and handed Bart a 6-weight streamer rod rigged with three feet of stout leader and a god-awful concoction of electric-green fur and Flash-a-bou, a veritable depth-charge of shimmer and light. It looked like a cross between a prostitute and a grappling hook.

"Tight to the bank, let it sink, three quick strips. Again."

Bart found his timing. He picked his spot along the bank.

"You just had a follow."

"Saw it. There!" He strip-set the hook at the flash of a pale mouth. Loose line burned through his fingers and the fish hit the reel like juice to a chop saw, teeth and pawl screaming to life.

Bart howled like a rock star. The fish ran with the current, capping that first giant run by breaking the surface and tail-walking madly across the water. Rainbow, a big one, flanks pink as an English rose.

The fish made two more good runs, with Bart reclaiming line after each, then a shorter burst when it finally saw the boat. Bart eventually steered it into the net.

"Good fish," I said. "Not your brown trout but not bad."

Bart grinned like a new moon. "Not bad at all. I think I like this place."

We fished on through the evening. Bart took a number of trout on the streamer, even a few of his big fabled browns. We reached the takeout by nightfall.

"About Teddy," he said. "Half the reason for this trip is to hook him on fishing, and I'm not the best teacher, if you follow…I don't have the patience. If you're any good at working with kids…" He seemed at a loss for anything else.

I nodded, for lack of an actual response.

Bart gave me his one-eyed wince in the failing light. The headlights of the lodge shuttle bobbed on the washboard road. "If we can get him interested it might save him from laptops and palm pilots." He laughed. "Might even save me."

I SAW THE ICEBERG EDGE OF BART'S IMPATIENCE THE NEXT MORNING. He and Teddy were on the lawn in front of the lodge, Bart ostensibly providing casting instruction. Teddy thrashed the rod around as though flogging an entire swarm of houseflies. Yellow line fell in impotent coils. Bart went red in the face.

Toni lingered on the porch, watching above the false horizon of a fitness magazine. She looked at me as I walked by. "Sure you're up for this?"

I tried for a reassuring grin, but it felt more like Bart's contagious wince. "We'll make it," I said.

Teddy's fly line had gone totally haywire by the time I reached him. Bart strode off toward Toni on the porch.

"Hey, sport," I said.

"Kinda made a mess here."

"You'll catch on. It's not the easiest thing to learn."

Teddy looked away.

A bit later we tooled down the highway, trout boat bouncing jauntily on the trailer behind. Everybody seemed to have cooled out. Teddy asked about the wooden beaver-slides, looming like dinosaur skeletons in the meadows.

"They look like catapults," he said. "For knocking down castles."

"They're about that ancient," I said. "But they're for stacking hay. Like that." Three giant haystacks sat at the far edge of the meadow, massive and primitive as mammoths. "The Big Hole's old-school."

We stopped for gas in Wisdom. Teddy studied the mural on the wall of the mercantile. "What's the fish with the sail?"

Bart was building a leader in the passenger seat. "Whitefish, not a very realistic one. Who'd want to paint a whitefish?"

"Actually that's a grayling," I said.

"Like Alaska grayling?"

"Yeah, Arctic grayling. Same basic fish."

Bart frowned. "This ain't the Arctic. Ought to paint that out and put in a brown."

"Actually there are a few native grayling in the Big Hole. Kind of a remnant population in the upper river."

Bart went back to his leader.

We put the boat in below Melrose to fish the lower river, the famous brown trout water. I put Teddy up front with Bart's spare rod. He climbed in clutching the ever-present laptop, locked now in a plastic hard case. He arranged the computer carefully between his feet.

"Leave that in the car," said Bart.

"It'll get stolen. Or melt in the heat."

"Then you shouldn't have brought it."

Teddy looked out across the water. "Think we'll catch a grayling?"

"Not if we can help it," said Bart. "We're about browns today."

Teddy looked at me.

"Not likely, sport. Don't see many this far down." On account of the browns, I thought, though I didn't say so.

For two hours Teddy mainly ran interference on Bart, thrashing his rod around with the world's worst timing. I lost count of the times Bart's streamer collided in mid-air with Teddy's vagrant fly line. Twice Teddy hooked me in the hat brim. I prayed to God that some witless, mentally handicapped trout would miraculously get itself hooked on his fly, but it never happened.

To make things worse, Bart himself wasn't exactly fishing like a house afire. He hooked one small brown on the streamer, but otherwise spent most of his time either disengaging his tackle from Teddy's, or steaming over the amount of time he'd squandered in the process. I could feel actual heat blasting from his end of the boat.

Finally things came to a head. "I wonder when the rain will come," Teddy mused.

Bart snorted. "There's not a cloud anywhere."

Teddy gave a partial shrug. "Computer said so."

"Oh man," said Bart. "Oh man. I ought to throw that thing in the river."

"Correct me if I'm wrong," said Teddy, "but wouldn't that pollute the trout stream?"

Bart went silent for two bottomless, nauseating seconds. I thought he might jump up and pitch Teddy himself overboard. Then this: "I should have left you with your mother, because you're exactly like her."

"A little rain would be all right with me," I ventured. "We need all the help we can get." Nobody answered. I started rambling. "Back in the late eighties the drought got so bad the upper river dried up completely—sure hate to see that again."

"Did you work here then?" Teddy asked.

"No, I was in grad school in Missoula. Got a master's in English, just so I could spend two more years fishing in Montana."

"Master's in English," said Bart, now apparently sniping at me. "What can you do with that?"

I heaved into the left oar to steer around a wet boulder. "You're looking at it."

Bart chuckled, an audible release of wicked, pent-up steam.

Teddy frowned. "You said the grayling live in the upper river?"

"Yup."

"And that's what dried up?"

"Yup."

"So what did the grayling do without any water?"

I saw a bronze flash in the depths along the bank, like the swing of a pendulum in a darkened room. Brown trout. "I don't know," I admitted.

An hour later a freak downpour drenched us to the bone.

I PICKED UP BART BEFORE FIRST LIGHT THE NEXT MORNING. We had a change of venue, off for the upper Beaverhead and then back to the lodge by dinnertime, a plan Bart described as "keeping the illusion of the family vacation."

No sign of Teddy. "Too early for the kid?" I said.

"Something like that," Bart mumbled.

On the river he caught fish like a machine, first with a caddis pupa and later with the big streamer.

"This is a great day but I'm feeling a little guilty," he confessed, when we stopped for lunch.

"Teddy?"

He nodded. "I'm an instant Nazi the second we get on the river. It never fails. What am I doing wrong here?"

I wanted to tell him that when it came to fishing he did nothing wrong at all, and that maybe this was the problem. But I'd known Bart two days, just long enough to peg him as the sort of autocratic perfectionist who would brook no criticism, even one draped in a compliment. I said nothing.

We rolled into the lodge that evening, to a sight that left us both momentarily speechless: Teddy on the front lawn, fly rod in hand, studying his back cast as it unfurled behind him. "What on earth?" said Bart.

Teddy scurried over when he spotted us, yellow line hopping behind him through the grass. He was yammering before we were out of the rig. "I want to catch a grayling and I want to catch one now, before the water goes any lower. Can you help me do that?"

He told us that grayling had been stranded here by a wall of glaciers during the last Ice Age, cut off for a hundred centuries from their Arctic family in the north. He told us grayling had lived all over Montana before dams and brown trout, and that the upper Big Hole was the only place ancient enough for the last few fish to survive. Nobody knew how many grayling were left, or how much more drought they could stand. Maybe they'd wink out by the end of summer, or the summer after, wink out like the mastodons and saber-toothed cats and bison herds, ten thousand years gone like a mist on the breeze. He'd learned all of this on his computer.

"I've been trying to cast all afternoon," he said. "I think I'm starting to get it. Can we catch a grayling without hurting it?"

"More or less," I said.

"Can we go now?"

"I think you should," said Toni, coming down off the porch. "It's all he's been talking about."

Bart looked at her. "What about the family dinner plan?"

She gave him a hard look back. "The plan changed."

We drove downriver a few miles, turning off through a rickety wooden portal onto gouged and rutted two-track. I rarely fished the Big Hole so far up, rarely encountered grayling at all outside the odd stray specimen that wandered down into the middle stretch to take some unsuspecting client's dry fly. The client would invariably assume he'd caught a whitefish.

Bart reached for his own rod when we parked. "No browns here," I said.

He started to reply, then caught my eye. He slid the rod back into the car.

Teddy slipped into the slow water of the upper river, sucking in a breath at the cold but stepping out nearly to his waist. Bart and I followed. "Hard to imagine with no water at all," Teddy said, his voice little more than a whisper.

Whatever casting improvement he'd made on the lawn didn't quite translate to water. He handled the rod like a whip to a nag, then tore his line back off the water with equal force. Before long I heard the fly crack off the tippet on a bad back cast. Bart winced like he'd just been vaccinated.

"Bring that line in, sport," I said. "Let's do something different."

Fish had begun to rise upriver, rings dotting a wide bend with the even distribution of rain. Brookies and small cutts, from the look of things. Tiny mayflies swarmed the air, but I found what I wanted on the surface of the water: caddis, wanton and unabashed as hedonists at a pool party. I added tippet to Teddy's leader and tied on the biggest elk-hair caddis I thought we could get away with. "Shorter casts," I said. "Let the rod tell you when."

We moved to the tail of the bend. Teddy's first casts put the closest risers straight to bed, but a few minutes later he got a reasonable drift in a fresh spot and a fish rolled up and took. Teddy gave an audible gasp, then jerked back belatedly on the rod. Line and fly shot out of the water before settling slack again on the surface. Teddy's head whipped around, eyes big as his oversized glasses.

Bart pinched two fingers together. "That close."

Teddy had two more near misses in the next half-hour, both fish spitting the fly before he could set the hook. By now the sun had dropped behind the mountains. A wash of odd, almost prehistoric light lingered across the valley, across the weathered lumber of the beaver-slides and the mounds of hay in the distance. Mosquitoes buzzed everywhere, interfering with Teddy's already belabored casting. Putting this particular kid on a vanishing species was very likely the biggest challenge of my entire career.

"That," I said, "is a grayling. They make that splash with their dorsal."

The same fish rose again as if on cue, a big, powerful interruption in the water's ordered flow, a rise unlike any we'd seen tonight. I told Teddy to move upstream five steps, then put the fly 10 feet above the rise.

He got into position and began to cast. Something had clicked at the sight of that suctioning rise—with Teddy so intent on that single ring of water he ignored the rod altogether, and by ignoring the rod he got it right. Line snaked behind him like a live thing, then reversed itself and traveled forward, once, twice. Bart started to speak and I gripped his upper arm, hard, to keep him quiet. His torso jerked through the motion of the cast.

Teddy's fly settled and began to drift. I thought for a fleeting moment how so much came down to a single, crucial tangle of animal hair and curved steel, crawling inch by inch across generations, entire epochs even, only to siphon at the last possible second into the rising maw of Teddy's chosen fish.

Bart whooped. Teddy raised the rod and the line came tight. The fish made one hot run before giving itself up to whatever superior force loomed on the other end of the line. Teddy reeled it close, and I took the fish with the giant sail and held it just below the surface of the river. The grayling wasn't large, 11 inches or so, but it had the finest features of a trout and a few all its own—the leopard-spotted sail, the tint on its flank the exact lavender of Big Hole sky just this side of sunset. This fish belonged to this place. It had for a very long time.

Teddy touched the grayling with one tenuous finger. He looked at Bart. "Not a brown."

"Nope," said Bart. "But it's a beauty."

I slipped the hook from the corner of its mouth and opened my fingers. The grayling held for the briefest moment, testing its gills before simply melting into deeper, darker water.

We splashed up out of the grayling's home, onto the wet rocks along the waterline and into the sage. Teddy still held his rod. "Fishing's complicated," he said.

"In a way," I said.

"Do you think they'll make it?"

I looked down at him, then at Bart, who was not wincing. "I hope they do," I said.

Teddy nodded. "I hope so too."

Date Night

By Fred Haefele

Summer 2013

THREE DAYS PAST THE WAKE, it was more like a party than anything; a spontaneous get-together at a bar called the Trestle, just before the rail yards, north of town. The gang ordered martinis, not Russ's favorite drink, but it was in honor of Miles, everyone's favorite hilariously self-destructive hedonist. By the third round, things got a bit loud, but nothing untoward, just a group of old friends who'd been through the wringer and now felt entitled to a break. Nearly as Russ could tell, this was how he found himself massaging the knee of Patty Liddell, a well-preserved public defender who, for her part, was polite enough to not even notice. Meanwhile, at the end of the tables they'd rearranged, his wife Nika sat so close to Marvin James he peered frankly down her cleavage, like he was on some kind of field trip. Pretty much everyone there could out-drink Russ, so he tried to pace himself. But the stories kept coming—the one about Miles' "four and a half ex-wives," the one about a particularly strange night in an Algerian slammer—and the laughter felt so good after all the sadness, and any attempt at self-preservation seemed out of place.

By the time the party broke up, it was twilight; a luminous April evening in the West. There was snow on all the peaks yet, a delicious freshening in the air. Outside the Trestle, a few friends lingered on to watch a sunset the color of pink lemonade spill out across the rail yards and overtake the eastbound freight, chugging stolidly toward the divide. Somehow, several of them ended up in Marvin's Subaru, where a reefer the size of a panatela was passed till they smoked themselves senseless, flung the doors open, rolled out into the street, coughing and chortling like some Cheech and Chong outtake.

Back on the sidewalk, Russ found alien landscape where his hometown used to be. It was a mistake, getting into Marvin's car, though it seemed a good idea at the time. The only thing he knew with any clarity was, there was no way in hell he and Nika would make it home. Even allowing they did, they'd need to finesse J.J., the new babysitter whom they'd promised, word of honor, they'd be home two hours before. He thought of calling a taxi, but didn't trust himself on the phone. In the course of these ruminations, he got deeply lost in the sunset, so that when he finally looked around, the rest of the party vanished, it was only him and Nika.

"Holy cow," he mumbled, finally.

"We've sure done it this time," said Nika, almost wistful. She gazed briefly upon the sunset.

"Let's get out of here, Russ." She said. "We've been standing around this joint for hours."

The two of them walked towards his pickup, a block away. They got in, closed the doors, buckled up as if they were actually going somewhere, but Russ could only sit like a pole-axed Hereford, trying to walk himself through whatever might come next.

He turned to Nika. "How many of those gin-bombs did you have, anyway?"

"Actually," she said. "Just two."

"Is there any way you can drive?"

"Probably," she said. "I could try, I mean."

"All we can ever do," Russ said, thoughtfully.

"Is to try," she nodded.

They pondered this revelation for a brief eternity.

"Well," said Russ finally. "At least we got *that* settled. Let's do this; easy does it, one block at a time, that kind of thing. If it ends up being too weird, we'll just park the truck and walk."

Nika frowned. "Well," she said. "I'll give it a shot for a block. But first," she said, kicking off her heels, "these shoes have got to go. Can't drive in them anymore than I can walk."

"Why does a person have such shoes?" said Russ.

"If you need to ask, I can't explain," she said curtly.

Russ slid towards her, she scrambled over him, ended up behind the wheel. She brought the seat forward, hiked her dress past her sun-browned knees and started the truck, her toes cunningly prehensile on the pedals.

Russ watched, fascinated. Wow, he thought. A barefoot woman, driving a stick-shift pickup. Was anything in the world more erotic?

Before he had a chance to give the question proper consideration, a police cruiser pulled smartly in front of them, braked for the amber light they would surely have otherwise made and came to a stop with a kind of dreadful finality. There was much to take in about a cop car, Russ saw, especially when you got this close: the 5/16-inch, heavy-duty channel steel bumper, and the diamond mesh of the felony cage, the pump action riot gun clamped niftily to the dash.

"Oh God, Russ." Nika suddenly whispered, her eyes on the mirror. "There's one behind us, too!"

Russ shot a glance behind him, felt his heart sink. "Guess we're going down, babe," he heard himself say.

It was a line straight out of a bad cop show, and he couldn't believe he said it. Instantly there was a roiling sensation in his stomach. A great bubble of merriment rose up inside, burst out of him like swamp gas in a manic laughing fit.

Nika turned ashen. "Christ," she said. "Jesus, please, Anything but that! Quick, Russ, turn on the radio!"

Russ nodded his head, set his jaw manfully. He composed his face to a rubbery scowl, but he could feel that it was futile, like trying to put a stopper in a geyser. He stabbed the radio's On button and instantly the cab was flooded with the chorus from Strauss's *Merry Widow*. It was his mother's favorite operetta, music so blithely at odds with the morbidity of their situation the two were instantly and disastrously undone, Nika clinging to the wheel just to keep herself upright.

"OK," she finally managed. "You're right, hon. We're going down."

"It was *your* idea," he gasped. 'Oh, quick Russ—the radio!'"

Increasingly, he was aware the truck was actually shaking with their laughter—or did he just imagine this? One way or the other, it didn't matter. They were stuck at a light between two cops, who, if they didn't leap out and cuff them on the spot, simply weren't doing their job. There would be lawyers, counselors, slammer time and disgrace. Not to even mention Family Services.

There was nothing left but for the cops to hit their top lights, drag them out and read them their rights. The worst part was, when they stuffed him in the cruiser, he'd probably get a good laugh out of that, too.

"Kill the music!" Nika commanded. "Russ, it's our only chance!"

Russ looked at his wife, dumbstruck. Why did she have to say that: "Russ, it's our only chance?" Now everything was a line from a cop show. Still, he did as he was told, switched it off. But the abruptness of the silence made their laugh suppression suddenly audible; a lot of snorkeling, farting noises, more hilarious than anything before. The floodgates were thrown full open, things would simply have to run their course.

On they crept in this grim caravan, fists to their mouths, their faces streaming tears. When they thought they could stand it no longer, the two cruisers lit their displays and with a whoop of siren, sped out suddenly to the west, left the two of them limp with wonder.

"My God," said Russ. "Someone needs arresting more than us?"

"It's a *miracle*," Nika murmured.

"That," said Russ, "or we're invincible."

There were a couple good signs when they finally arrived home: no petulant children gibbered from the tree house, no frantic-looking sitter paced the fence line. When Nika pulled in and parked the truck, Russ finally dared look at his watch. Just 10 minutes had elapsed since they left the Trestle. In that time, they'd run the gauntlet of sex and terror, hilarity and reprieve. They'd arrived home unscathed, if you didn't count the chorus from *Merry Widow*, now lodged in Russ's brain pan like a tick.

Nika fished a Kleenex from the glove box, dabbed her eyes and composed herself for J.J., the mere mention of whom had inspired another laughing fit just minutes before. J.J. was a pretty, birdlike redhead. They'd hired her because she'd seemed particularly attentive, a quality which now seemed certain to work against them.

"Do you think we're trashy parents?" Nika asked.

He considered this. "No more than most," he said.

"Wow. *Thanks*, Russ."

"I mean, probably not. Trashy parents are always last to know."

"I think you can shut up now," Nika said.

He began to laugh.

"Just stop," said Nika, slipping back into her shoes. "Knock it off now, Russ. OK?"

She was right, of course. They'd already had more fun than was probably good for you. Still, she really turned him on, he had to face it.

And they hadn't yet been spotted, so hypothetically, at least, the party wasn't over. In the dusty shadow of the Douglas fir, Russ looped his arms around her, pulled her to him.

She kissed him tentatively, then began to cry.

"I just miss him, Russ," she said. "I tried, but I can't believe Miles is gone."

Russ loosed his grip, wiped a tear from her cheek with a finger. "Neither can I," he said finally. He realized then that in the back of his mind, he'd managed to hold the idea it was some elaborate kind of prank.

Christ, Russ thought. How irrelevant can I get? He was embarrassed not to know his wife any better than this, and he held her as she wept quietly against his chest, marveled how sheer the membrane was between such completely opposite things.

From inside the fence came the chirrup of children's voices. Walt and his towheaded friend, Turtle, popped through the gate, grinning maniacally about something.

The boys charged at Russ and Nika, hugged their legs like they'd just got off some lifeboat, "Mom! Dad!" Walt cried out. "Oh my God, we love you. We *missed* you!"

Russ had never seen this particular con and briefly, he was thrown by it. "So what do you guys want?" he finally said.

They'd already decided it was risky to approach J.J. together, so Nika bravely turned to face the music.

He ended up spread-eagled in the handsome Guatemalan hammock Miles had left him. He lay completely still, felt the air begin to stir, watched the leaves on the weeping birch ripple with the wind. He felt so full yet so spent, so relaxed, but so aware, and it occurred to him, out of nowhere, this made an ideal time to pray.

Not a particularly religious man, Russ reasoned that, just because he had no affiliation or clear idea whom it was going to, it didn't mean he couldn't pray anyway. Besides, he recalled hearing that the heartfelt prayer of a righteous man was one of the most potent things on earth. But how would such a prayer go?

"Please watch over my friend Miles, Lord, he's as good as they come."

It was kind of banal, but it would have to do. Now all that was left was to send it out. Aloft. Whatever. He decided an effective prayer required more than sprawling in your yard like a wino, so he sat up, placed his feet on the ground, touched palms together like a child readying for bed.

"Dear Lord," he began. "Take care of my old friend Miles ..."

But before he could even finish, a plume of smoke gathered at his fingertips, coiled into a massive silver column, then powered its way upwards, straight to heaven. Russ was so astonished, he nearly fell out of the hammock. He knew little about prayer, but he sensed he'd overdone it.

H E TURNED TO NIKA. She lay on her stomach, reading Ian McEwen by the muzzy light of the Marriage Saver book lamp he'd bought for her 40th birthday. They were wiped out, the two of them, but he couldn't yet put aside the mysterious events of the day—its antic gravitas, its dilation of the appetites.

"Yeah," said Nika, when he told her about his prayer. "That was bitchin' weed all right." She frowned. "God, Russ. I hope we didn't blow it with J.J. —do you think we shocked her?"

"Look," said Russ. "I'm 56, you're 44. We're a hundred years old, between us. I say it's time we had some fun."

"That's one way to look at it," she said. "I don't know, hon. I think you should have taken her home."

"Why's that?"

"I got the feeling she was goofing on me."

Russ thought about it. "Maybe. But they say impaired dads are twice as threatening as a mom."

"Who says?"

"That's just common knowledge."

"You need to do better than that, Russ."

"OK, I read it somewhere."

"Where?"

"Emily Post?"

"Of course," she said.

He was stung by the way she'd dismissed his smoke vision. He made it a point not to walk around hallucinating, so he knew well enough what he'd seen; it was his prayer made visible, probably a gift of some kind, though one he didn't necessarily deserve or understand.

He placed his palm at the small of her back, gently rocked her hips, zeroed in on her sore spot, between the third and fourth lumbar vertebrae. He pressed it firmly with his fingers, began to hum the *Merry Widow* chorus, until he lost himself in the task. He thought about Miles, and the great beyond. Was it really all that great, and what was it beyond? Did Miles actually now look *down* on his friends?

When he thought about his prayer, he had to laugh. The irony was, when he was alive, Miles probably saw that stuff all the time. Miles probably thought if you weren't wasted enough to launch a moon shot prayer, then why bother?

You really had to give it to Miles, thought Russ. Even when he was dead, he was larger than life. Russ thought about his nine-year-old son, who represented, depending on who you talked to, a remarkably foolhardy or hopeful undertaking for a guy in his 50s. How soon might he be looking down on his family, giving the big thumbs-up, or whatever a person does in that position?

Nika sat up abruptly. "Are you having an affair?" she said.

For a second, Russ imagined she was talking to someone else.

"*What?*" he said at last.

"Well?"

"Sorry," said Russ. "For a moment, I thought you were joking."

From where had she plucked this idea? Had she noticed him groping Gretchen?

Quickly his mind wheeled to the defense; in the first place, it wasn't groping, it was more like *patting*, a significant difference. In the second place, there was nothing going on with him and Gretchen, low sparks between old friends at the most, and if pressed, he would point out she'd sure made Marvin's day, with that spring cleavage tour she'd conducted. Really, the truth was—and he actually thought he might tell her this—that he'd patted Gretchen's leg because her own was unavailable. It made perfect sense, it was probably even true, but it was likely to be a very hard sell.

"Has this day not had enough drama?" he said.

"You tell me."

"OK, it has," he offered.

"Why not answer the question?"

He tried to measure her seriousness. He could not.

"I'll answer, but I need to know why you're asking. Come on, what's the red flag here. Do I disappear for hours?"

"No."

"Call you by another woman's name?"

"No."

"Leave sports bras lying around?"

"You seem really distracted. That's all. "

"Cripes, Nika. Why can't it be something else? Maybe I'm thinking about Miles in heaven. Maybe I'm listening to the footfalls of my own mortality. Anyway, the answer to your question is no. No, I'm not having an affair."

In the 20 years they'd been married, he'd been completely, perhaps tediously faithful. This had not been the case with his first marriage, in the brief course of which he'd discovered himself to be a particularly inept philanderer and a bad liar to boot, unable to remember whom he'd told what, which compelled him to make up stories people couldn't believe if they wanted to. Nika's question made him wonder if it was she having the affair, in which case she'd need him to be having his own, if he understood how such things worked. She'd certainly kept her looks, but with two young children and a full-time job, if she was so far ahead as to pull it off, it was almost admirable. Besides, there was nothing he could do about it anyway.

The truth was, he *had* thought about making a play for Gretchen but it was mostly contextual; part of a collective understanding that, like the reefer and martinis, the night should embody the kind of jailbreak bacchanalia that had long been Miles' signature. Glumly, he realized he was out of his league; he'd got as smart as he was going to be some years ago, and the thought depressed him. Damn, he thought. What's going on here? It was only a party. A big, sloppy, feel-good party. Everyone has forgotten about it and gone to sleep except for me.

It was getting on towards midnight, and he didn't want to sully things with more speculation. With its Bombay gin, raucous friends, numinous sunsets and adventures in ganja-land, the day seemed a kind of gift; it was, in a way, he and Nika at their best, if not their smartest. Still, they'd come through it together, handled everything the universe dished out, and that was a good enough way to leave it. ◄

A Second Kiss

By Milana Marsenich

Fall 2010

IN THE COPPER MINES OF BUTTE, dirt, rock and wood crashed quickly down and closed off whole rooms. It happened often and without warning, ruining men known for their courage, known for their brute strength and steadiness. The summer of 1969, the summer of a thousand untold love stories, the summer that Leo died, life had taken one of those landslide shifts. The rocks flew, one by one: jail, Leo's mom, Rebecca, killing the Gardens' dog. It wasn't really that the first caused the next, except probably in the case of Leo's mom. It was more like a slide of bad luck, like drawing dead in a poker game, where no amount of determination unseats you.

I met Leo on my 13th birthday when he got his nose broken by my brother, Rick. Rick started all male relationships with disdain, hatred and a fight, starting at the bottom of possibility to avoid disappointment.

Growing up a girl in a mining town, where things would get rough soon enough, even if I didn't know it, I had my own method of dodging disappointment. I hid in my back porch cubby. I read National Geographic, studied nature, and excluded myself from sure-to-fail things such as friendship or romance.

In the third grade I went on a field trip to the Lewis and Clark Caverns. I counted 208 bats in the chamber room, before I dropped deeper into the limestone caves to awe over the stalactites and stalagmites. In fourth grade, I climbed Timber Butte and collected rocks. Back on the flats, near Silver Bow Creek, I wondered what combination of elements flowing out of the Berkeley Pit painted the water like leather. I pondered these mysteries alone and I liked it that way. So, when Leo got his nose broken and turned it toward me, I walked forward with ambivalence.

Leo was three years older than me, had large dark eyes and black wavy hair that swung down his back. He was tall and leggy, with smooth, rich skin. His arms hung from his shoulders like vine beans, the muscles shining and growing. The muscles might've had a mind of their own, kind and innocent, afraid of their own strength, like maybe they'd let Rick win the fight.

After the fight, Leo sat silently on our living room couch with an ice pack on his nose, his dark eyes turned sullenly toward the floor, his black hair curling out of control. Shadow, our 2-year-old black lab, licked Leo's palm, leaving a syrupy slime at the center. Rick brought Leo ice cream, which melted into pink and white swirls in a chocolate soup, which I later tossed down the drain.

Mom took Leo to the doctor. They adjusted his nose, she said, which I guess finally got a yelp out of him. She tried to take him to his home, explain and apologize to his mother, but he wouldn't let her, didn't want to worry his mother. Fighting is every boy's right. His mother might try to stop him and then he'd fight with her. Best to let it be, he said. He got out of the car at Second and Montana. Mom could still see him in the rear-view mirror near the Dairy Bar as she dropped over the hill to the flats.

MONTHS AFTER MY 13TH BIRTHDAY, we walked to a church near the junior high school where people waited to be dunked into a tub of cold water.

"Come on," Leo said, and dragged me to the front of the line.

Unlike me, Leo had never been baptized.

To my father's later dismay, I went in first, the cold water burning my face. I came out gasping for breath, my long black hair pasted to my head. When Leo went under, I looked around for Jesus. I saw him shining in the blue and red sun of the stained-glass window.

"Born again. A double birthday for you," Leo said as we left the church.

My father didn't see it that way. "You need one baptism for the remission of sins," he said. "You've been baptized already and this is just getting your hair wet." He crossed his arms in the final gesture. I figured he knew what he was talking about and he was probably right, since in our house that was almost always the case. I also figured that Jesus knew my circumstances and wouldn't begrudge my request.

FOR MONTHS AFTER THE BAPTISMS, Leo did a very annoying thing and called me "Birthday Girl." One day, close to my 14th birthday, I tossed an invisible football to him.

"The birthday girl has a name," I said.

"A birthday name," he said. "Look, I see it in the clouds."

I looked at the sky. "A birthday is one day, every year, and then it passes, like all others. And, in case you haven't noticed, I'm not really a girl anymore."

"I've noticed," he said, holding the invisible football to his chest.

"Birthdays are special," I said. "You get presents and cake. Grand-parents call you up. Brothers are nice. You get cards in the mail from your mother's high school friends. A birthday's a celebration."

"I celebrate you every day."

"Stop it," I cringed.

"Each day with you an adventure."

"My name, Lindsey."

"A wild new frontier."

"L-I-N-D-S-E-Y."

Leo dropped the invisible football, walked over to the large willow tree where I stood and wrapped his arms around me. He pinned my chin to his chest, caught my shoulders in his armpits. I tried to push him off. He locked his arms. I struggled. He tightened his grip. Shadow barked and jumped. I wrapped one leg behind Leo's in a way I'd seen on TV, pushed him over it and we both tumbled to the ground. When we hit the grass his hands loosened and I jumped up. I wiped my palms on my T-shirt and brushed the dead grass off my jeans. I walked across the yard, picked up the invisible football and threw it at him.

"Lindsey," I yelled at him. "It's my name. Use it. You moron."

I ran inside and locked myself in the bathroom.

BY THE BEGINNING OF THE NEXT SUMMER, the summer we killed the Gardens' dog, the summer Leo died, we spent most of our free time together. People often mistook us for boyfriend and girlfriend or brother and sister. Being brother and sister was easy to clear up. I had a brother and Leo had three sisters. I'm still not sure how Leo felt about being boyfriend and girlfriend, but the possibility fermented into a mysterious mess in my growing 15-year-old heart.

"Last night Eddy asked me if you and I were dating," I said. The wind blew my hair in my face. I wore my favorite grass-stained jeans and Rick's new T-shirt. We stood at the edge of Harding Way, beside Leo's gasless Ford Fairlane, hitchhiking.

"Let him wonder," Leo said.

I nodded. Wondering. I didn't need to know anything yet, I rationalized, since, in an age of wild freedom, tempered by designated dating ages, I hadn't yet reached my parents' dating age of 16. I still had nearly a year to go when Leo's truck tipped upside down, flipping him under it, and rolled over the top of him.

An old farmer in a beat up Chevy passed us.

"Look," Leo said.

A smooth-headed soldier in uniform, with his sleeve pinned to his shoulder, stood about 10 yards up the road, his good arm out, thumb up. The farmer stopped for the soldier. The soldier nodded toward us, shook his head and refused the ride. The farmer pulled forward and stopped. After a minute, he backed up and the door opened. The soldier got in and the truck backed toward us.

"Get in, if you don't mind riding in the open," the soldier said. "He'll take you to town."

"What'd you say to him?" Leo asked.

"Nothing. Just commented on the fact that I just spent a year in 'Nam. Fighting. Boys and girls running 'round here? Can't be much harm in that."

The farmer dropped us at the YMCA.

We thanked both the farmer and the soldier and, in near unison, they gave us a nod of welcome. Leo had just graduated high school and signed for the draft. He didn't want to go to Vietnam. To use Leo's cliché, death had a sad, dark smell and he could smell it on the horizon. The smell filled his nostrils, throat and ears, he said, and he was certain that he'd die over there. If he died, there'd be no one to take care of his mom and his sisters. The draft was solid. No matter how he tried, he couldn't find a way out. With three young girls and an absent father, Leo's family had no money for college. Most money Leo made went to his mother for expenses.

He'd just started working at the Berkeley Pit, a huge open-air copper mine that constantly gnawed at the town. It had already chewed up Meaderville, and most of McQueen. Every day the pit grazed toward Helena. We couldn't begin to imagine the final fate of the Berkeley Pit. None among us could've known that the pit would fill with thick water, heavy with metals, arsenic, cadmium, and sulfuric acid. In 1969 we couldn't have known that nearly 20 years later a flock of snow geese would think they'd found a home for a night, only to die in the open water. None of us could've imagined such a flight of bad luck.

Inside the YMCA game room, I dropped two quarters into the pinball machine and handed the first turn to Leo.

He took the flippers and nodded his head toward the boy's bathroom.

"Who is it?" I asked.

"Shhh. Don't let them hear you."

"The attendants must smell it."

"Not pot." He flipped the silver ball into the maze. "Glue."

"Stupid. Did you tell them about Denny Lee last week? He's gone. Won't eat. Doesn't talk. He just lays there." I watched the silver ball bounce off of the sidebars and ring up the points, 100,000; 200,000; 500,000, then slip hopelessly beyond the reach of the flippers.

Leo knocked the machine with his palm and sent it into tilt.

"Tried. They wouldn't listen. We've got better things to do anyway."

"Did you get some?" I asked.

"Have no fear. Lightning Leo is here." He took a swipe at me like he'd just pulled a long sword from his belt.

I jumped back to avoid the invisible sword. "From your mother's liquor cabinet?"

"I don't need to steal from Mom. It's in the car. Rick can take us for gas." He put on his green army coat and motioned to the door.

Across the street, at the Masonic Temple, a strobe light deleted and added about 200 teens in time with a local rock band's version of "A Whiter Shade of Pale."

When the band took a break, the bright lights revealed Rick. "Let's get out of here," he said. "They're about to scare up the druggies."

"Whatever you say, captain. We need your wheels though. Mine are stuck out on Harding Way, out of gas. Take us to her and the rewards will be great." Leo shook his keys like a magic genie.

"Guess you got to stay, Sis," Rick smiled. "You're not allowed to ride in cars with boys."

"Mom and Dad won't know," I said.

Rick shrugged. "Your life."

ONCE WE GASSED UP LEO'S FORD FAIRLANE WE ALL DROVE TO CLARK Park, stopped near the baseball fields and broke out the beer. Rick ran to the middle of the first diamond and fell to the ground staring at the stars. Leo and I climbed the nearest tree.

"I hate mining," Leo said, shifting his long legs to get a better foothold. He pulled two shivering beers from a pocket of the green army coat and passed one to me.

"Work. It's a necessary phase." He flashed a grin that nearly knocked me off the branch.

I popped the can and took a drink of my beer.

"This is crazy," he said. "I know we just got here, but we should go. I've got to work afternoon shift tomorrow. And I'll need to help Mom with my sisters in the morning. She hasn't been feeling well. Besides, your parents won't like you out so late and you'll be paying in time all summer."

"You and Rick join a conspiracy? I can handle my parents. Let's just stay until we finish our beers. You'll still get plenty of sleep."

"Yeah," he said and stared off toward the lights on the hill. Finally, he leaned close and whispered, "I want to kiss you."

"Kiss me? You're like a brother."

"Like a brother."

If I'd been older I might have known my own heart and reached out a hand to touch his back, or I might have said something to console us both, to repair my blunder.

He jumped out of the tree and I let him go.

I took a hard drink from my beer, tipping the can way back, closing my eyes and enjoying the cold burn in my throat, baptizing myself a third time. Behind my eyelids, I could see Jesus in the flashing red and blue of the stained glass again. I left my eyes closed for a long time before I realized that the din of blue and red came from a police car. At least a moment passed before I realized that the car was parked right below me, in the baseball field parking lot, next to Leo's Ford Fairlane. I opened my eyes slowly, with a prayer, experiencing the kind of denial most people have when faced with some serious, unretractable mistake. This would make handling my parents much more difficult.

THE POLICE TOOK US TO JAIL. My parents took their own sweet time getting us out. We spent the night. I didn't know it then, but this was the first rock of the landslide. Rick and I were grounded, except for the funeral. Leo was 18 and charged for contributing to the delinquency of minors. He didn't make it home that morning in time to help his mother with his sisters. Leo didn't make it home in time to help his mother at all. She had suffered a seizure while we were in jail, passed out on her back and choked on her own spittle. By the time Leo arrived to wash up for work, his mother had passed from this life to the next. His little sisters had watched her go.

After his mother's funeral, Leo drove his sisters to Portland to stay with an aunt for a month. She couldn't afford to keep them forever and they decided the girls would live with Leo. Being head of the household would at least keep him from going to Vietnam.

He told me all of this in a letter. He sounded happy, upbeat in the letter.

I'd convinced him to stay that night in Clark Park and it haunted me. If we'd left when he suggested, we'd have missed both the cops and jail. Leo would've been home when his mother seizured and he could have turned her on her side—a simple move—and she would've lived. Her life was so close to being saved.

WHEN LEO RETURNED TO BUTTE WITH THE GIRLS, it took him two weeks to call.

"Want to go to the drive-in movie tonight?" he asked.

"How are you?"

"I miss you."

"But your mother's death, how are you handling it?"

"Fine," he said.

"You sound cheerful."

"Good luck, bad luck. It's all luck. What a man does with it shapes his heart."

"Have you been reading again?"

"Saint Catherine of Siena. You want to go to the movies or not?"

"I'll talk Rick into taking me and meet you there." Rick wouldn't refuse. He knew I blamed myself for the death of Leo's mother.

At the Starlight Drive-In, I left Rick with friends and climbed into Leo's Ford Fairlane.

"Are you OK?" I asked.

"I'm fine."

The movie started and I moved close to him, like a girlfriend would. He was holding the popcorn and I was hungry. After I'd eaten several mouthfuls, he put his arm around me.

"Is this OK?" he asked.

"Sure."

"More popcorn?"

"Sure."

"You liking the show?"

"Sure."

Leo smiled sweetly, hugged me really tight and kissed me soft and slow, right on the lips. If I didn't say it before, Leo was strong, had rich beautiful skin, and a smile that could knock a girl right out of a tree. Whatever I knew about the movie up to that point disappeared like the popcorn. I couldn't even tell my parents about the movie when I got home. "A-a western," I mumbled, hoping they wouldn't ask for details.

The next day Leo came over and we played a game of invisible football on the front lawn. Shadow chased and tackled us. I never told anyone how I shivered all over when Leo kissed me that night, and I never went to the drive-in movies alone with him again.

So I SHOULD HAVE BEEN RELIEVED WHEN HE SHOWED UP ONE SATURDAY afternoon with Rebecca. I half ran, half skipped down the steep sidewalk that led from the Butte Newsstand, where I'd been killing time, to the corner of Park and Main. As soon as I spotted Leo, I broke into a full-fledged run and from about five feet away took a flying leap toward him. He caught me, twirled me around and put me down, dizzy and happy.

"I want you to meet my friend, Rebecca," he said, smiling. He took the hand of a girl with the wildest red hair I'd ever seen. She wore a flowing red sundress and stunningly pure make-up. At that moment my happiness disappeared. The dizziness overtook me and my heart sank. She was beautiful.

"Nice to meet you," Rebecca said, with a smile as brilliant as her hair. She reached out to shake my hand.

"Sure," I said to the pair of smiles, obliging the handshake.

"Rebecca's from Portland," Leo said, still smiling.

"That's nice," I said.

"She's an artist. You're gonna love her work," he said with a smile big as a tree, a smile like a kiss, a stupid luck smile.

I would not love her work. "Did you move out here?"

"I wish she would."

"How old are you? Let her answer," I said.

"Seventeen," she said.

"Sweet 17," Leo said. "Hey. Let's go to the Gardens. I hear The Company's gonna take its big teeth right through the children's swing sets. Right up through the pretty little pansies."

322

"You work for The Company," I reminded him.

"Only a necessary phase," he reminded me. "Rebecca's visiting her grandmother for the summer. She's agreed to take care of the girls while I work."

"Hey, you guys. Come on, you're gonna miss the bus." Rick stood across the street, one hand up, motioning the bus to hold.

I dropped my nickel into the glass box that held the Saturday fare. I felt sick. Rebecca was taking care of Leo's sisters. I looked north. Although I couldn't see them, I knew that huge orange trucks, with tires bigger than me standing on my brother's shoulders, crawled down the sides of the Berkeley Pit.

The bus started toward the hill and Rick, Leo and Rebecca laughed about something that I closed my ears to. I sat in front of them in my boy's T-shirt and my grass-stained jeans, my hair a mess and I wouldn't dream of putting on make-up. Leo evidently really liked Rebecca and I was nothing like Rebecca.

The bus jerked and bounced a load full of already bouncing kids. The fumes made me even sicker. I crossed my arms and sank low in my seat.

The bus pulled up between two white pavilions and let us out. We followed popcorn and cotton candy smells to the midway. Leo walked past the plastic fishpond to the ball toss and picked up three baseballs. He threw them at three balanced clowns, knocking each, in turn, down to the wooden floor. He won a number one prize, which he could trade for number two and number three prizes when he won again later, which of course he would, because he always won. He chose a bright pink, feathered hair barrette that he gave to Rebecca. She immediately put it in her wild red hair, making it even wilder, making me feel even drabber.

Rick stuffed his hands into his pockets and gave me one of his "What do you want me to do" looks.

"Nothing," I said out loud.

"What?" Leo asked, walking toward the roller coaster.

"Nothing," I said, following.

From where we were we could see the pansy-filled gardens shaped like huge butterflies. On the grounds above the butterflies were several picnic areas, with swings, slides, teeter-totters and laughing kids.

Past the merry-go-round's colorful clay ponies, and the electric airplanes, we bought tickets and lined up for the roller coaster. We climbed into the yellow car, onto the black vinyl seats, Leo and myself in front, Rick and Rebecca in back. The ride attendant gave the car a shove and the chugging pulley grabbed it with a jerk and dragged us to the highest tier where it threw us to the mercy of the tracks. My stomach jumped as we flew around the corner. At the first drop I felt a complete loss of control. Down we went and up. The rise and momentary danger freed something wild inside of me. Down we went again, and back up and around, finishing the top tier of the tracks and dropping to the lower tier. We flew around a corner, dropped to the ground and soared back up the other side. At the crest of the last drop, just as we started the downward surge, I saw the dog: a brownish red curly haired Chesapeake.

He must've weighed a hundred pounds. Casually, he stepped onto the tracks and looked up. He stood completely still, staring green-eyed right at us when we hit him. For five helpless seconds we tried to stop the collision. We yelled, prayed, waved our arms. Nothing worked. We went through him like water and finished the ride.

We jumped out of the car and ran over to see if he was still alive.

"Nope. He's deader'n a rock," the ride attendant said. "Just stupid, bad luck."

I couldn't take the smell of the bus fumes for the ride home, so we walked, the landslide well on its way. At Continental Drive we split up and went in opposite directions. Rebecca and Leo turned toward town; Rick and I headed for the flats. I was seething inside. I shouldn't have gone to the Gardens that day. Leo shouldn't have brought Rebecca with us. Or better yet, he should've waited on Rebecca, until I was 16. At least that way I'd have had a chance to date him. It was wrong. Leo. Rebecca. That poor, poor dog. The whole day was just so wrong. Leo should've given me a chance for a second kiss.

"Go have your fun," I turned and yelled at them. "It's a free country."

"What?" Leo cocked his ear toward me.

"You moron."

AWEEK LATER MY DAD SHOOK ME OUT OF A SOUND SLEEP.
"Lindsey, honey, I've got bad news. There was an accident at the pit last night. Leo lost control of his truck. I'm sorry, sweetheart," my father said, "Leo died in the accident."

My father was an honest man, but I knew he was lying. Someone had made a mistake. Later, when I saw Rick, his face told me that this was the landslide's grand finale. Dodging the last few flying rocks and getting used to the newly structured ground was all that was left.

THAT YEAR I FINISHED THE SUMMER IN FRONT OF THE TV WITH NO NEED of grounding. The bones sharpened in my face and clothes hung crookedly on my uncertain body. After Leo died, brute strength and steadiness held my insides in place. It was a necessary phase.

Rick finished school early, signed for the draft and moved to Portland with Rebecca. Leo's sisters moved to Portland with their aunt. I combed my hair and put on make-up. I washed my blue jeans and they remained grass-stain free. The war in Vietnam ended and, as luck would have it, left Rick safe by two simple numbers.

The Anaconda Mining Company ran a bulldozer through the pansy butterflies of the Columbia Gardens. They mined the land for copper, eventually leaving a large unattended hole in place of the children's laughter. Twenty-eight billion gallons of poisonous water filled the Berkeley Pit. They found 342 dead snow geese from the errant flock that landed there. We all drank the bad water.

One fall night, a couple of years after Leo died, I dreamed that he called my name. He smiled that huge, knock-you-out-of-a-tree smile and tossed an invisible football. He walked over gently and kissed me on the cheek.

Live, the kiss said, live.

That morning I drove my dad's Suburban up Harding Way and took Shadow for a walk in the woods. Her black coat glistened in the afternoon sun. We hiked a long way back into the trees and, while we walked, I planned my first trip to the West Coast. Far off the trail, where red pine needles covered the forest floor, we found a clear mountain stream. Shadow drank freely. I splashed cold water on my face. Through the large arms of a blue spruce, I saw Jesus and Saint Catherine of Siena. I read the clouds. The words floated there, in the autumn sky, like fallen leaves. Good luck. Bad luck. It's all luck. What I do with it shapes my life. ◀

Orphan

By Pete Fromm

Spring 2010

MY DAUGHTER WILL LOOK YOU STRAIGHT IN THE EYE, no room for doubt, let alone argument, and tell you she's an orphan.

This after raising her myself, playpenning her in my shop in the beginning, then letting her wander half-built homes sporting a tool belt instead of any Easter dress while I banged in cabinets. Best we could do. My fault, maybe, making a joke of it, saying to write "Half-Orphan" in the ethnicity block on the college apps, that it might get her minority status, rake in those perks.

It's the "whole"-orphan thing that grates. Her mother vanished like a puff of smoke a week before Midge's first birthday. But I didn't go anywhere. Just lived through the police scrutiny, turned prime suspect for lack of any other kind. Gwen takes off for a girl's weekend in Glacier, just her and her new friend, maybe even more hippy than the last new one, and I called her in missing after the weekend plus a day.

They found her car just where she said she'd be camping, and not one thing beyond that. Ever. So, they zero in on me, and I can't even remember the new girlfriend's name. Have to read the paper for that. Just like anybody.

Even for the cops, then that one asshole reporter, I can't play distraught, can't spend my days stapling up fliers, trudging Glacier's backcountry. I've got a one year old who still needs a party, chocolate frosting to smear all over her face, who, hell, needs to just plain eat. And none of my jobs are calling, saying they'll be happy to hold up the floor guys, the painters, waiting on me to track down my wayward wife before scabbing together their goddamn curly-maple fronted cabinets.

The cops ask, so I tell them my best guess is she just took off, though I appreciate everyone's efforts, the rangers combing the mountains, everybody talking Night of the Grizzlies all over again. Gwen and motherhood. If she'd stuck around, they'd have replaced oil and water. After dropping Midge, she never seemed to take more interest in her than wondering how this had happened, pondering this tiny person like you might an asteroid come suddenly to rest in your living room. Breastfeeding lasted three days. Said it hurt, the teeth. Midge didn't have any more teeth than a worm. I brought home one of those pumps, and when I got it set up, tried explaining how it worked, she asked where I planned on using it, on which of my body parts. This wasn't exactly how I pictured it going.

The detective, nodding along, like every bit of it made sense, said, "You think maybe she switched teams?" His partner flinched, looked out the window.

I said, "You mean crossed over to Canada?"

He took a breath, started talking more slowly, annunciating like he was at a spelling bee, and I explained that I got it, that the Canada line was a joke. You've never seen anybody not smile so wide.

"I don't know," I said. "She could have. She didn't much like this team." The detective said, "Are you joking again, Mr. Dawson?" His partner, still looking out the window, said, "And now she and her girlfriend both disappear?" like he'd dug this black fact up from the bottom of the skankiest cesspool.

"Seems so," I said.

Still staring out the damned window, like he was waiting for Gwen to come strolling up hand in hand with what's-her-name, he said, "What do you suppose we'd find if we tore up your basement?"

"Maybe my coping saw," I said. "I sure can't lay my hands on it."

And now Midge, who guys on the job used to call my barnacle—"Hey, Dodge, where's the Barnacle?" and out she'd peel from around a half wall, hammer in hand, like as not my hard-hat slopped around her ears—has gone over all these files, holds up my answers as sure-fire proof I drove her off. "You never even looked for her," she says.

"I was looking after you," I answer.

She's hired an investigator. One of those people who'll find your birth parents if you've been adopted. A whole agency of people who'll bring down some middle-aged couple's carefully constructed life, dredging up secrets, an offspring rising up out of the past like Lazarus.

I tell Midge that Gwen was no confused teen runaway. She was more runaway train, no brakes, 10 percent grade, pity anything in her path. And she was smart, she didn't leave behind a clue. Anywhere. No note to me, no farewell time capsule buried in the garden for Midge. I don't give Midge's investigator one chance in a thousand of turning her up now. A graying wild child on the Canadian team? Whooping it up with the draft dodgers who never came back? There wouldn't be so much as a single frayed thread stretched back over the years to me and Midge.

But Midge is wrapping up college, those half-orphan scholarships added to what I stashed away from all those cabinets, and, well, apparently there's not much you don't learn in college. Midge certainly hasn't missed a thing. Has got it figured flat out. Is pretty much pure obnoxious with knowledge.

I go down to Missoula for her graduation. Even though I've spent the spring working a job halfway between us, that much closer, I'm late, slip into the back of the auditorium. As strangers troop across the stage, I peel varnish off my thumbnail. I've been doing all the finish work on a ridiculous place looking out over the Missions, which are a range easterners think about when they think about mountains, white peaks knifing into the sky without the introduction of foothills. Just a view. The house is an homage to the owner's own wealth, enclosing more square footage than a small town, each room with its own theme; Wolf, Grizzly, Buffalo, Eagle, animals you could spend your whole life in Montana without ever glimpsing, except the eagle, steroidal magpies that they are.

I've never met him, but what I do admire is that he tried so hard to hold onto this place after the crash. Even from across the country. I only got the stop work order from the general a few days ago. I didn't have much left, doubt now that I'll ever get paid, so I've held onto the key, have imagined holing up here with Midge till she decides what she'll do with her life, a degree in economics. Maybe rebuild the world. I'll do the finish work. It's exactly what I'm still dreaming of when from a long, long way away I hear my own name called, glance up in surprise, see Midge striding across the stage. I'm not embarrassed to say I had to clear my eyes, the first person in my family to ever make it through school.

But afterward, when I make it through the throngs, she gives me a single back-tap hug, something you might lay on a total stranger, and tells me she already has plans for the night, the weekend. She says, "Thanks for coming." Thanks. Like it was a chore or something. I start to tell her about the house up in the Missions, how maybe we could squat up there, finish it for ourselves, swap rooms every night until we've worked our way through the animal kingdom. But some guy comes up, robed just like Midge, same flat cap, and when he puts his arm over her shoulders, she introduces me as Dodge. No mention of any parentage, and this guy, whose name skates right past me, shakes my hand as if maybe I'm some official at the U. They make their way off through the crowd, leaving me standing there until I make my own way out, spend a night alone without heat in the Otter room.

The next time I see Midge she stops by unannounced, demanding records. The guy waits out in the car. If it's the same guy. I wouldn't recognize him if I found him in my kitchen. I hand over all I've ever had of Gwen, a knot of maybe half a dozen letters from when I was working in Texas, half of those nothing more than postcards, one you'd be hard pressed to call anything but porn, a scrawled list of all she planned to do to me if I ever came back to Montana. There's a photograph, too, a Polaroid she asked some Japanese to take of us at the Grand Canyon, after she hitched down to take me home. She came walking out of the heatwaves into that Dallas subdivision like a mirage, and I went for her like any thirst-raved pioneer. The Canyon shot is pure tourist shit, a couple half-dressed specks standing in front of a blurred ditch the size of the east coast. Be hard enough finding Gwen in the picture, let alone finding her with it. We'd screwed ourselves silly that whole long unemployed drive back to Montana. Places like Abilene. Like Chickasha. Roswell. Kanab. Gunnison. Kemmerer. Butte. We could not stop, could not get enough. I was pure dazzled that she'd thumbed across a nation just to tell me she missed me, to get me to quit the best paying job I ever had. I zigzagged the West, hoping every minute of every day that we'd never get wherever we were going.

I watch Midge stare at the photo, something she's never seen. "What do you think you're going to find?" I ask. "She doesn't want to be found. Never did."

"How would you know? You never looked. Never lifted a finger to help anyone who did."

"If I thought she wanted to be found, I would have looked." I turn away from Midge, then back, her face too like Gwen's at that age, when we met. "It was this thing I had, this problem. Doing whatever she wanted."

Midge curls her lip like she doesn't know whether to pity me or swat me. Straight out of Gwen, too. "She might not even be alive. She and, and—"

"Miss Herron?"

"They could have fallen off a cliff, drowned in a river, there could have been bears, there, there—" I interrupt with a look. "Did any of that ever cross your mind?" she insists.

"It did," I say. "Didn't much care for it."

"So you just go on? Build some more cabinets?"

"There was you to think about."

She stamps her foot. Gwen would have thrown something. At my head. "You have no right to use me as an excuse."

I nod, work a second at a sudden kink in my neck. "I don't guess I ever thought of you as that."

"Well you could hardly call it parenting. Turning me into your apprentice."

"Is that a class you took? Nastiness 101?"

She jaws on something a second, but nothing comes out. Maybe she failed that class.

"Tell me," I say. "If you took off right now, how hard would you want me tracking you down?"

Man, it's a line that will haunt me, because I see that until that second the idea had never once occurred to her. I watch her stomp off to that car, slam the door behind her, and I don't see her again for months.

But she's no Gwen. Not in any way that means anything. Nothing more than looks. I drive down to Missoula that fall, figure the time, even the weather, will have cooled her off. I dial her same old cell number. She answers on the second ring. Not exactly making herself invisible. But just her hello rocks me back, puts me in any one of those last houses we worked together, me inside the cabinet, her calling down adjustments as we set another granite counter top.

"Found you," I whisper.

There's a moment's pause, an awful long moment if you want the truth, and then she says, "Took you long enough."

Instead of telling me where she lives now, she says to meet at a bar, the old train depot, and walking over I figure it's fitting enough, a place someone would have left town from back in the day. Or gone to meet someone, watching their lives pull back into the station.

When she comes in, peers around in the new dark, man, for a second

330

all there is is Gwen, stepping out of that Dallas heat, peering into the cool, shadowed shell of the model home, no idea how many of the others she must have looked into first, how many hoots and whistles and offers she must have put up with. I lift a hand, wave, but it's another second before her eyes adjust, then there's no smile, just her moving my way. It's early and the place is deserted. She slides into the booth across from me.

"Hey, Barnacle," I say.

She glances down at the table, then up to me. "Do you know what a midge is?"

"A word your mother liked."

"It's a tiny bug. Hatches in the dead of winter. Just like me."

I shrug. "Okay."

"You didn't know that?" she asks.

"No."

"Mom did."

I shrug again. "It's something she might have. Her interests were kind of all over the place."

"It wasn't a question."

"You asked if I knew."

"Mom knew. She told me."

"You weren't a year old, sweet pea, you couldn't," I start, but then it hits home, and I sag back, look at her, get out, "No way."

She nods. "Canada, just like you always said. B.C. Silverton."

I can't do more than a blank stare.

"North of Nelson." She waits. "Straight north of Spokane." She waits again. "Spokane," she says. "It's a city. In Washington."

I nod.

"It's not Mars. Not the dark side of the moon."

"Okay."

"Hundreds of miles. Not thousands."

I keep nodding, though it seems breathing is challenge enough.

"My whole life, Dad, only a few hundred miles."

I cling to that Dad like a life ring. "Might as well have been Pluto though, huh?"

"Yeah, might as well have been."

The barmaid finally notices us. I ask for a beer, and when Midge doesn't even look her way I say, "How about two?" but Midge says, "Water will be fine."

"Your agency?" I say, once we're alone.

"They helped," she says, as if she's defending Mother Theresa. "But it wasn't hard, Dad. She didn't even change her name."

"Our name?" I say. "Or hers?"

Midge looks away, after the barmaid, like she might suddenly be dying of thirst. "Hers."

The beer comes, the water, but we both just watch the sweaty glasses. There's frost on the lip of mine, actual ice. "When was all this?" I ask.

"This summer. Before school started."

"School? I thought you were finished."

"Grad school."

I sit back to go for my wallet. A kneejerk. "You need money?"

"Full ride."

"No shit. Well, look at you."

"The orphan thing."

Nobody could miss the left out half. No parent anyway. "So," I say, "was she surprised?"

"You could say that," she says without a trace of a smile.

"I can imagine," I say.

"Yeah."

I turn my beer back and forth on its pulpy cardboard coaster. "Pleased?"

"I'm not so sure you could say that."

"You two catch up? The missing years?"

"My whole life, you mean?" She doesn't touch her glass, hides her hands under the table. "She asked."

"And, what about her?"

Midge shrugs. "She's with somebody. I didn't ask."

I take a sip. It's cold enough to hurt.

"A guy, Dad. No switching teams as far as I know."

"I never thought that. That was the police."

She nods. "And no," she says.

"No?"

"No, she didn't ask about you."

I take a few breaths, say, "I wouldn't have expected her to."

"She said she knew I was in good hands. The best. She said she'd never have left me if she didn't know that."

"Big of her."

"She said I was better off."

"Only thinking of you then?"

"I think that's her story."

"And she's sticking to it."

Midge lifts her hands above the table. Reaches over and takes a sip of my beer. "Water," she says. "What was I thinking?"

I force a smile.

"I told her about that picture. At the Grand Canyon."

My smile turns real, which doesn't make me happy. Just the idea of that trip still doing it for me. Kind of pathetic, you know.

"She laughed. Couldn't believe you still had it."

"She remembered?"

"She said so."

A train rattles by, barely moving, but just freight, woodchips, no passengers leaping into anyone's waiting arms. We watch it through the wavery glass.

"So, you two going to keep in touch?" I ask, still looking out the window, waiting for the caboose. "Make up for lost time?"

"I don't think that's really her style."

"No, I wouldn't guess it is."

Midge leans back, eyes me for maybe the first time since she made me out in the gloom, came over to sit down. "Did you know she was going to leave?"

She waits for an answer, takes another sip of my beer, something to do with her hands.

"No," I say. She hands back the glass and I take it, but she's fast, our fingers don't touch. "I didn't think she could stay, but I never really saw her leaving."

"That makes sense?"

I shake my head. "Nope."

"And then just me, this baby?"

"Not this baby. The one baby in the world."

"But, you could have had so much more if you'd gone after her."

"More than you? You don't think you were enough? You left me lacking? In what way?"

"A partner," she says. "Like, Hello?"

"The Barnacle?"

She smiles. "Not that kind of partner. Don't play stupid with me, Dad. Nobody's better at it than I am."

I smile because I'm supposed to. She asks, "Weren't you so pissed off?"

"Pissed off? Maybe. I don't know. Sad is more like it. That she couldn't stay."

"Because of me?"

"You saw her, I didn't. But I'm guessing you saw somebody you could see was not likely to stay."

She gives a tiny shake of her head. "She's got this huge garden. She was out snipping heads of this kind of freak garlic with these huge curly-cue shoots."

"Peasant dress?"

"Blue jeans."

"Torn?"

"A little. But, yeah, pretty hippie. The old man with the gray beard. Lots of pot."

"And you can see her staying in Kalispell?"

"There's plenty of pot there."

"Not growing next to the house, mixed in with the tomatoes and garlic."

Midge sighs. "I couldn't believe I was looking at my mom. That that's what I'll end up like."

Man, it's killer not to ask what that's like. I've shredded half the coaster before I see what I've done. "You'll end up whatever way you choose."

"Like you?"

I pin the remainder of the coaster beneath the somehow empty glass. "Some of the choosing gets done for you."

"Or to you."

"Well, yeah, there's that too."

The barmaid makes her way back, moving slow enough I wonder what we're interrupting, and Midge orders this time, another single. The barmaid turns to me, but Midge says, "Really, just the one." I realize, a little late, that it's exactly how we drank Cokes when she was a kid, milk shakes, me just trying to do that much right, limit the bad shit by drinking half of it myself. This with the fast food bags scattered around us in some unfinished kitchen, our half-palace for a day, teaching her a trade I never saw a single woman in. Dad of the year stuff.

"I got more of you in me than her," she says, which makes me wish for a glass right now, something to hide my smile behind.

"It'd be a biological first," I say.

"Still," she says.

The barmaid appears like she's been dropped. Our new beer gets set down, and when we're alone again, Midge says, "I asked her about coming down, just for a visit."

I don't say a word.

"I said it might give you a little closure."

"Closure?" I say, wondering if this is a word they toss around at her agency. Like having the earth split wide open at your feet, swallow you whole, close back up over you.

"It might be good for you."

"We were together three years, Midge. Six months of that I was in Texas. And the last year I was already taking care of you, watching her build up the nerve to bolt."

"But, still."

"That leaves a year and a half. And half of that we were just on the road, traveling without a plan. The best half maybe."

"Are you saying I wasn't planned?"

"Planned?" I can't not laugh. "Gwen? Hardly. We worked at you like a vocation, but no, not planned."

"Maybe I don't need to know any more."

I look at her like she's just gotten off the train. "You and me? How many years are we going on now?"

She shakes her head. "Twenty-two, Dad."

I push the beer toward her, sliding it on its new coaster. "I don't want to see her again, Midge. Honest. I mean, I'm crawling over with curiosity, but—"

"You don't think it'd be good?"

I tap my temple. "How could it be better than what I've had up here? We've been on that road trip for decades."

"But, Dad?"

"And it hasn't held a candle to you. Not a day of it. What could I say to someone who's missed all that?"

She actually blushes. God, I could come across the table for her, sweep her into my lap.

"What did she say?" I ask. "When you asked her to come down?"

She takes the beer in her hand, takes a swig, wiping her lip with the point of her tongue. She lets her face fall flat a second, then tucks her still baby silky blonde hair behind her ear in a gesture I know by heart, can still see on the blackest nights. She lets out a laugh which is not hers, but a dead-on of Gwen, and she lowers her head just a degree, the perfect tilt, peering at me from under her blond brows as she shakes her head. "Oh, honey," she says, and I don't know where she gets the gravel, the pitch perfect timbre, but I am looking at my wife of so long ago as she says, "He has never told you a thing about me, has he?" ◣

CONTRIBUTORS

Ted Brewer is the author of travel guidebooks to Utah, Prague, and the Czech and Slovak republics. He's contributed to *Montana Outdoors*, *Geographical*, *Exquisite Corpse* and other publications. He lives in Helena.

Jennifer Graf Groneberg lives with her husband, Tom, and three sons on the Pronghorn Ranch north of Roundup. She has written one book, edited another, and photographs life on the grasslands of central Montana.

Malcolm Brooks is the author of the acclaimed novel *Painted Horses*, released in 2014. A carpenter by trade, he lives in Missoula, where he settled in his mid-20s. His passions include horses, fly-fishing and bird hunting.

Fred Haefele has received literary fellowships from the NEA and Stanford University. His books include the award-winning motorcycle memoir *Rebuilding the Indian* and the collection *Extremophilia*. Haefele lives in Missoula.

John Byorth is a historian and writer from Livingston. He has written for the National Geographic Channel and a wide range of publications, including *Men's Journal*, *Montana: The Magazine of Western History*, and *Nowhere Magazine*.

Jeff Hull is the author of the novel *Pale Morning Done* and an essay collection, *Streams of Consciousness*. His work has appeared in *The New York Times Sunday Magazine*, *The Atlantic*, *Audubon*, *Outside* and many others.

Tim Cahill is a founding editor of *Outside* magazine and currently serves as its editor at large. He's the author of several books, including *Road Fever* and *Jaguars Ripped My Flesh*. He lives in Livingston.

Allen Morris Jones is the author of *A Quiet Place of Violence: Hunting and Ethics in the Missouri River Breaks*; a novel, *Last Year's River*; and numerous published articles, essays, stories, and poems. He lives in Bozeman.

Glen Chamberlain is the author of *Conjugations Of The Verb 'To Be.'* In March 2016, *All I Want Is What You've Got* will be released. Chamberlain has won numerous awards, including a Pushcart Prize, The Rona Jaffe Prize, and the Gilcrease Award.

Ed Kemmick is the owner and chief writer of LastBestNews.com. He worked for newspapers in St. Paul, Minn., Butte, Anaconda and Billings, spending more than 20 years at *The Billings Gazette* as an editor, reporter and columnist.

John Clayton's book *Stories from Montana's Enduring Frontier* is a collection of essays on Montana history. He also wrote *The Cowboy Girl*, a biography of writer Caroline Lockhart. He lives in Red Lodge.

Alan Kesselheim has written for *Montana Quarterly* from its start. He has written 11 books, most recently *Montana: Real Place, Real People*, with photographer Thomas Lee. He teaches at Montana State University.

Pete Fromm's latest novel is *If Not For This*. He has a degree in wildlife biology from the University of Montana. His new wilderness memoir, *The Names of the Stars*, will be published in Fall 2016. He lives with his family in Missoula.

William Kittredge retired as Regents Professor of English and Creative Writing from the University of Montana in 1997. Over the past three decades he has published numerous books and written for more than 50 magazines.

CONTRIBUTORS

Craig Lancaster, of Billings, is the author of five novels, including the High Plains Book Award-winning *600 Hours of Edward*. His most recent book, the novel *This Is What I Want*, was released in July 2015. He's the *Quarterly*'s design director.

The writing of *Montana Quarterly* Editor Emeritus Megan Ault Regnerus has appeared in *Runner's World*, *Fit Pregnancy, Brain, Child* and other magazines. She lives in Bozeman.

Butch Larcombe grew up in Malta, Montana. He was the editor of *Montana Magazine* and the managing editor of the *Helena Independent Record*. He lives in Helena with his wife Jane and Harry, a dog.

Gail Schontzler has worked for the *Bozeman Daily Chronicle* since 1983. She has a master's degree in journalism from UC Berkeley, and has won several state and regional awards for reporting on subjects ranging from abortion to MSU.

Thomas Lee is the *Montana Quarterly* senior photographer. He accepts commissions for speaking engagements and commercial, editorial and fine art imagery at www.ThomasLeePhoto.com and www.ThomasLeeTrueWest.com.

Maryanne Vollers, author of *Lone Wolf* and *Ghosts of Mississippi*, started writing about music when she was an editor at *Rolling Stone* magazine. She lives in Livingston with her husband, William Campbell.

Milana Marsenich is a Montana native who currently lives and works in the Flathead Valley. Her work has appeared in a handful of magazines, including *Big Sky Journal*, *Feminist Studies* and *The Polishing Stone*.

Jeff Welsch, the sports editor at *The Billings Gazette*, has authored five books, including three with his wife, Sherry Moore. They share a home on the Gallatin River with their chickens and healthy populations of trout, deer and turkeys.

Scott McMillion is the editor of *Montana Quarterly*. His work appears in magazines around the country. He's the author of the award-winning book *Mark of the Grizzly*. He lives in Livingston with his wife Jennifer and a cat named Norman.

Daniel Person is a freelance writer based in Washington State. Before freelancing, he worked as a reporter and editor for newspapers in Hardin, Bozeman, Spokane and Seattle.

Myers Reece is a frequent contributor to *Montana Quarterly*. His essays, fiction and journalism have appeared in newspapers and magazines across the country. He lives in Kalispell with his wife and two dogs.

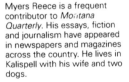